IMAGES
of America

WEST WARWICK

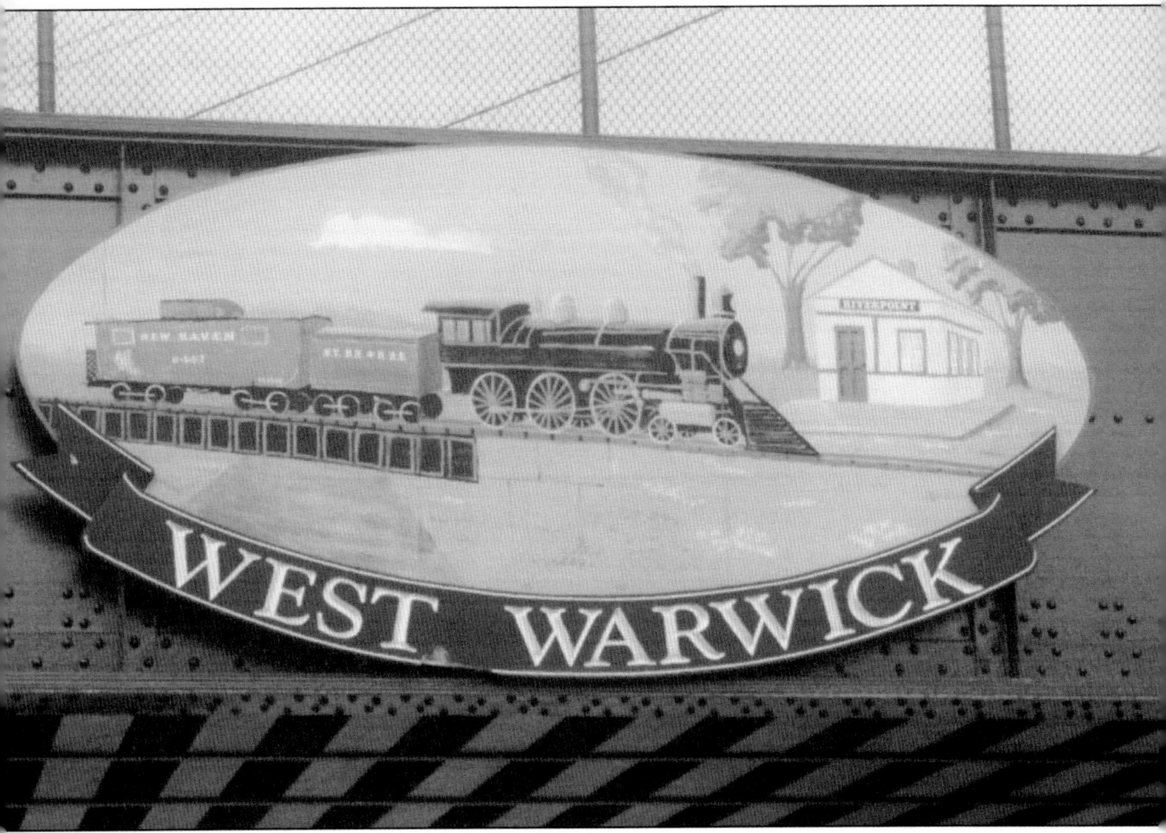

This beautiful painting is on a large plaque attached to the restored railroad bridge over East Main Street. It displays the days when the New York, New Haven & Hartford Railroad crossed the bridge as it approached the River Point Depot on the way to Providence. See pages 123–124 for more information. (Courtesy of Gerard Tellier Jr.)

On the Cover: The newest town in Rhode Island, West Warwick, was incorporated on March 14, 1913. When this photograph was taken on the Fourth of July the same year, people had a great deal to celebrate. Leo St. Onge Sr. is shown in a parade that passed in front of his father's Star Clothing House, later known as St. Onge's, on Main Street in Arctic. (Courtesy of Gary St. Onge.)

IMAGES
of America

WEST WARWICK

Raymond A. Wolf

ARCADIA
PUBLISHING

ISBN 978-0-7385-7520-9

Published by Arcadia Publishing
Charleston, South Carolina

Printed in the United States of America

Library of Congress Control Number: 2010940355

For all general information, please contact Arcadia Publishing:
Telephone 843-853-2070
Fax 843-853-0044
E-mail sales@arcadiapublishing.com
For customer service and orders:
Toll-Free 1-888-313-2665

Visit us on the Internet at www.arcadiapublishing.com

To my mom, Helen O. Larson, who, for over 60 years, loved shopping in Arctic.

Contents

ACKNOWLEDGMENTS

The driving force behind the creation of this book is the memory of my mom, Helen O. Larson. She was a devoted shopper of Arctic's retailers for over 60 years. She was also a frequent contributor of the Poetry Corner in the *Pawtuxet Valley Daily Times* for many years.

I wish to thank Gerard Heroux of the Pawtuxet Valley Preservation and Historical Society for his help in digging through the numerous files to find many of the photographs that appear in this book. I want to express thanks to Gerard Tellier Jr. for allowing me to include documents and photographs from his collection of Phenix memorabilia. Thank you also for introducing me to Gerard Heroux and Larry Soucy. Many thanks go to Larry Soucy, Armand Boucher, and Charles Despres for sharing their knowledge and photographs. Of course, the story of West Warwick would not be complete without the cooperation of Denis Roch and his unique collection of material on the Majestic building. Denis, I am grateful for your help.

I want to express thanks to Donald Carpenter, who I remet at a Hope Historical Society meeting. He was gracious enough to allow me to include material from his extensive collection of old West Warwick photographs. Donald and I used to attend school together. However, beyond that I want to express my deepest appreciation for the hours he spent proofreading the draft before it was shipped to the publisher and became the book you now hold in your hands. I also want to express my appreciation to Jenn Carnevale, who has proofread my books, *The Lost Villages of Scituate*, *The Scituate Reservoir*, and at the present, *West Warwick*. Jenn has earned the title of being my resident proofreader, and I really appreciate it.

I would be remiss if Gary St. Onge was left out of my acknowledgments; he not only spent time going through his archives with me, but he also introduced me to his dad, Leo St. Onge Jr. Leo and his wife, Marion, opened their home with the greatest hospitality as we went through items they had not seen in years. Marion even made lunch for me on two occasions. Thank you Leo and Marion, you are a magnificent couple. It was in your home that I first announced the date of my retirement from TJ Maxx.

Finally, I wish to extend a great big thank-you to Rob Burton, the Tree Guy, for cheerfully allowing me the use of his bucket truck. Without it, I could never have captured the photographs on pages 95, 99, 102, and 104. In conclusion, I wish to thank the extraordinary team I work with at Arcadia Publishing: Hilary Zusman, assistant editor; Lynn Beahm, publicity manager; and Beth McKenna, senior regional sales manager.

Unless otherwise noted, all images appear courtesy of the Pawtuxet Valley Preservation and Historical Society archives.

INTRODUCTION

The population of the western portion of Warwick decided to secede in 1912. In 1913, they incorporated as West Warwick. The town has a total area of eight square miles and contains the North Branch and the South Branch of the Pawtuxet River. The town is made up of nine villages along both branches of the river. The villages are (in alphabetical order) Arctic, Centreville, Clyde, Crompton, Lippitt, Natick, Phenix, River Point, and Westcott. The chapters are presented in this order.

The property owners along the river would build mills and erect housing for their workers to rent. Soon, the mill owners would build company stores where workers could purchase everything they needed. Some owners would even build their workers a church. This is how nine villages sprang up along the banks of the Pawtuxet River Branches. Most of this happened in the early 1800s; the Lippitt Mill began construction in 1809 and was completed in 1810. The Centreville Bank was granted a charter in 1828.

For an interesting exercise, obtain a Rhode Island state map and lay it opened flat on a table. Take a yardstick or similar straightedge, and draw a line from Pascoag in the northwest corner of the map to the southwest corner of Newport. Now, draw another line from the northeast corner of Pawtucket to Westerly in the southwest corner of the map. Interestingly, they cross each other in West Warwick—and in Arctic, which in its day was considered the retail capital of central Rhode Island.

The following paraphrased and quoted excerpts from a letter dated Monday, February 19, 1979, from Mary C. Petrella of Natick to Leo St. Onge Sr. of Arctic explain how people lived in the early 1900s. She remembers walking with her mother the distance from Natick to Arctic, called Jericho by the Italians, in all kinds of weather. She tells about her father and mother buying all their furniture from J.B. Archambault and paying him 25¢ a week, which was recorded in a passbook. Her mother made 35¢ an hour working in the Warwick Mills in Centreville, and when she received her paycheck, the first thing she did was put a quarter aside for Archambault and another one for the John Hancock representative. He collected $1 a month on her father's $250 life insurance policy. She continues, "It was a sacred duty this weekly payment of one's bills." She writes about going to bed with doors unlocked. She mentions the three-seater outhouse—two for adults and one for children. They felt rich if they had a ton of bituminous coal and a cord of wood. She remembers the double-runner Speed-Away sled. She writes about her mother scrubbing clothes in a large galvanized tub with a huge bar of Octagon soap and another tub for rinsing. She writes, "If we were poor, we didn't know it, everyone was in the same boat." She explains she was born in 1924 and lived through the Great Depression. She remembers her father had come to America in 1900. Her father worked two jobs so she could get her bachelor of science degree from Rhode Island State College in Kingston and her master of arts degree from the University of New Hampshire in Durham. Dr. Cartier would mail spectacles to school for her. She says, "During summer vacations, I worked for Majestic Hardware and Sinnott's Department Store. One summer, I worked in Anthony Mill as a bobbin girl in the weave shop from 2:00 p.m. until 11:00 p.m." She concludes her letter by saying she hopes he enjoyed her letter as much as she enjoyed writing it. After signing "Cordially yours, Mary C. Petrella," she adds a postcript: "I remember purchasing Pendleton suits and sweaters at St. Onge."

Enjoy the trip you are about to take through history. The author's mother wrote the following poem in July 1991 at age 80:

The Great Depression
by Helen O. Larson

Our country had a crisis
many, many years ago
And how we survived it
I will never know

Many nights we went to bed hungry
hunger pains all night long
We don't know what happened
to cause our country to go wrong

Soup kitchens sprung up here and there
people could have soup once a day
It will be forever embedded
in my memory to stay

My brother got a job shucking corn
the man paid ten cents an hour
So many times my mother wished
she had a bag of flour

One day I found a crust of bread
my mother said to me
You break it right now and share it
your brothers are also hungry

No money for food or clothes
or to see a movie show
How we got through the depression
We will never know

We couldn't take a bus
to pass away some time
The fare was only a nickel
just half a dime

Lucky we didn't get sick
a doctor we couldn't afford
Someone was watching over us
I'm sure it was the Lord

Then one day all that changed
an election took place
And Franklin Roosevelt ran
and he won the race

All the mills started up
and we got a raise right away
My friend came to me and said
thirty-five cents an hour they'll pay

We were getting twenty-five cents an hour
and now with the extra ten
We knew we would celebrate
though we didn't know when

As I write this poem
dear God I ask you
Don't ever again let your people
go through what we went through.

One

Arctic

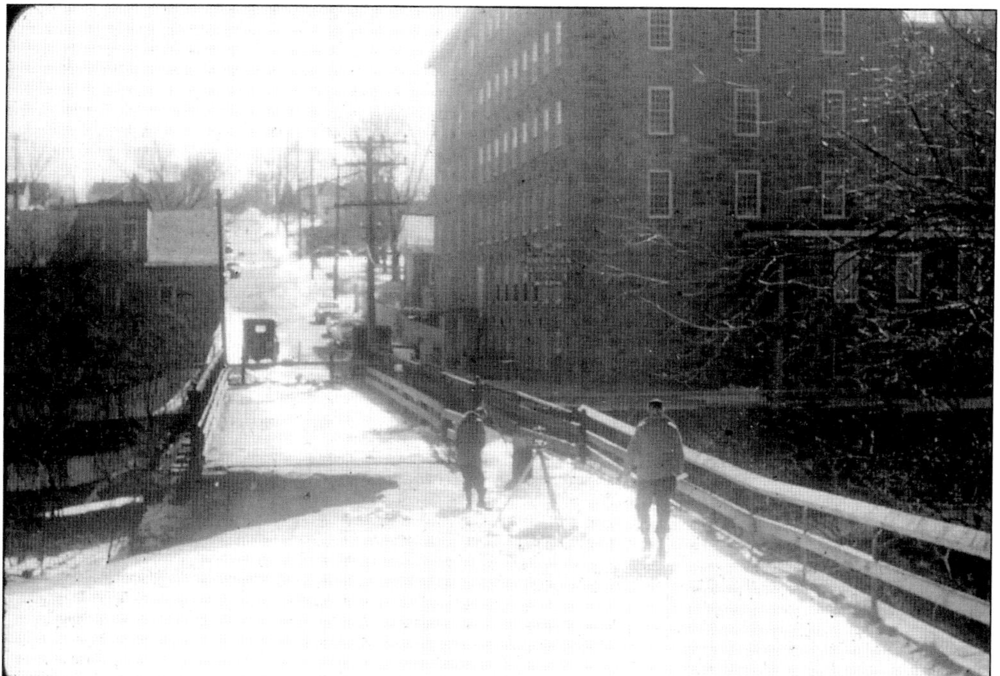

The Arctic Mill was built in 1852 alongside the South Branch of the Pawtuxet River. Henry T. Potter was born in Johnston on October 1, 1821. He built the mill of granite and laid out the village in Warwick when he was 31 years old. This photograph, which appears to be from the early 1900s, shows Factory Street has been washed out just before the bridge crossing the Pawtuxet.

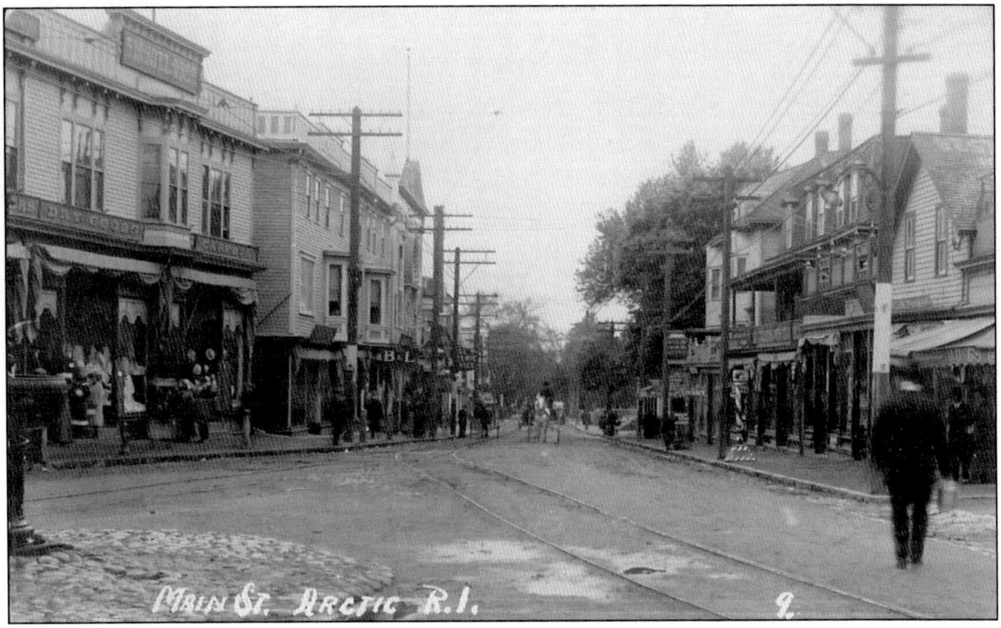

This postcard shows an early view of Main Street taken from the Square looking toward Centreville Bank. Sinnott's Department Store, which carried dry goods and clothing, is on the left. The building was later occupied by the Boston Store and after that by Maxine's. Mastro Electric presently calls it home. Note the hitching posts in the images from this postcard series. (Courtesy of Gary St. Onge.)

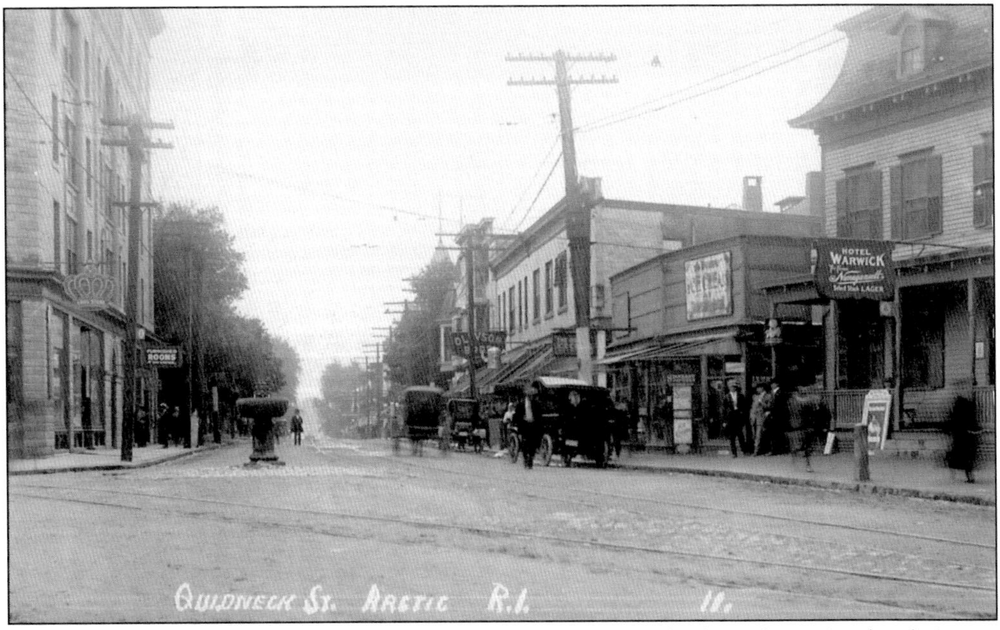

The next postcard in this series was also taken from the Square looking down Quidneck Street, now known as Washington Street. It appears to be early 1900s, as the modes of travel are walking, horse and carriage, automobile, and trolley. The Majestic is on the left, and the Hotel Warwick is on the right advertising "The Famous Narragansett Select Stock LAGER." The hotel was built in 1889 and in 1923 became the site of the F.W. Woolworth store. (Courtesy of Gary St. Onge.)

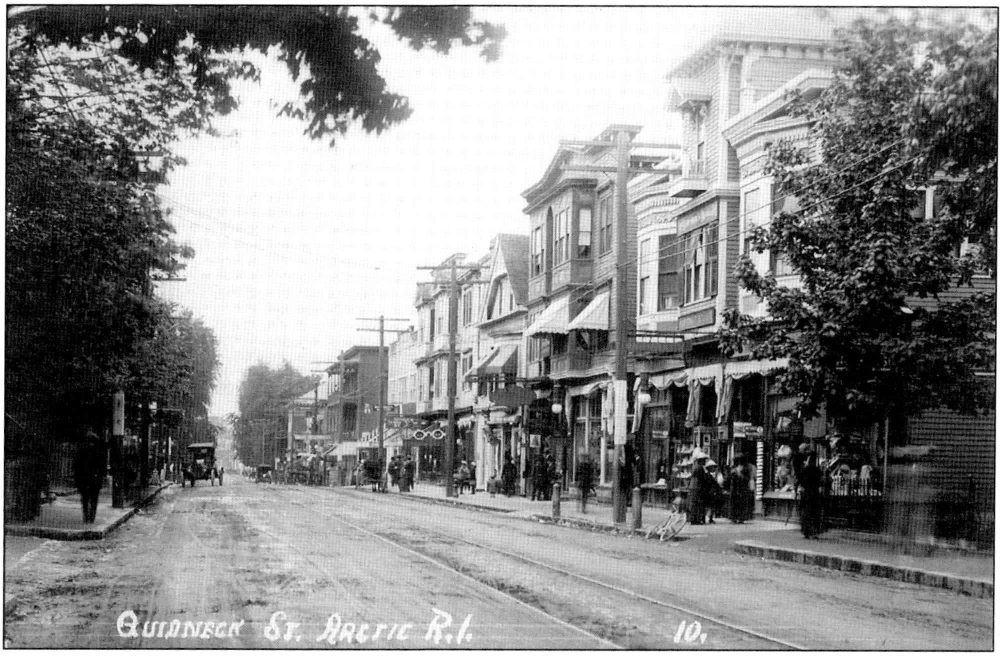

The photographer has relocated further down Quidneck Street for this postcard, which shows a great lineup of stores. The J.J. Newberry Company built its one-story commercial block here in 1921. The St. John's Church, built in 1874, is located on the left. (Courtesy of Gary St. Onge.)

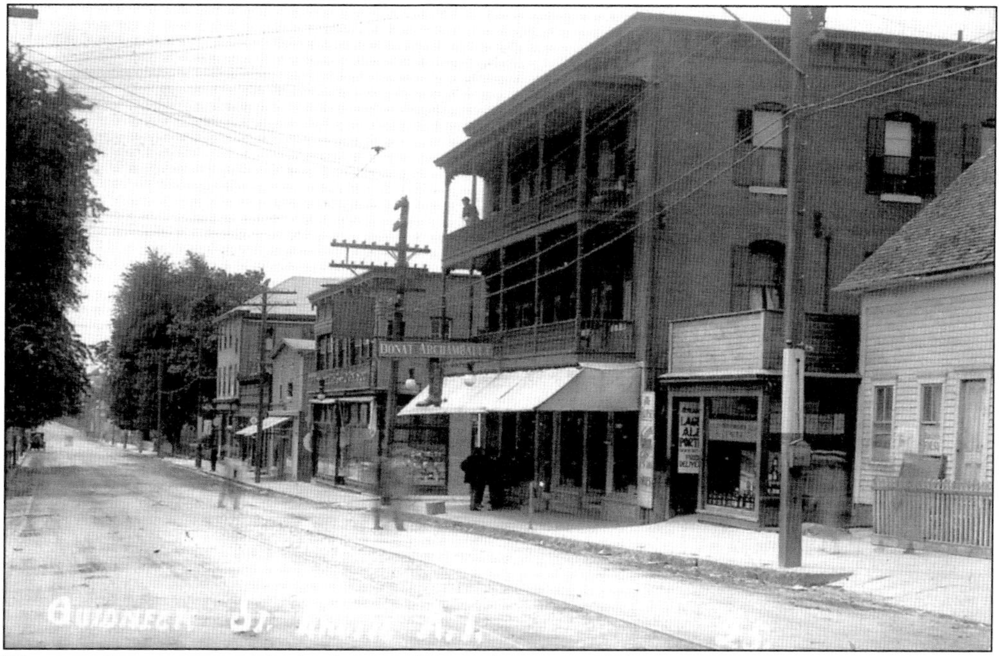

This is a close-up view of the background from the postcard above. The next building after Donat Archambault's store was built in 1910 by Archambault's father, Lucien, and occupied by F.W. Woolworth's five-and-dime store until 1923. (Courtesy of Gary St. Onge.)

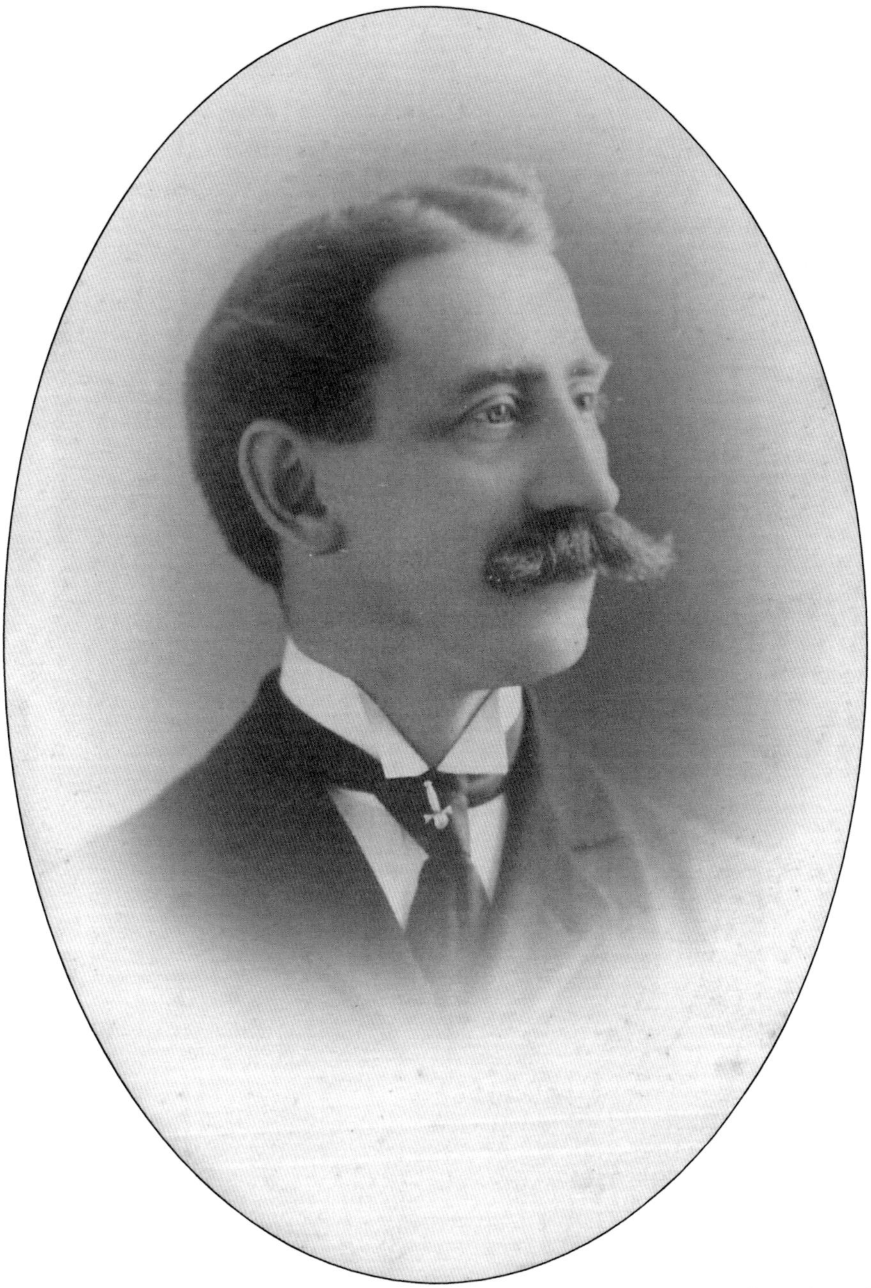

This portrait of Stanislas St. Onge was taken in 1885. He came to America from Canada with his family around 1860. At age 10, he worked in the Lowell cotton mills six days a week from 6 a.m. until 6 p.m., collecting pay of a dollar per week. At age 14, he worked as a handyman for J.L. Chalifoux, a local merchant. In a few years, St. Onge became head clerk, and in 1888, he was manager of a new store in Manchester, New Hampshire. Later, he was paid $65 a week to manage a store in Birmingham, Alabama. Good friends in Boston and New York suggested he ask for a $10-a-week raise; he did and was fired immediately. With his life savings of $2,000, he moved his family to Rhode Island and on August 18, 1894, established the Star Clothing House. (Courtesy of Gary St. Onge.)

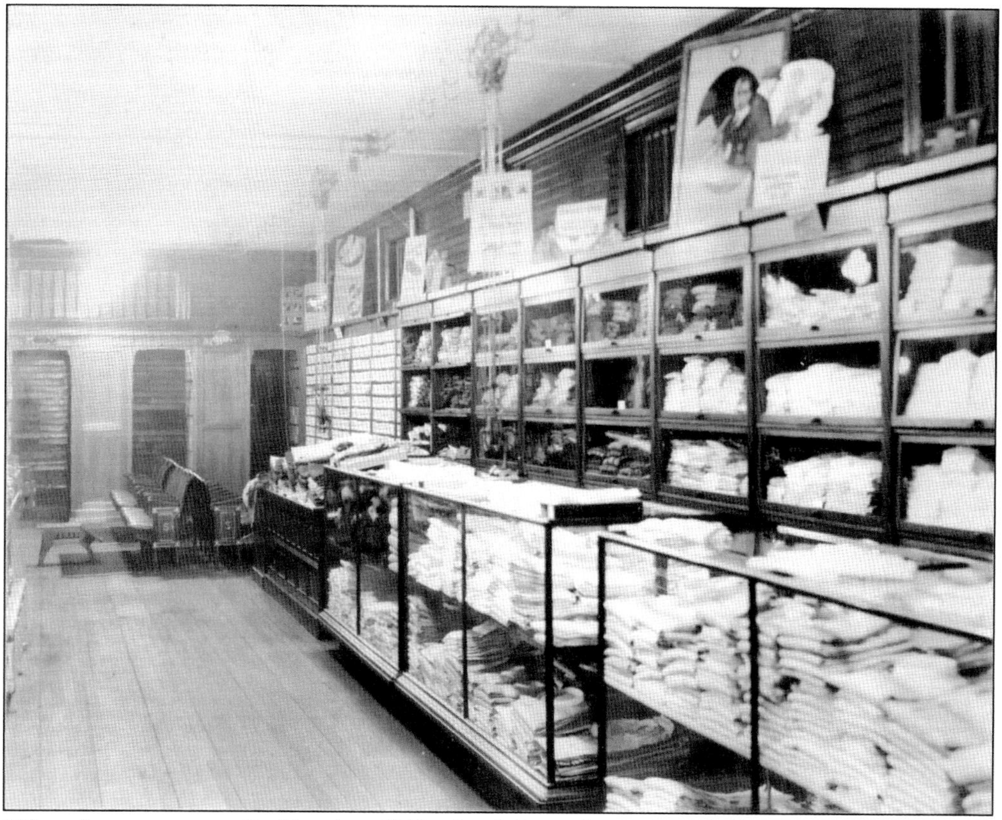

When the store next to St. Onge's at 45 Quidneck Street became available in 1898, he took it over and doubled his selling space. In 1906, he bought a building at 1223 Main Street. He completely remodeled it and moved the Star Clothing House there in 1907. Son Leo St. Onge Sr. took over the business in 1922. The photograph above, taken in 1926, shows the system of tracks on the ceiling that carried customers' money to the office. The photograph below, from the early 1930s, shows men's suits displayed behind glass doors. (Both, courtesy of Gary St. Onge.)

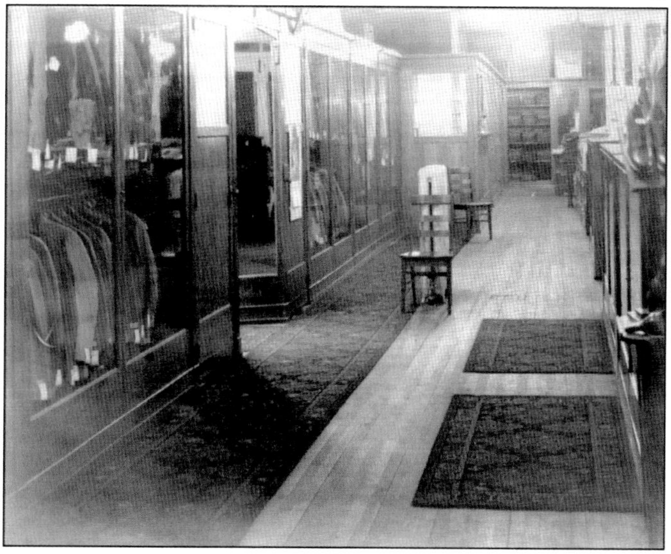

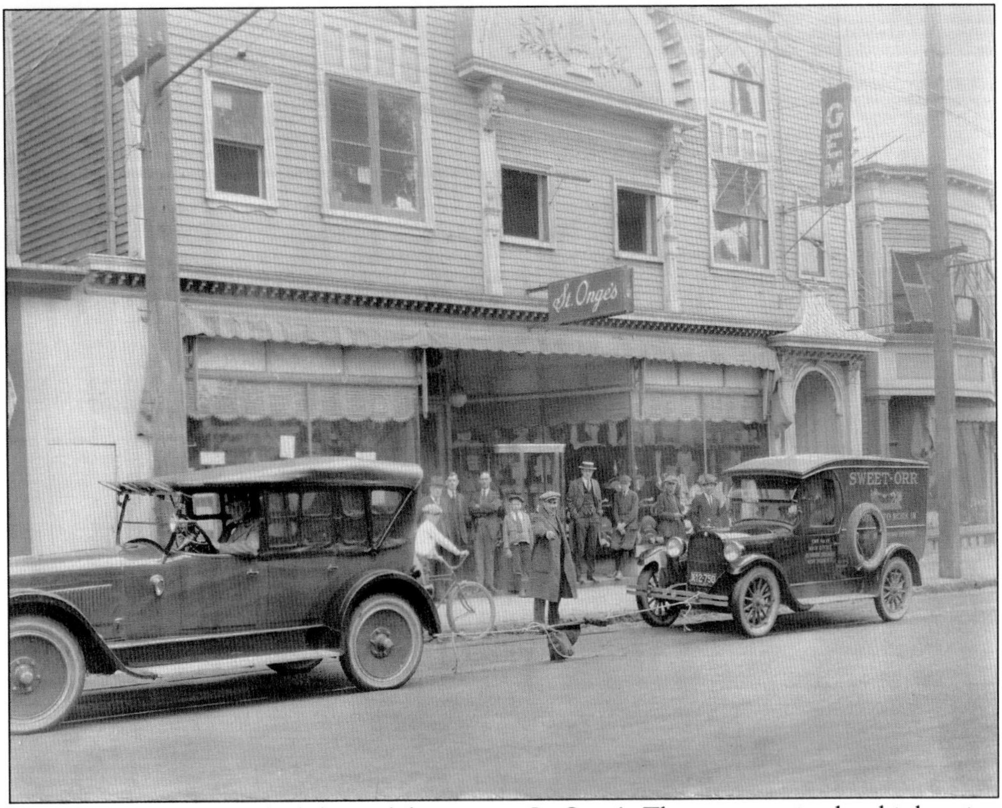

In 1922, Leo St. Onge Sr. had changed the name to St. Onge's. The store remained at this location at 1223 Main Street until 1967. The crowd in front of the store is watching St. Onge using a pair of Sweet-Orr workpants to tow the delivery truck, which had the logo, "Clothing to Work In," painted on the side. The promotional stunt demonstrated how durable Sweet-Orr work clothes were. The Gem Theatre was located above St. Onge's.

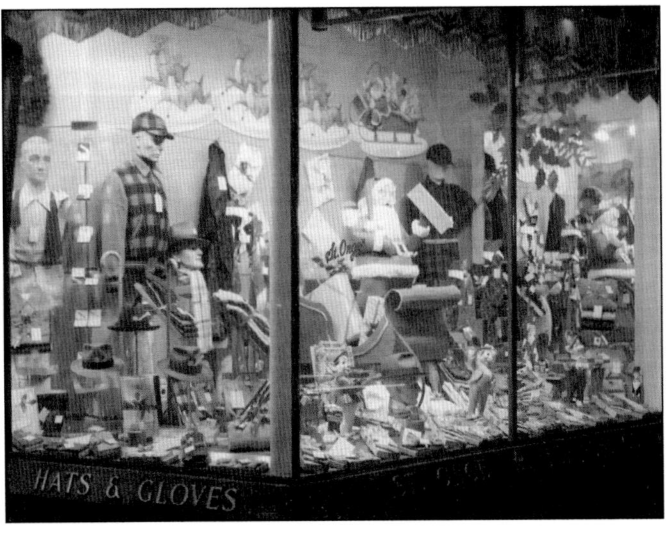

Taken during the Christmas season of 1955, this photograph brings back memories of how busy Arctic used to be. The following verses are from "Birthday of a King," written by Helen O. Larson in 1998 at age 87: "Stores are filled with gifts, and all kinds of toys / Everywhere you look, these are Christmas joys. And as the day is ending, and we put all things away / We must always remember, it was the Savior's birthday." (Courtesy of Gary St. Onge.)

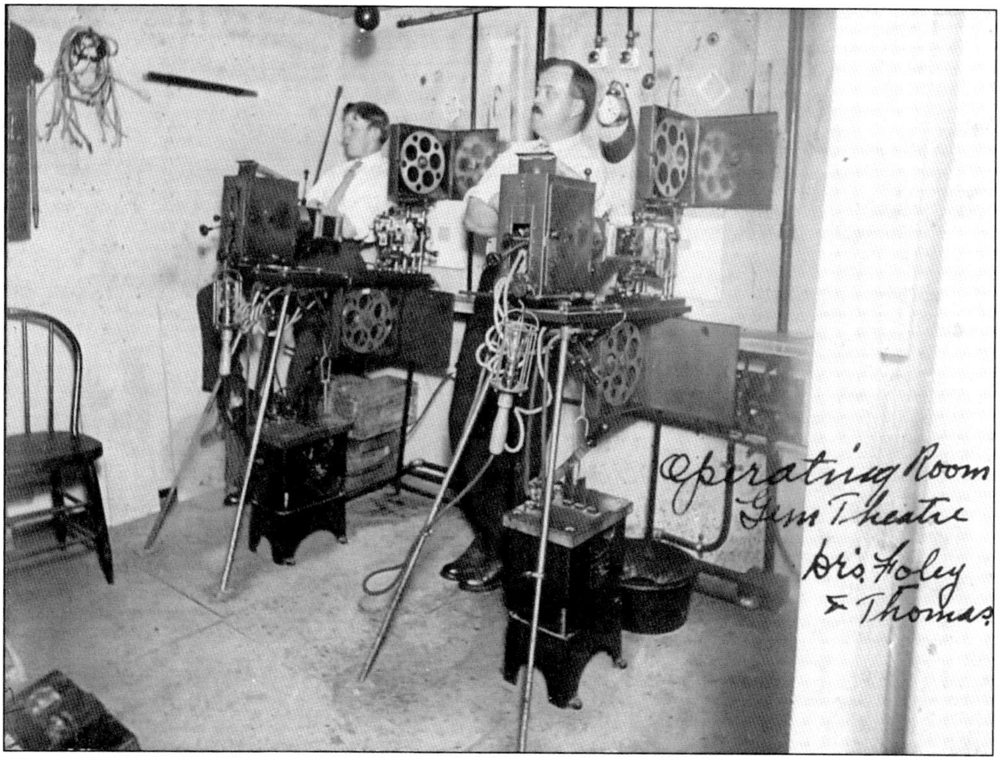

This is the projection room of the Gem Theatre, located over St. Onge's store. Operators Foley (right) and Thomas Dennigan are pictured with their projectors. Motion pictures used to come on two reels. When one reel was finished, they would turn on the second projector, hopefully without mishap or delay.

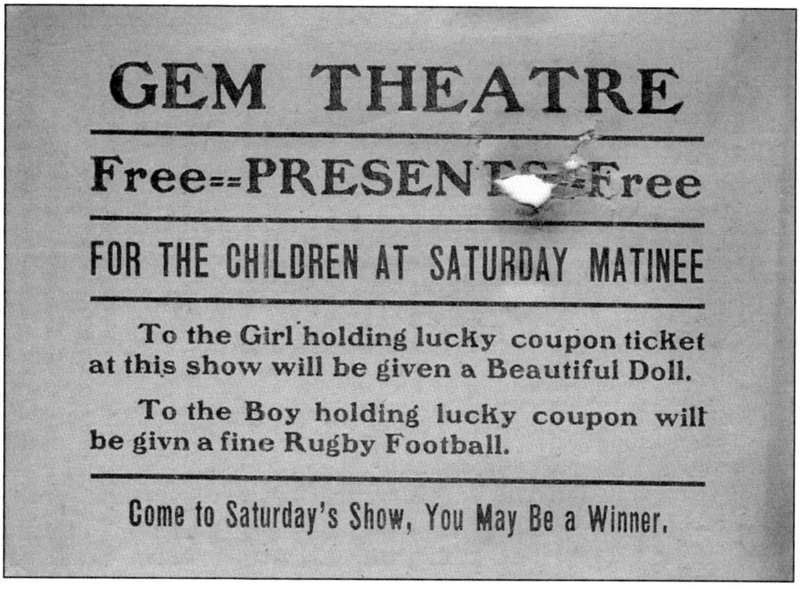

GEM THEATRE

Free==PRESENTS==Free

FOR THE CHILDREN AT SATURDAY MATINEE

To the Girl holding lucky coupon ticket at this show will be given a Beautiful Doll.

To the Boy holding lucky coupon will be givn a fine Rugby Football.

Come to Saturday's Show, You May Be a Winner.

To entice the children to attend the Saturday matinee, the Gem Theatre would from time to time give prizes to the girl or boy holding the winning ticket. (Courtesy of Gary St. Onge.)

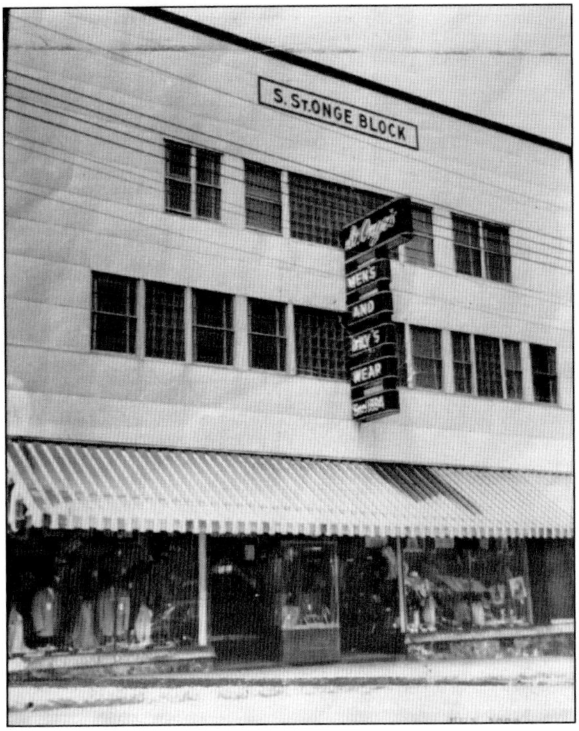

In 1953, Leo St. Onge Sr. turned over the business to his two sons, Leo Jr. and Paul. After Paul passed away in 1965, Leo Jr. continued the family tradition of expansion. When Sears moved out of Arctic to set up in the new Midland Mall (now known as the Rhode Island Mall), he saw an opportunity. On May 1, 1967, St. Onge moved into the old Sears building next door at 1227 Main Street and renamed it the S. St. Onge Block. (Courtesy of Gary St. Onge.)

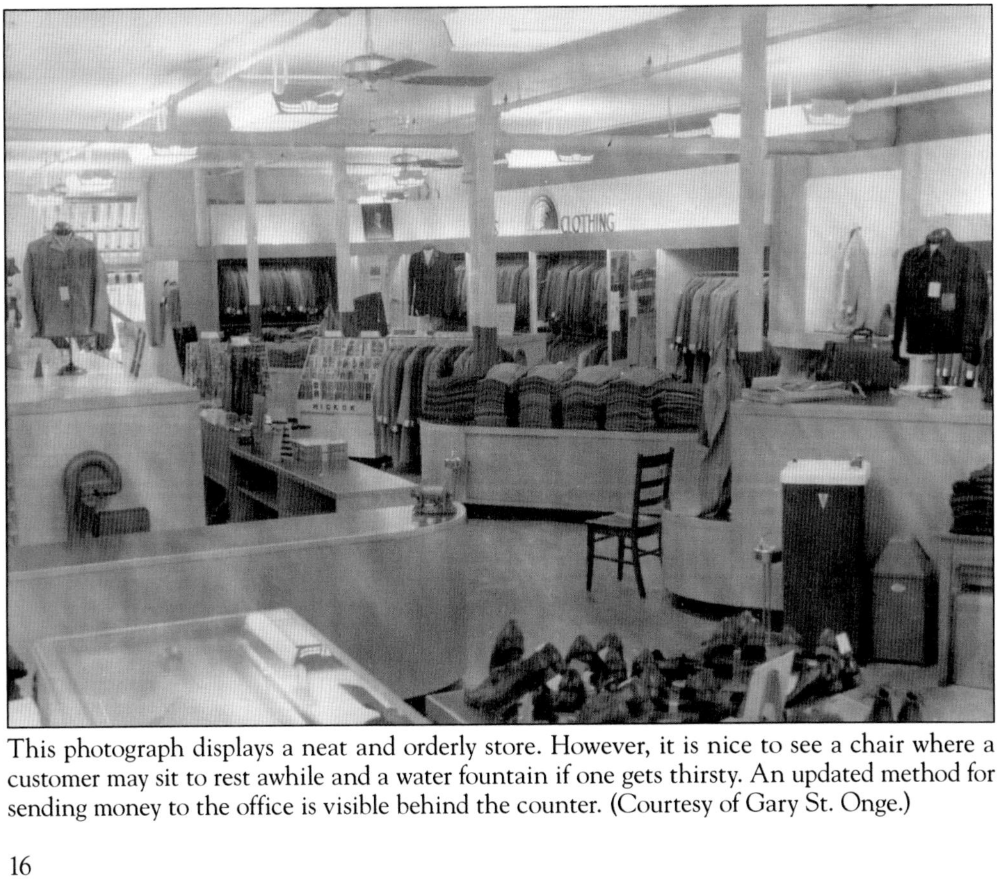

This photograph displays a neat and orderly store. However, it is nice to see a chair where a customer may sit to rest awhile and a water fountain if one gets thirsty. An updated method for sending money to the office is visible behind the counter. (Courtesy of Gary St. Onge.)

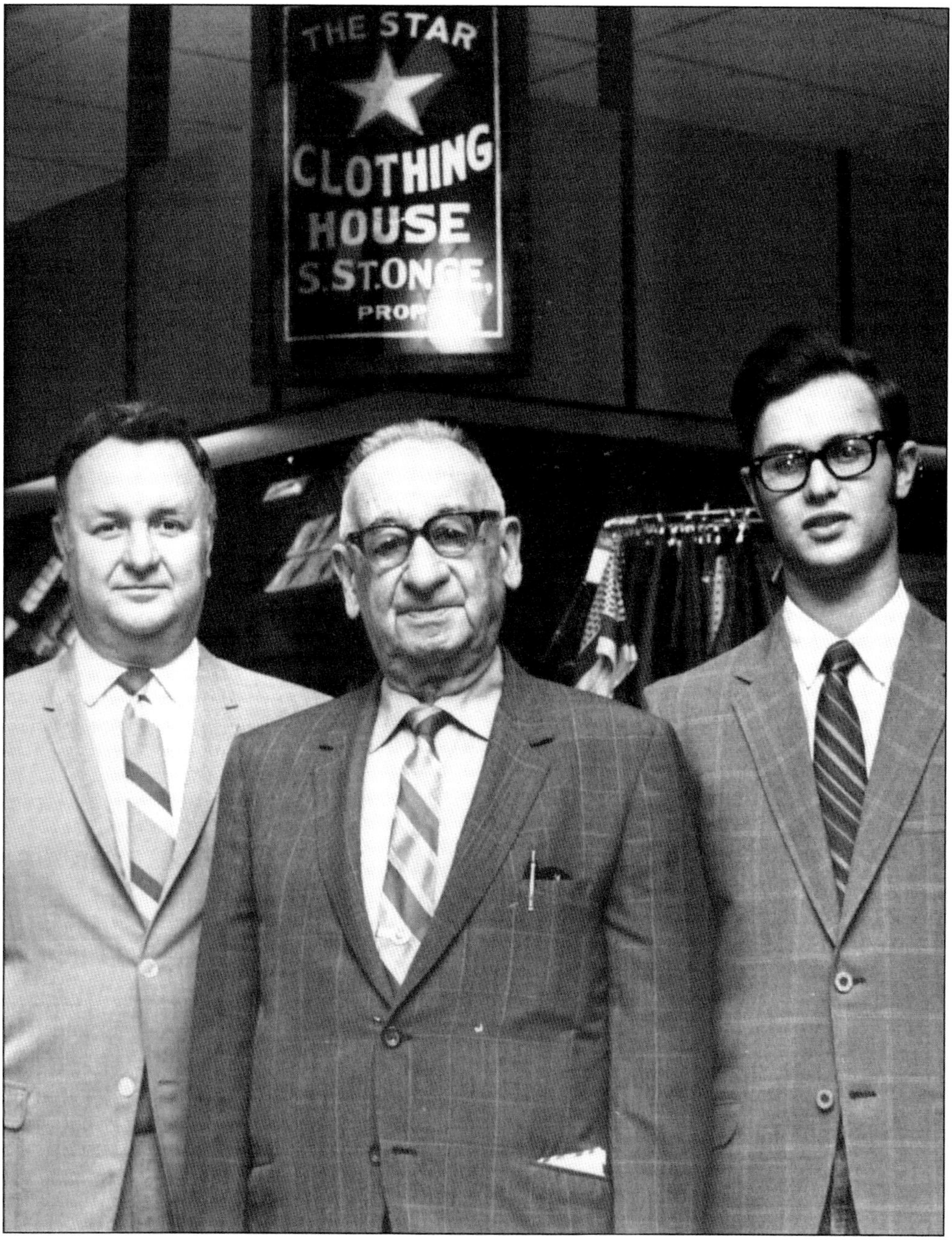

This photograph, taken on July 29, 1969, shows Leo St. Onge Sr. standing proudly in front of his father's (Stanislas St. Onge) original sign announcing the start of the Star Clothing House. To the left is son Leo Jr., and to the right is grandson Gary. In August 1972—just three years after this photograph was taken—a fire destroyed the building. Leo Jr. rebuilt and moved into a new and larger building on February 1, 1973. However, the fire was the beginning of the end. The St. Onge family business, which had been in Arctic for 87 years, is no longer; it closed on April 30, 1981. Even though Leo Sr. retired when he was 62, he visited the store every day until he was 90. (Courtesy of Gary St. Onge.)

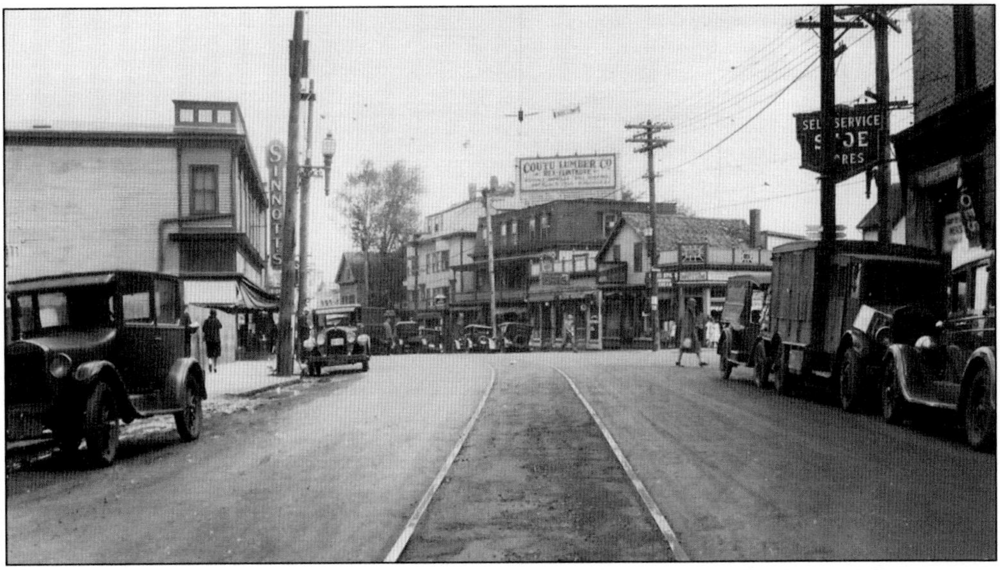

This 1929 photograph of Arctic Square was taken from Quidneck Street. The Sinnott's Department Store is on the left, and Self Service Shoes in the Majestic is on the right. Coutu Lumber Company had a large sign on the roof of an eatery. Suspended on wires above it is a small sign that reads, "FARE LIMIT." Riding the trolley beyond that point would cost extra. The following verses are from "The Man on the Bench" by Helen O. Larson: "He said the girl he was to marry, was killed by an auto one night / Now he would never see his sweetheart, dressed in bridal white. I said I am sorry, it's so hard to take I know / And we don't always understand, why some things have to be so." The bench was located right next to the Majestic.

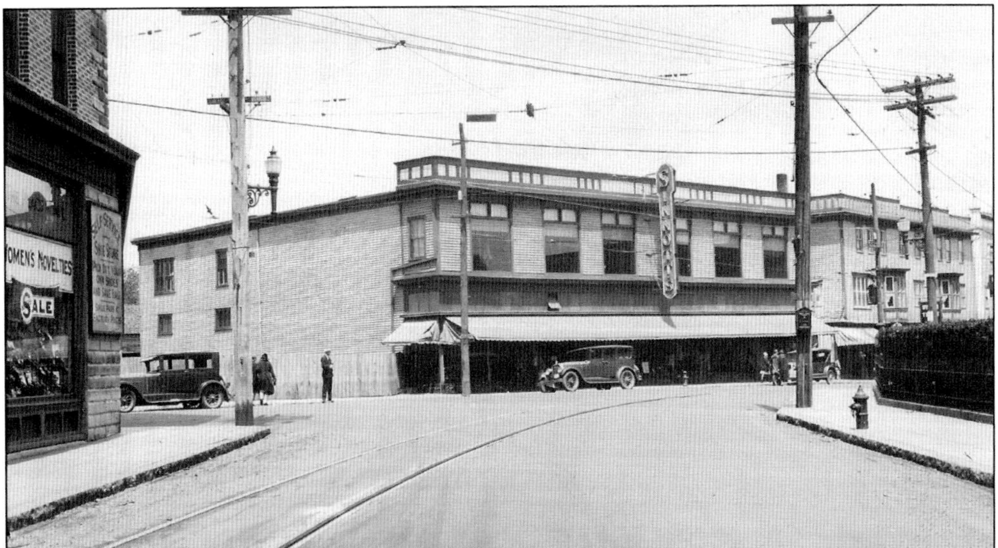

This is the view one would see in 1930 traveling into Arctic Square from Centreville on Main Street. The Majestic building is on the left with Self Service Shoes on the corner. The Sinnott building (center) was constructed in 1889 and enlarged in 1897. Note the old-style streetlights. The following verse is from "Is Arctic Dying" by Helen O. Larson: "I walked past Service Shoe store, where my shoes I used to buy / There was a lump in my throat, and I began to cry."

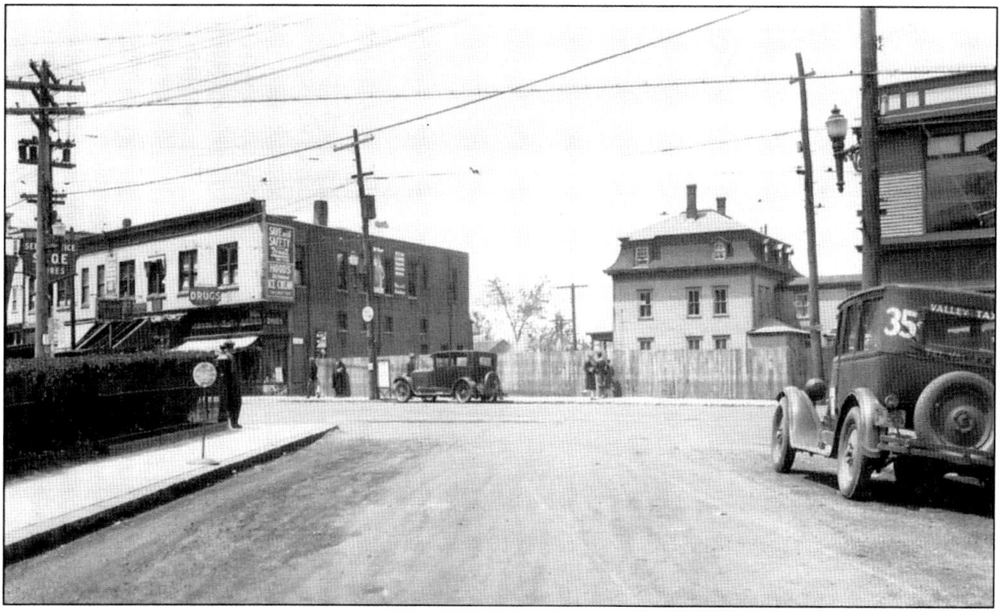

Taken in 1930, this view of Arctic Square shows the J.V. Smith Rexall Drug Store in the building on the left. The same building appears in the photograph at the bottom of page 10. The Union Trust Company built a bank branch in the empty lot behind the parked car and fence. The Valley Taxi Stand is on the right. The license plate was P-826, and the fair was a whopping 35¢.

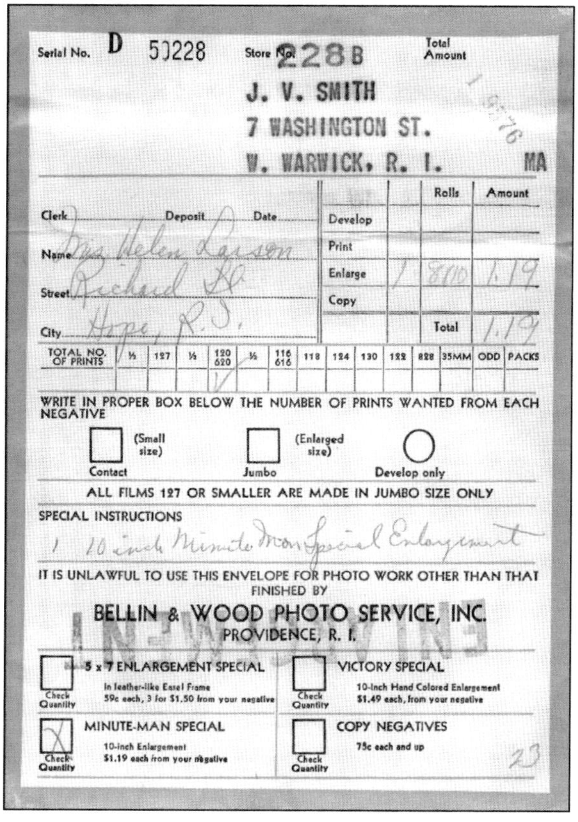

Serial No. D 5J228 Store No. 228 B Total Amount

J. V. SMITH
7 WASHINGTON ST.
W. WARWICK, R. I. MA

Clerk Deposit Date
Name Mrs Helen Larson
Street Richard St
City Hope, R.I.

		Rolls	Amount
Develop			
Print			
Enlarge	1	800	1.19
Copy			
		Total	1.19

TOTAL NO. OF PRINTS | ½ | 127 | ½ | 120 620 | ½ | 116 616 | 118 | 124 | 130 | 122 | 828 | 35MM | ODD | PACKS

WRITE IN PROPER BOX BELOW THE NUMBER OF PRINTS WANTED FROM EACH NEGATIVE

Contact (Small size) Jumbo (Enlarged size) Develop only

ALL FILMS 127 OR SMALLER ARE MADE IN JUMBO SIZE ONLY

SPECIAL INSTRUCTIONS
1 10 inch Minute Man Special Enlargement

IT IS UNLAWFUL TO USE THIS ENVELOPE FOR PHOTO WORK OTHER THAN THAT FINISHED BY

BELLIN & WOOD PHOTO SERVICE, INC.
PROVIDENCE, R. I.

Check Quantity — 5 x 7 ENLARGEMENT SPECIAL — In leather-like Easel Frame 59c each, 3 for $1.50 from your negative

Check Quantity — VICTORY SPECIAL — 10-Inch Hand Colored Enlargement $1.49 each, from your negative

Check Quantity — X — MINUTE-MAN SPECIAL — 10-inch Enlargement $1.19 each from your negative

Check Quantity — COPY NEGATIVES — 75c each and up

Arctic residents used to bring their film to J.V. Smith to have it developed. This is what Helen Larson did when she wanted to get a 10-inch Minute Man Special enlargement, for which she paid $1.19. J.V. Smith's would then send it out to the Bellin & Wood Photo Service, and hopefully, the photograph would come back in about a week. The following verse is from "Is Arctic Dying" by Helen O. Larson: "I passed J.V. Smith's, where cards I used to buy / What's happening to this old town, and I drew a deep sigh." (Author's collection.)

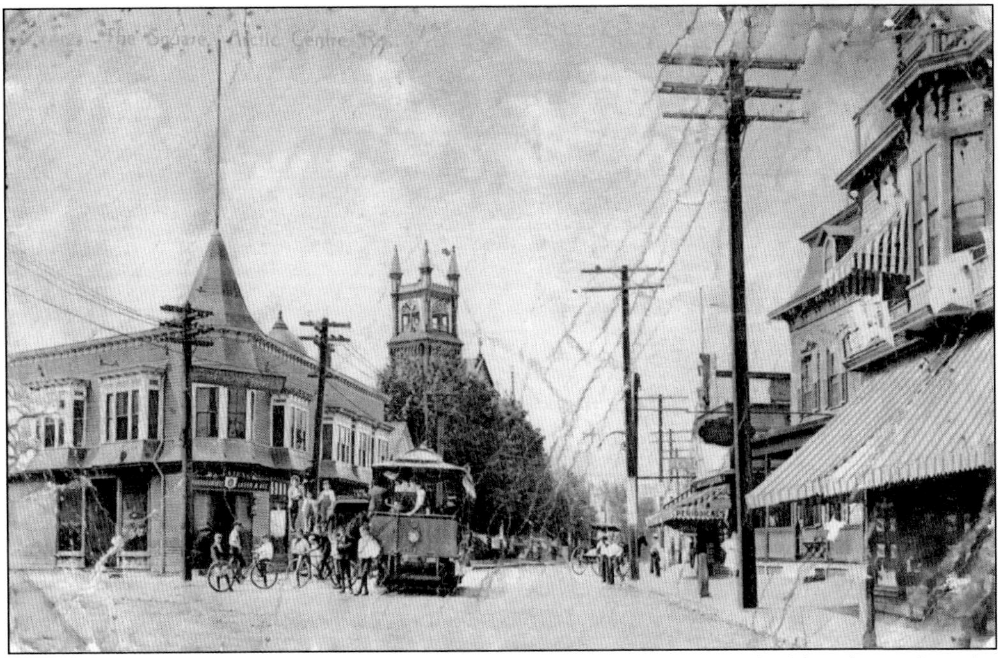

This postcard is a view of the square in the late 1800s. It shows the first building located on the corner of Quidneck and Main Streets. The sign just below the roofline reads: "Arctic Centre, Bowling and Pool Rooms," and the sign above the door advertises Narragansett Lager Beer. The tower of the first St. John's Church can be seen in the distance.

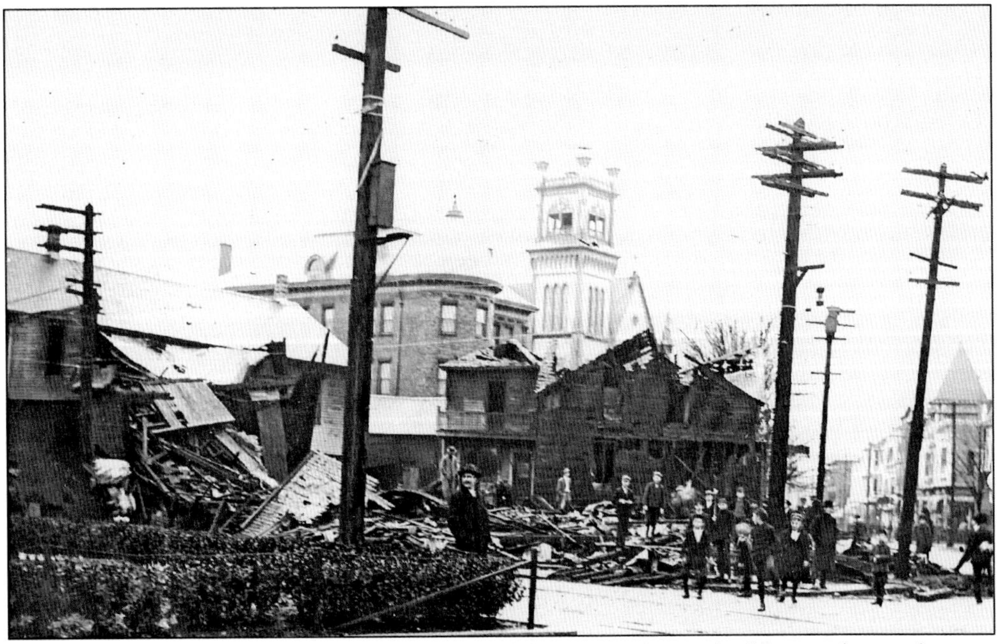

On the night of November 3, 1900, fire consumed the Arctic Centre building, reducing the two-story structure to ashes. Joseph Archambault, the owner, estimated his losses at $17,000. The man with the top hat is Fred Proulx. He was the bartender at the Hotel Warwick, located across the street and visible in the photograph on the bottom of page 10.

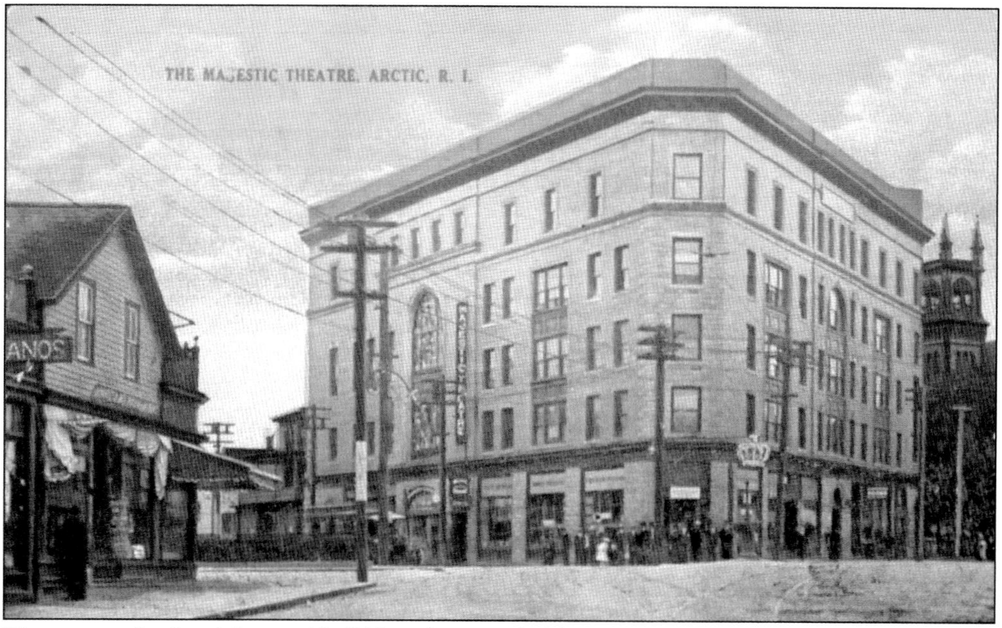

This postcard is dated August 18, 1919, and was mailed from Arctic to Norwich, Connecticut. After the fire of November 3, Archambault was asked what he was going to do. It is said that he replied, "I'm going to build the biggest building in western Rhode Island. One that fire will never destroy. It's going to be a skyscraper." He constructed the new five-story building using brick, concrete, and steel girders. He named it the Majestic, as it had risen majestically out of the ashes.

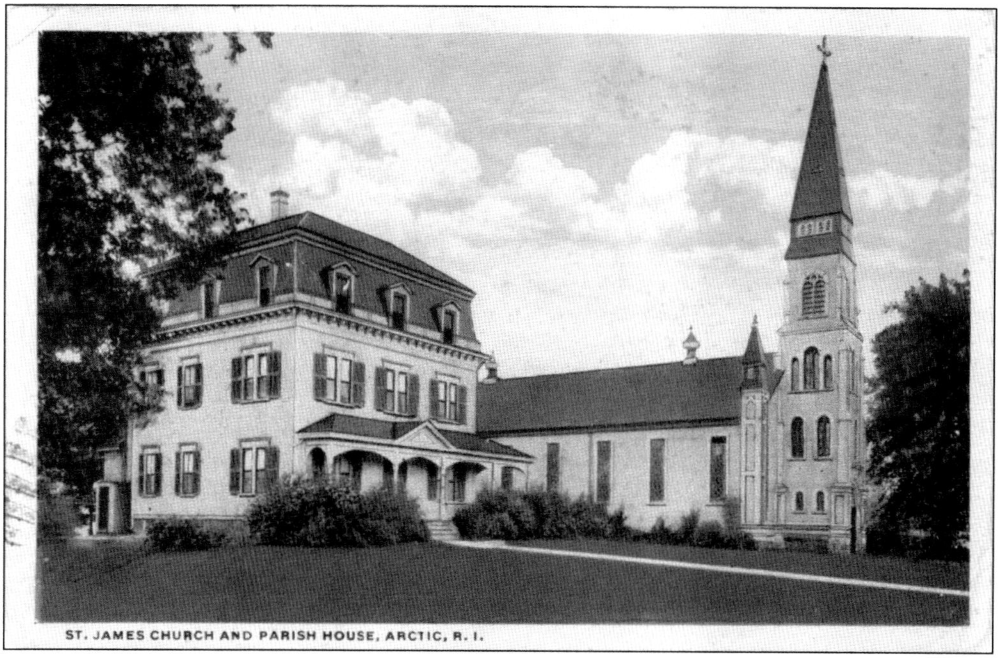

This postcard was mailed in February 1922. It shows the first St. James Church, built in 1889, and the parish house, which were opposite the Majestic building. The original church was leveled in 1959, and a second was built in 1960. The St. James congregation joined St. John's on September 13, 2003, and the vacant church was demolished in 2006. (Courtesy of Lawrence G. Soucy.)

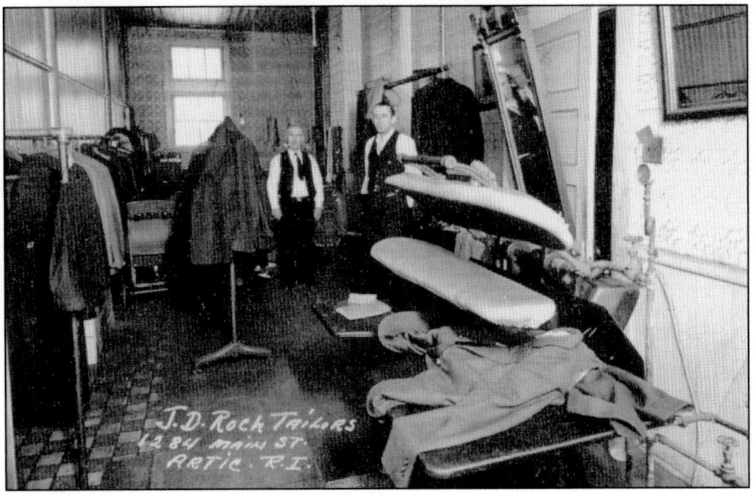

Joseph D. Roch Sr. (left) owned a tailor shop at 1284 Main Street next to the Majestic building. Joseph Jr. (right) would go to the bowling alley at the Majestic on his lunchtime to bowl a game. Notice his business attire in the picture below, which was taken the same day. (Courtesy of J. Denis Roch.)

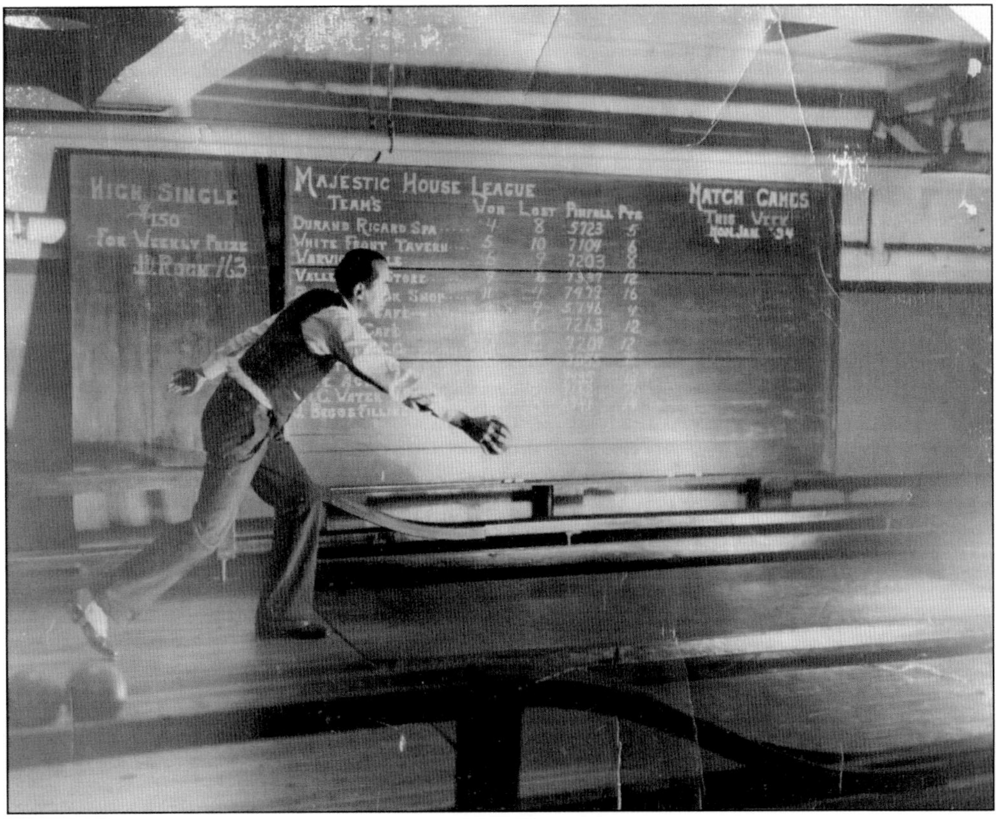

This bowling alley was located in the basement of the Majestic. Joseph D. Roch (above) won the weekly prize of $1.50 when he bowled the high single of 163 in January 1934. The teams listed on the board were Durand Ricard's Spa, White Front Tavern, Warwick Mills, Valley Farm Store, Roch Tailor Shop, Frank's Café, Ruzzo's Café, Crompton Community Club, Scotty's Five, Five Aces, Warwick and Coventry Water Co., and J. Begos Filling Station. (Courtesy of J. Denis Roch.)

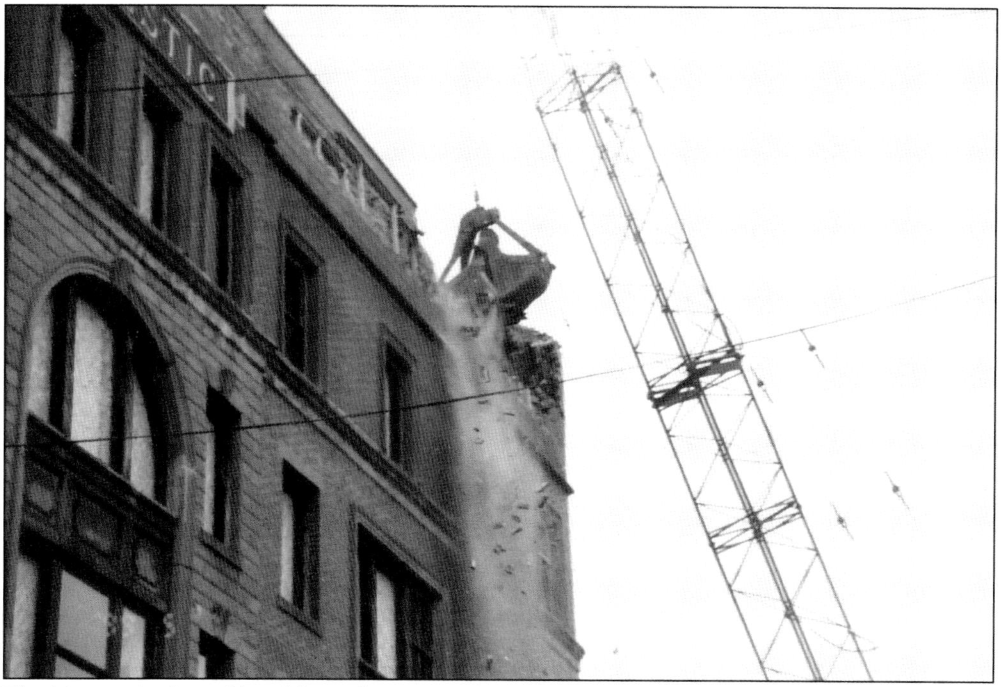

The Majestic had stood humbly on the corner of Main and Washington Streets since 1901. However, this day, May 8, 1999, marks the end as the Coventry Building and Wrecking Company's crane takes a bite out of the Majestic's top corner. (Courtesy of Gerard J. Heroux.)

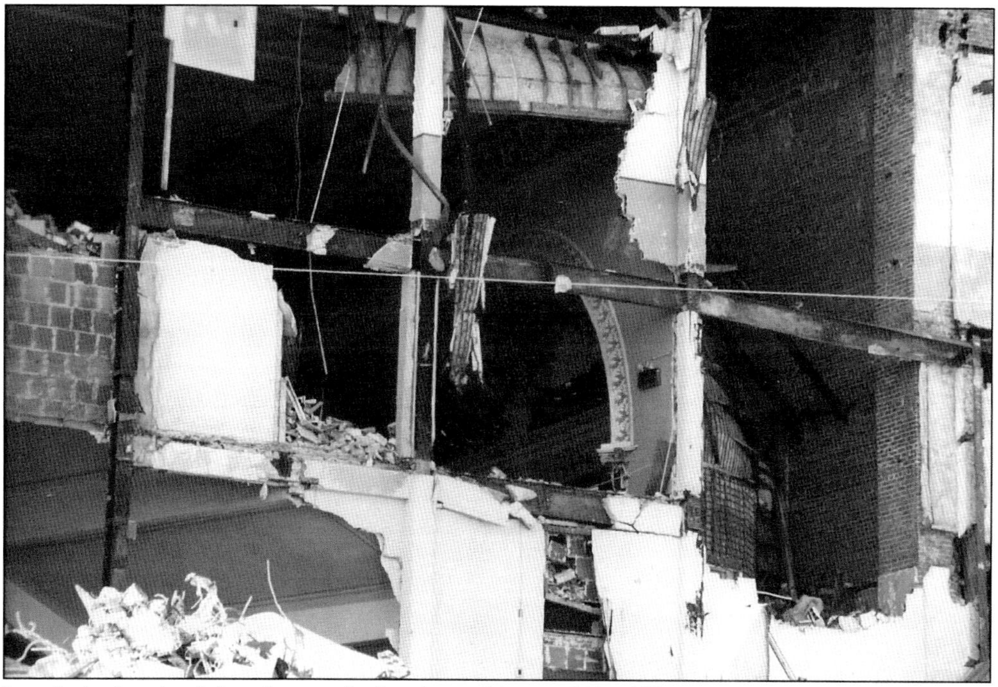

Joseph Archambault kept his word when he said he would build his Majestic with brick, concrete, and steel, as this photograph attests. Part of the Majestic Theatre, which consumed the inner second, third, and fourth stories can be seen in this view. (Courtesy of Gerard Tellier Jr.)

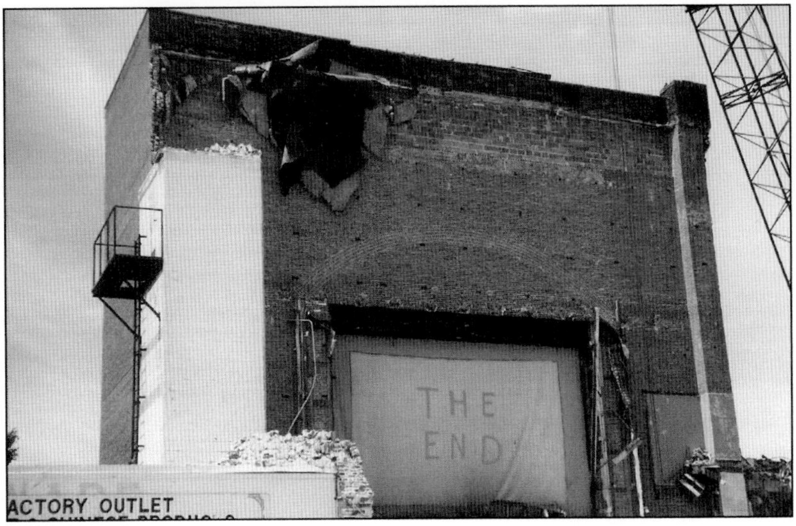

This photograph shows one end of the building still standing a bit defiantly on May 9, 1999. Someone has nailed a sheet on the stage wall that announces the end of an era. (Courtesy of Gerard Heroux.)

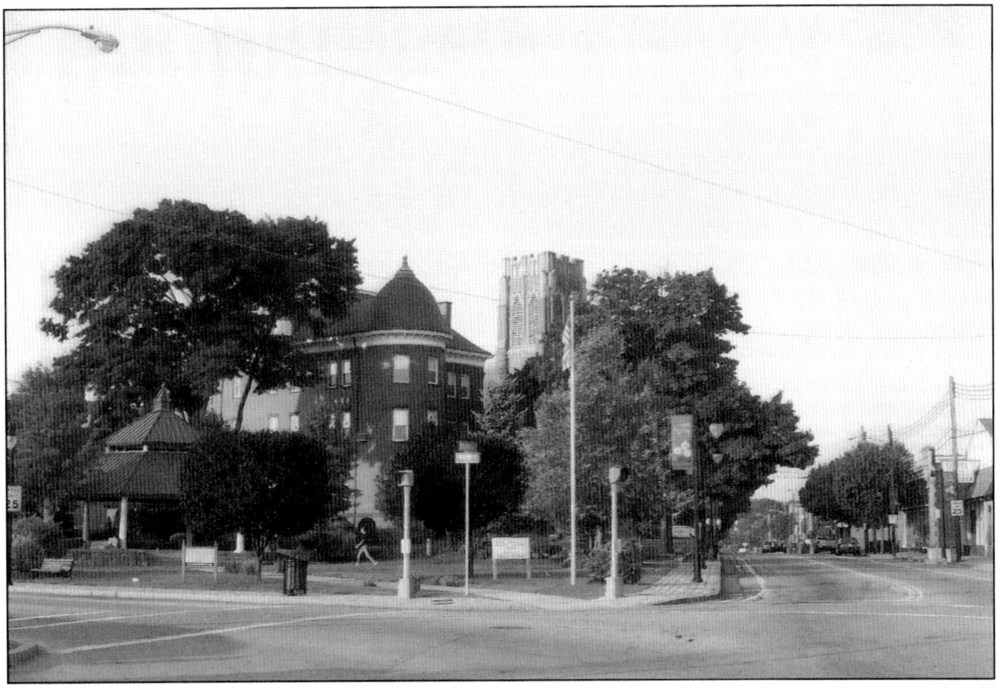

The grand Majestic building is no more. It has been replaced by this park. Joseph Archambault was right when he said fire would never destroy his new building. However, he did not foresee this happening. The second St. John's Church tower stands lonely, now missing its soaring companion beyond the trees in this photograph taken on August 31, 2010. The following verses are from "Is Arctic Dying" by Helen O. Larson: "My heart was so sad, as I walked down Main Street one day / The town looked deserted, so I brushed the tears away / Is the shopping centre called Arctic, going to die all the way / I hope someone does something, so this beloved centre can stay." (Author's collection.)

This advertisement was in a booklet commemorating West Warwick's Golden Jubilee in 1963. The author's father bought all the windows and doors for the home he was building in Hope at the lumber company. Champlin's gave him the carpenter's apron below in 1942. Champlin Lumber Company is no longer, but the apron lives on after 68 years. This was during a time when residents had to dial VA-1 to make a telephone call. Notice the date at right; Champlin's had been established longer than the town of West Warwick. (Below, author's collection.)

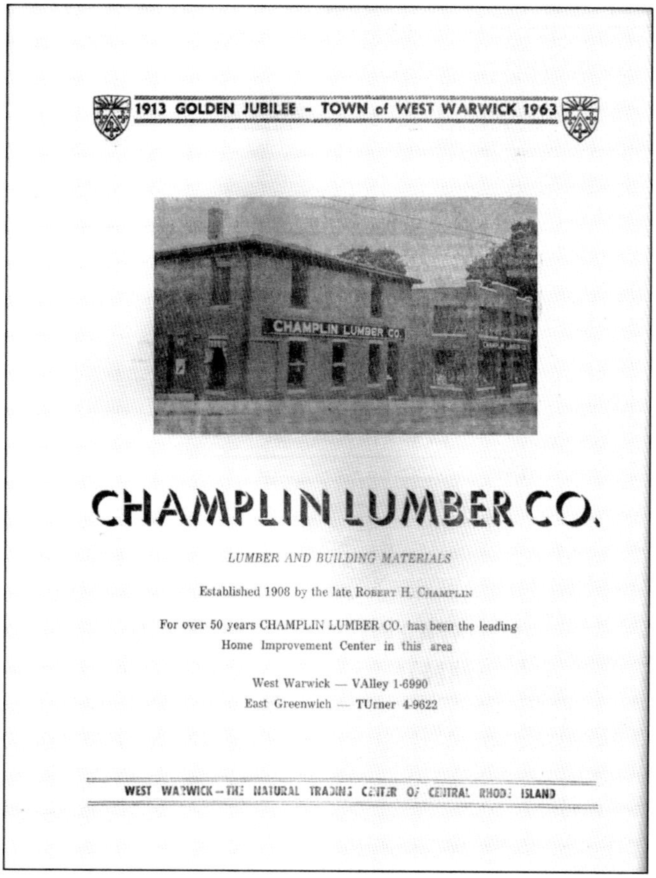

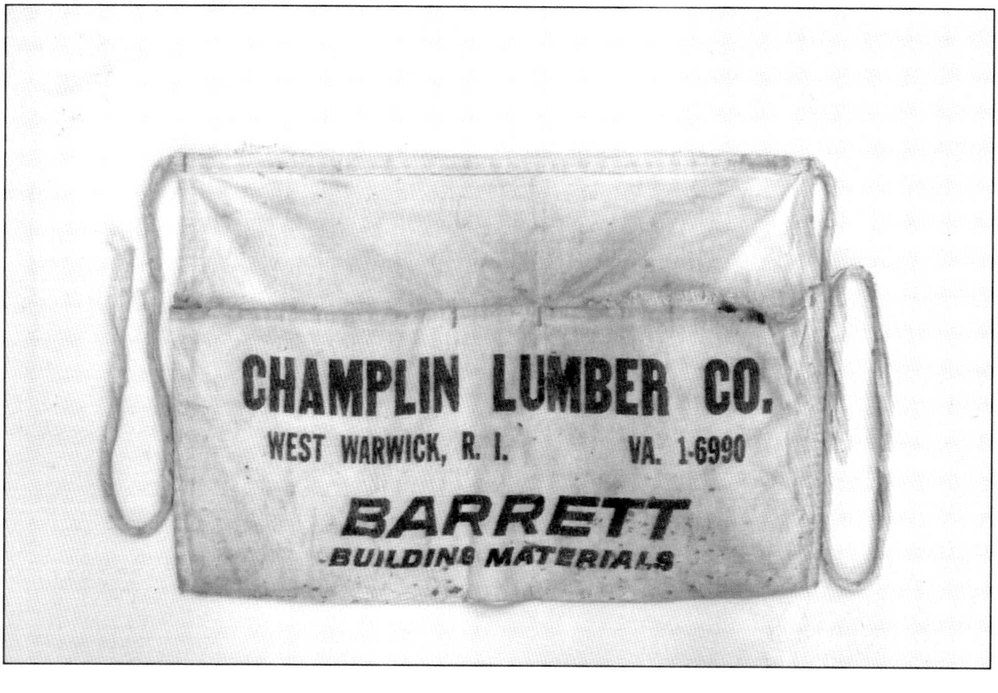

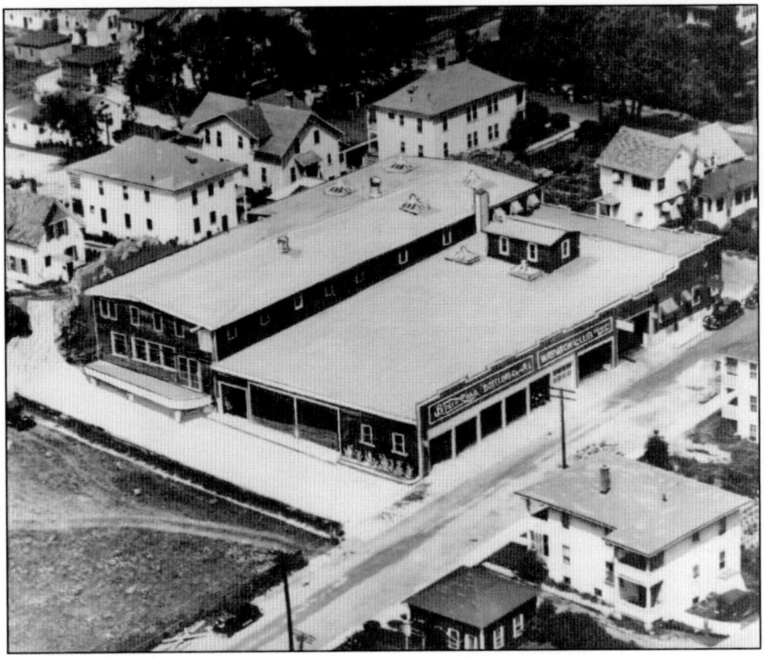

Pepsi-Cola Bottling Company of Rhode Island and Warwick Bottling Works were located in this facility at 108 Pond Street in the back of Arctic. Pepsi-Cola began in 1896; Warwick Club Ginger Ale Company began in 1930.

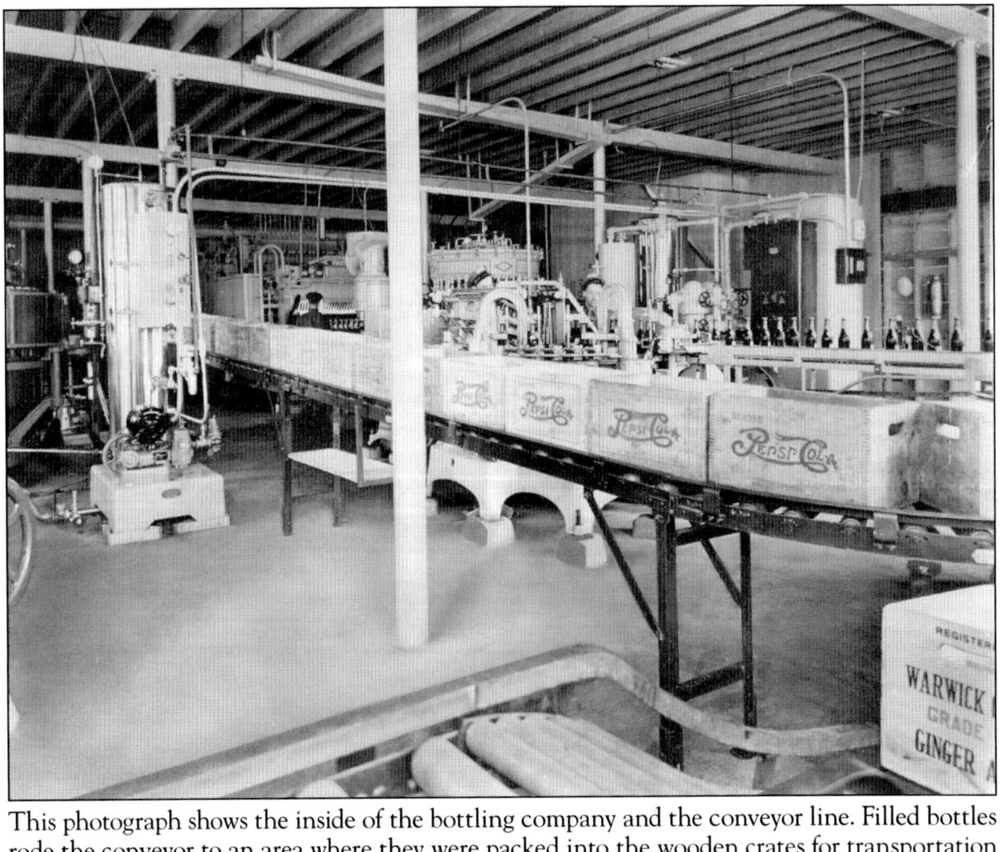

This photograph shows the inside of the bottling company and the conveyor line. Filled bottles rode the conveyor to an area where they were packed into the wooden crates for transportation to the stores. In the lower right corner is a Warwick Club Ginger Ale crate.

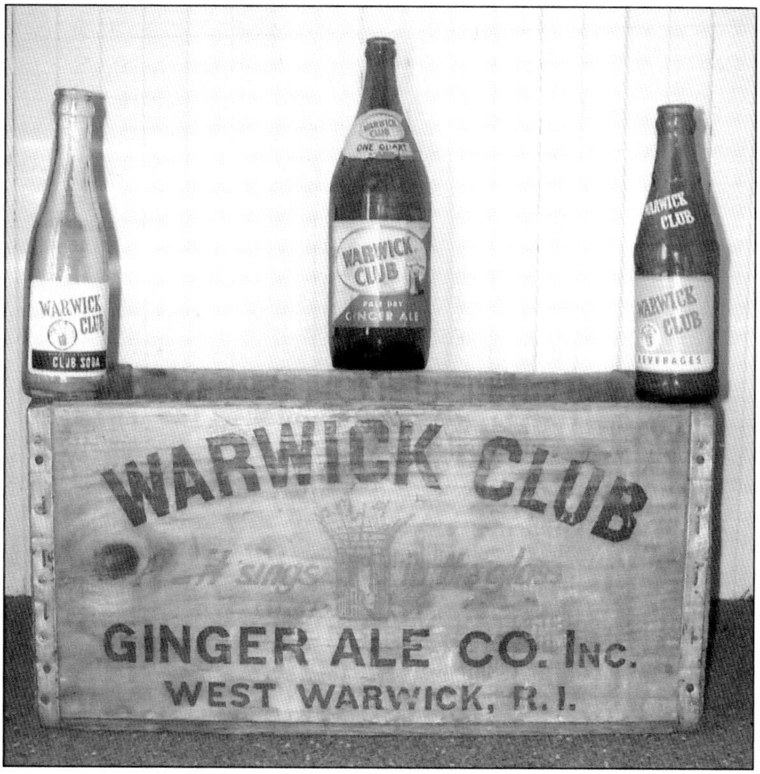

Friends Ernest "Kit" Archambault and Adolph "Skee" Jusczyk drove trucks for Lou Clark, owner of Warwick Club. They longed to partner and go into business for themselves, and in 1953, they did. They named their company the Pawtuxet Valley Bus Lines (seen on page 36). (Author's collection.)

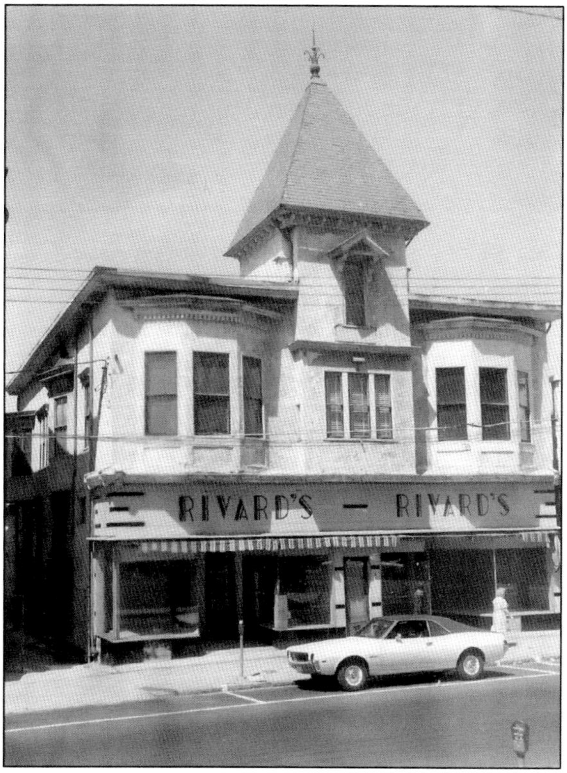

Stanislas St. Onge started the Star Clothing House at 43 Quidneck Street in 1894. He later expanded to 45 Quidneck Street next door. The hitching posts in the photographs on pages 10 and 11 have been replaced with parking meters for cars. This photograph was taken in August 1968. The following verse is from "Is Arctic Dying" by Helen O. Larson: "Another store closed, a while ago / It was Rivard's Clothing store, Mr. Rivard always said a cheery hello."

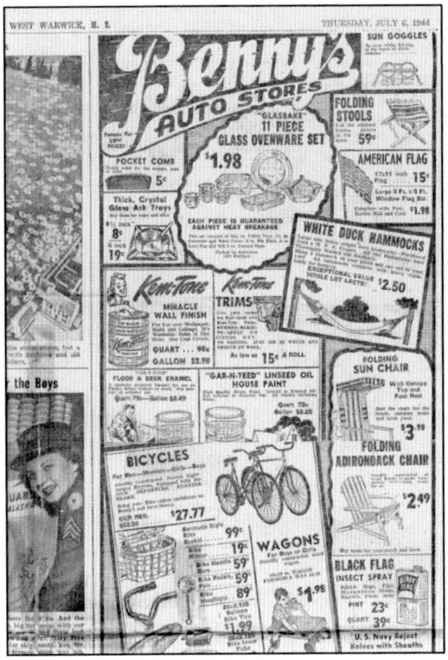

This ad appeared in the *Pawtuxet Valley Daily Times* on Thursday, July 6, 1944. A bicycle was discounted from the regular price of $32.50 to a sale price of $27.77. A gallon of Kem-Tone paint cost $2.98. A pocket comb was 5¢, an ashtray was just 8¢, and an 11-piece glass ovenware set cost $1.98. A popular item during the war was the American flag; a 17-by-11-inch flag cost 15¢, and a large three-by-five-foot window flag set—complete with the pole, holder, ball, and cord needed for mounting—was $1.98. The following verse is from "Is Arctic Dying" by Helen O. Larson: "I walked past Benny's, where my husband used to go / Why are they all moving out, it shouldn't be so." (Author's collection.)

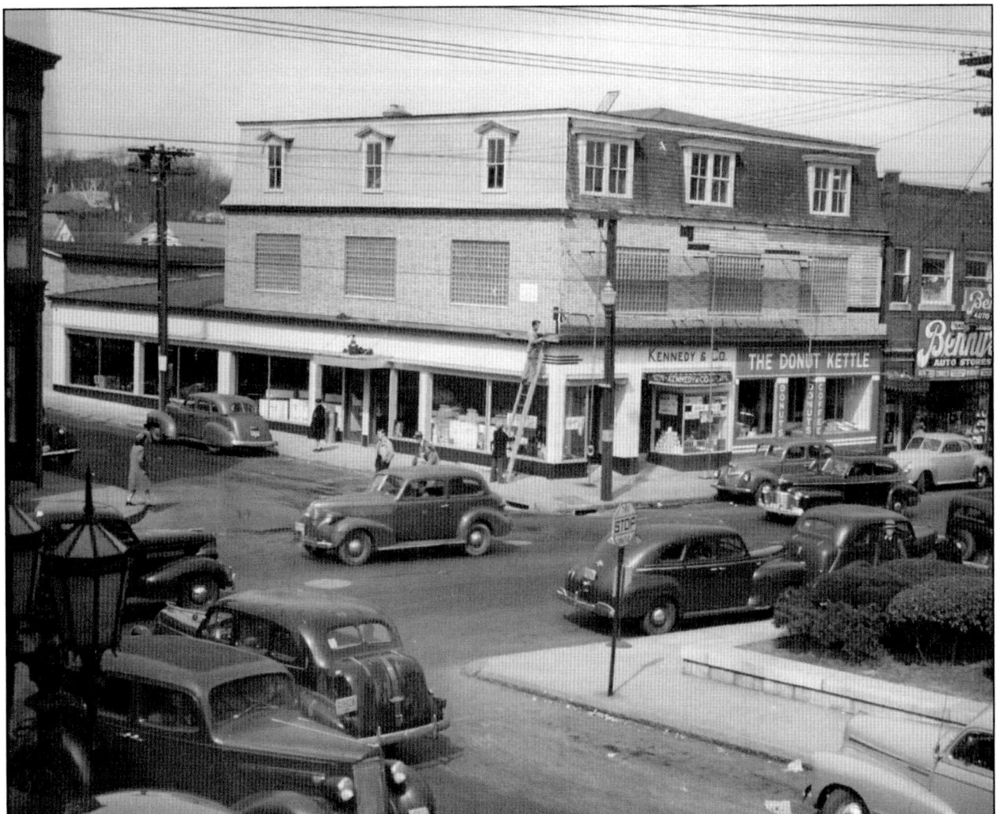

This photograph from the late 1940s gives a view of Main Street, Cursin Street, and Bank Street before it became one way. Kennedy's, the Donut Kettle, and Benny's Auto Store were at 1213 Main Street, across from the Centreville Bank building.

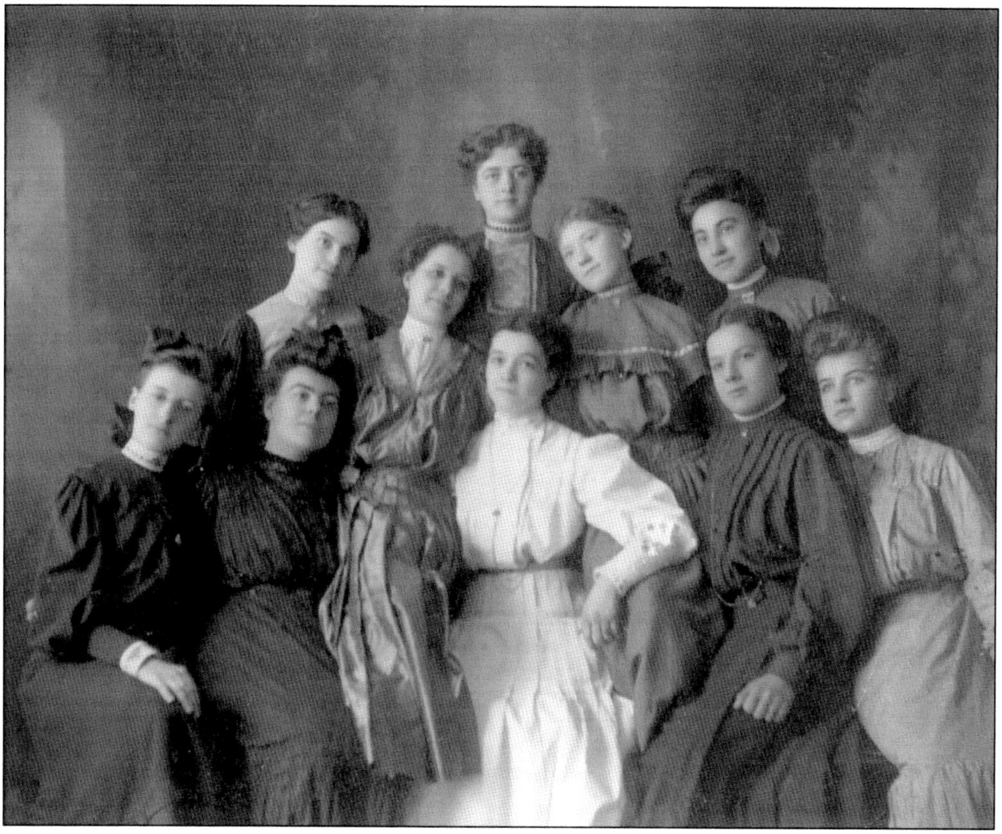

The photograph above of the Bedard's Clothing Store sales girls was taken in 1906. The clothier was located next to where Donat Archambault erected the J.J. Newbury building on Quidneck Street in 1922. From left to right are (first row) Catherine Brodeur, Hectorine Chenevert, Marie Anne Bacon, Florida Tellier, Diana Lincourt, and Alice Frenette; (standing in second row) Ernestine Tellier, Antoinette Sevigny, Miss Desmarais, and Cordelia Fontaine. Between 1865 and 1900, a great number of French Canadians immigrated to the United States and settled in Arctic. Pierre Bedard lost so much of his Canadian clientele that he decided to follow them and subsequently opened his clothing business in Arctic. Ernestine Tellier married Joseph Smith, the druggist at J.V. Smith Rexall Drug Store (seen on page 19). Diana Lincourt married Richard Hughes Sr. Their son, Richard Hughes Jr., is a contributor to this book. Pierre and his sales girls (below) pose for the camera on August 11, 1906, in front of his store.

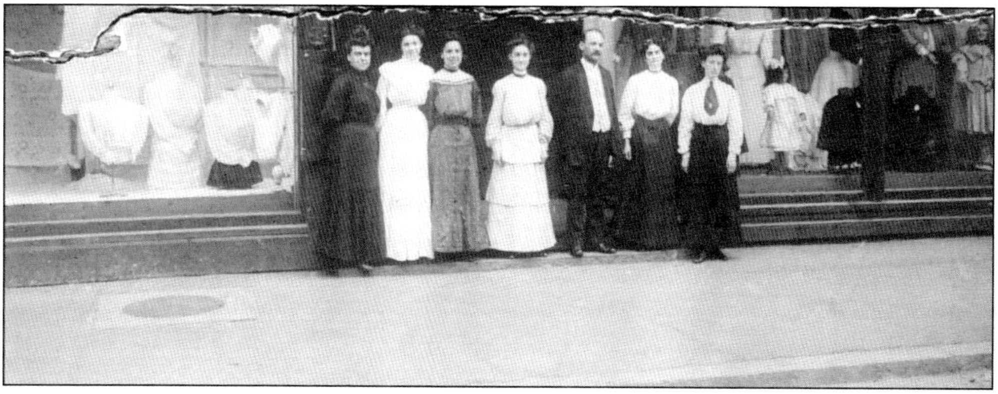

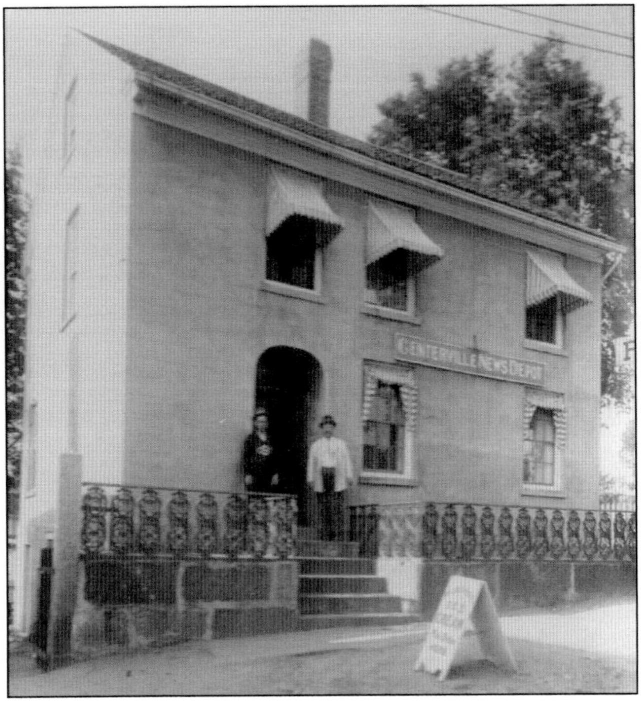

In June 1828, the Rhode Island General Assembly granted a charter to John Greene and Sylvester Knight to create the Centreville Bank of Warwick. In 1865, it was in the best interest of the bank to take out a charter to become the Centreville National Bank. To better meet the needs of its customers, the Centreville Savings Bank was incorporated in 1888; this allowed the bank to offer more services. The bank was located on Centreville Road between Christ the King Church and Bridal Avenue. When the bank moved out, the Centreville News Depot moved in. The man in the white coat is Frank Shippee. The sign states "ICE CREAM for sale here."

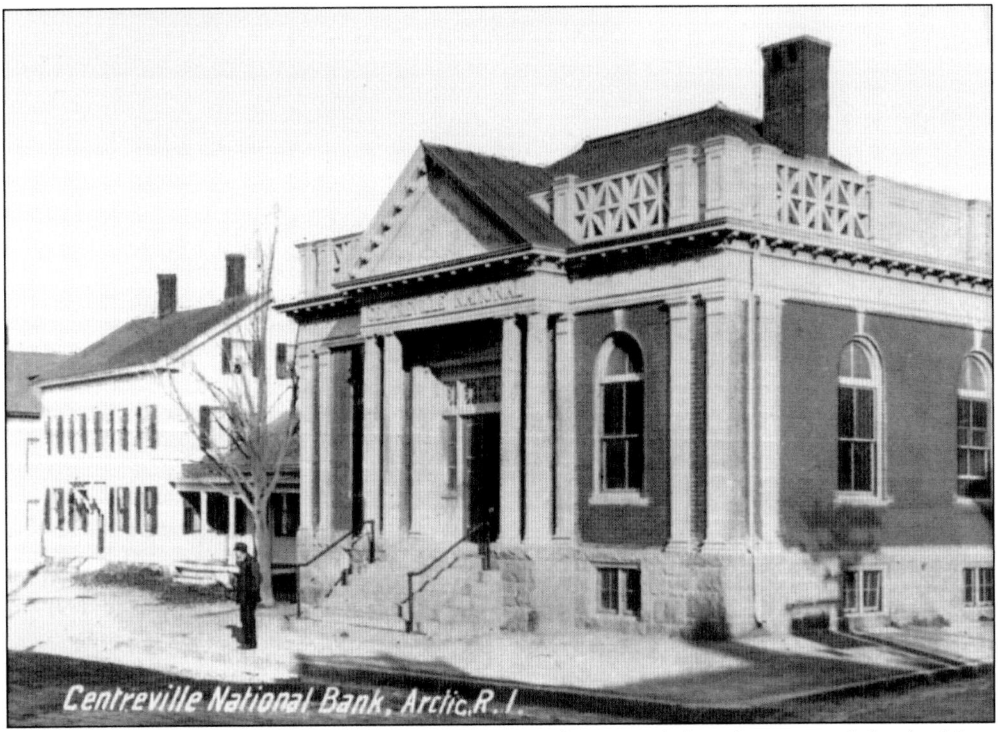

The Centreville National Bank's services were so well received that they erected this building in 1901 and relocated. The bank chose the corner of Main and Bank Streets in Arctic. When Main Street was widened in the 1920s, the building was demolished. The bank bought the house next door to create a lot spacious enough for a new, larger bank.

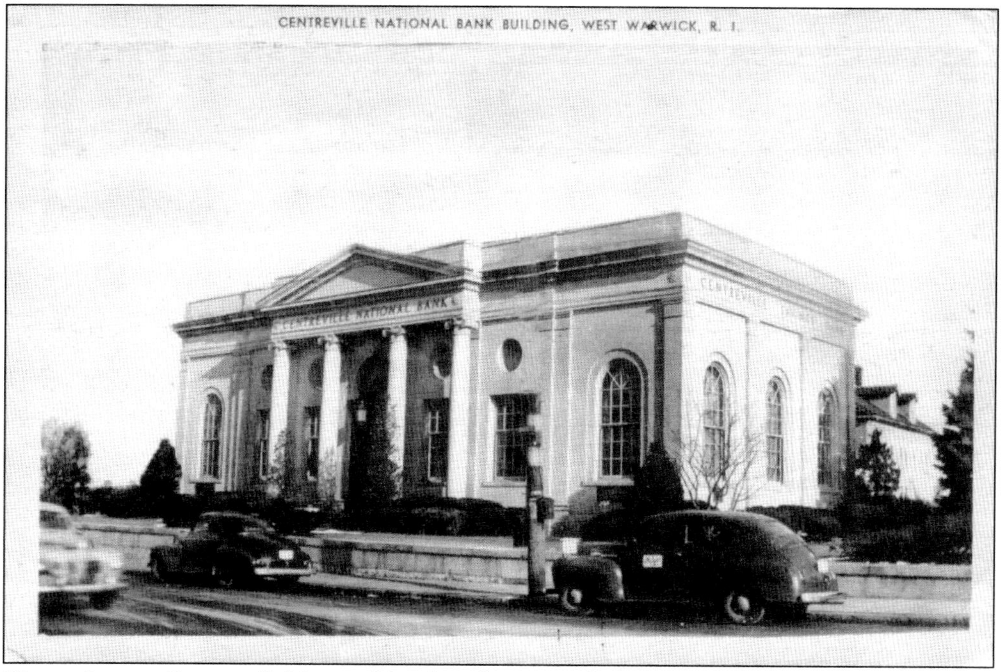

This is the new Centreville National Bank and Centreville Savings Bank constructed of Indiana limestone. It was dedicated on October 6, 1928. During the planning and design of the building, the decision was made to set it back from the road. This postcard was mailed to New Hampshire in 1953.

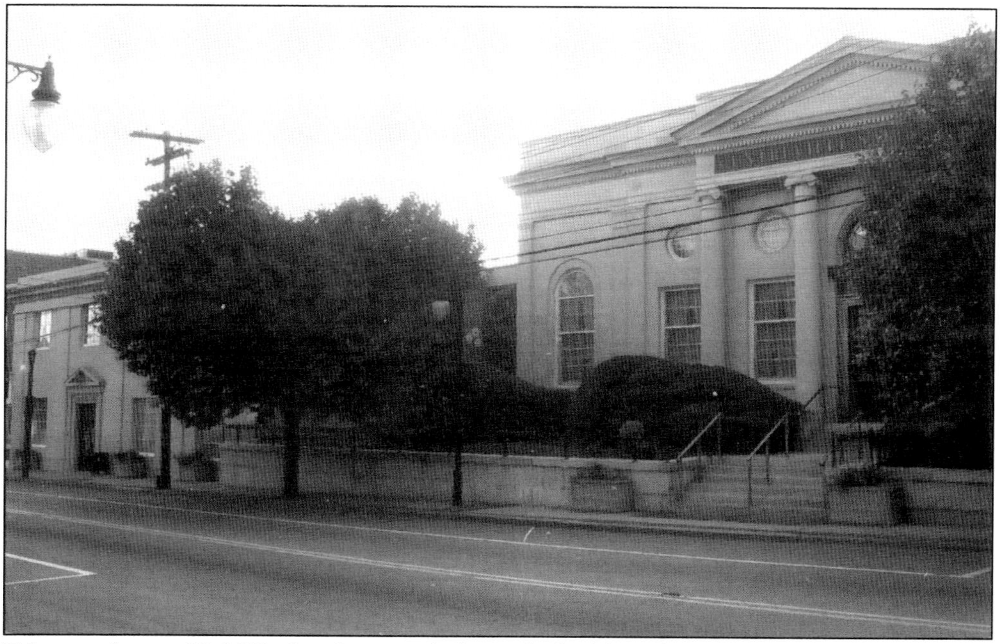

Taken on August 30, 2010, this photograph shows the building that was added in the 1950s (left). All services are available at this street-level branch, which opened in November 1988 to make the bank accessible in compliance with the Americans with Disabilities Act. The trees are nearly hiding the structure connecting the new building to the main branch. (Author's collection.)

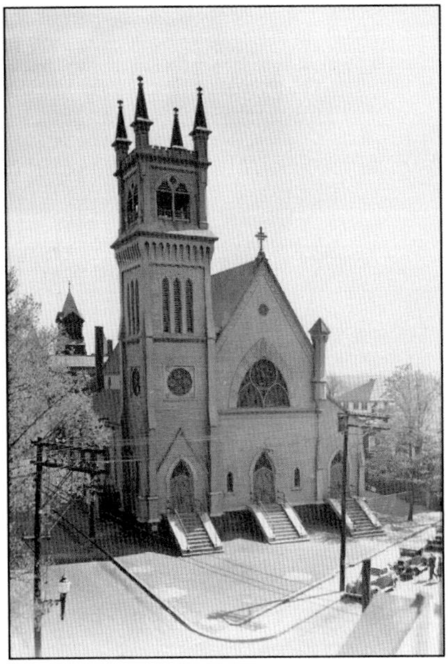

St. John's Church was built in 1874 and torn down in 1938 when the present one was built. The school in the rear was added in 1957. In 2003, the St. James congregation (see page 21) united to form SS John and James Church. The following verses are from "When the Church Bell Rings" by Helen O. Larson: "At 11 o'clock today, the church bell will ring / Calling the people to worship, Christ the King. They will walk in the church, and sit on a seat today / They will assemble together, to worship and pray."

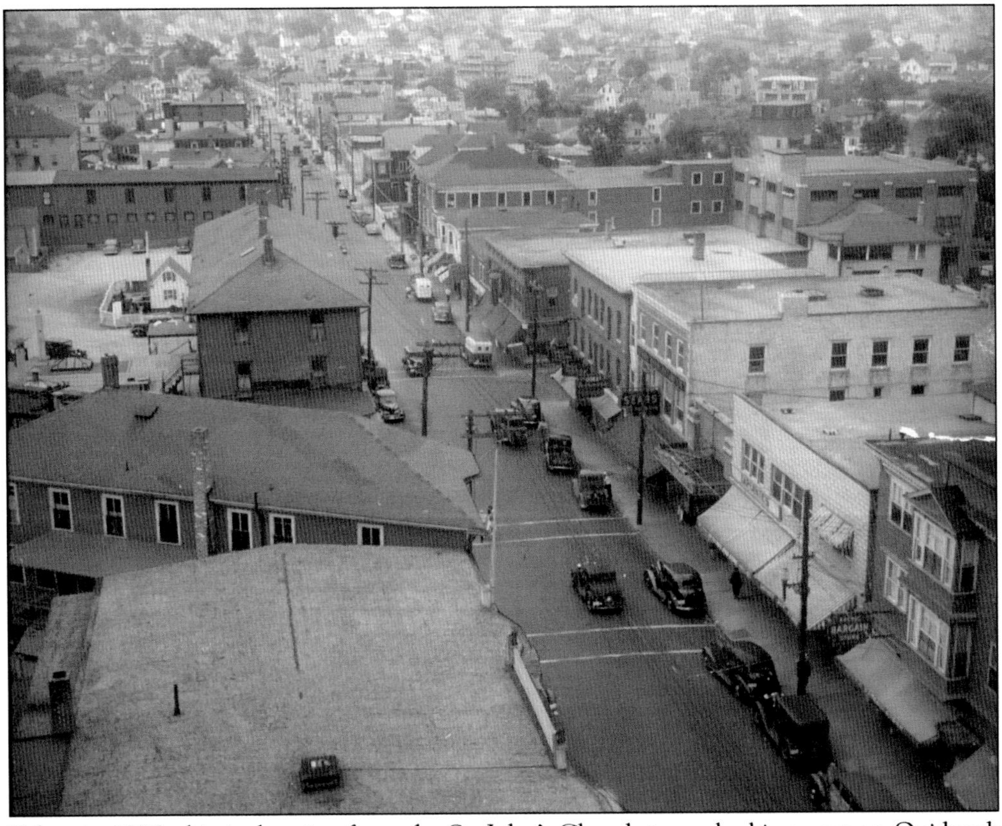

Taken in 1946, this is the view from the St. John's Church tower looking west on Quidneck Street. The Arctic Bargain Store is in the lower right corner. Next to it, from front to back, are the Brouillard building, the Palace Theatre marquee opposite Brookside Avenue, Sears, Donat Archambault Clothing, Valley Liquor Store, and a small shop on the corner of Crawford Street.

This view from the St. John's Church bell tower looks south down St. John Street. The light-colored building (top center) is the Odeon Theatre. Fr. Joseph R. Bourgeois of St. John's created it in 1909 after visiting the Odeon Opera House in Paris. The old St. John's School was in the building on the right. The house on the left with the porch was the home of Dr. Jeannette D. Vidal. It is interesting to see cars parked on both sides of the street—some headed in the wrong direction and three parked in the crosswalk.

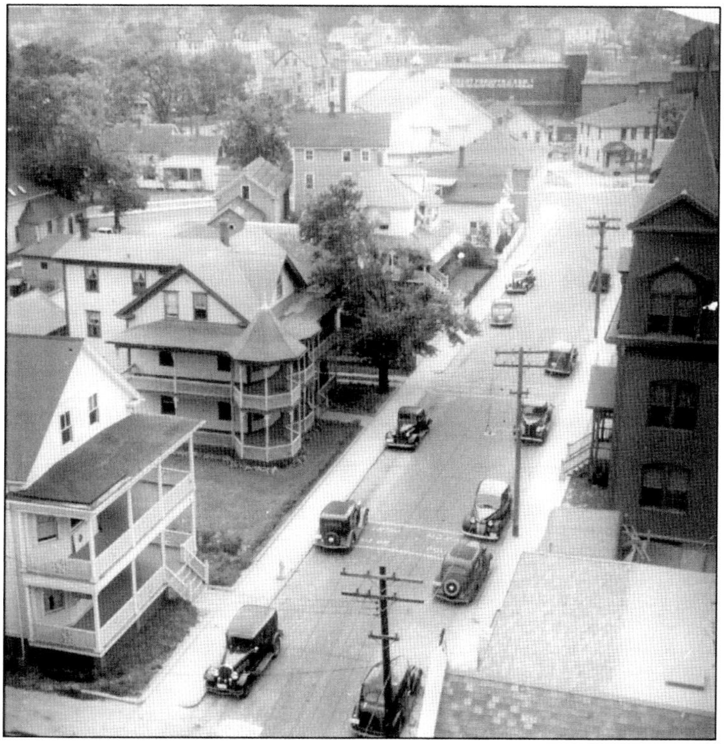

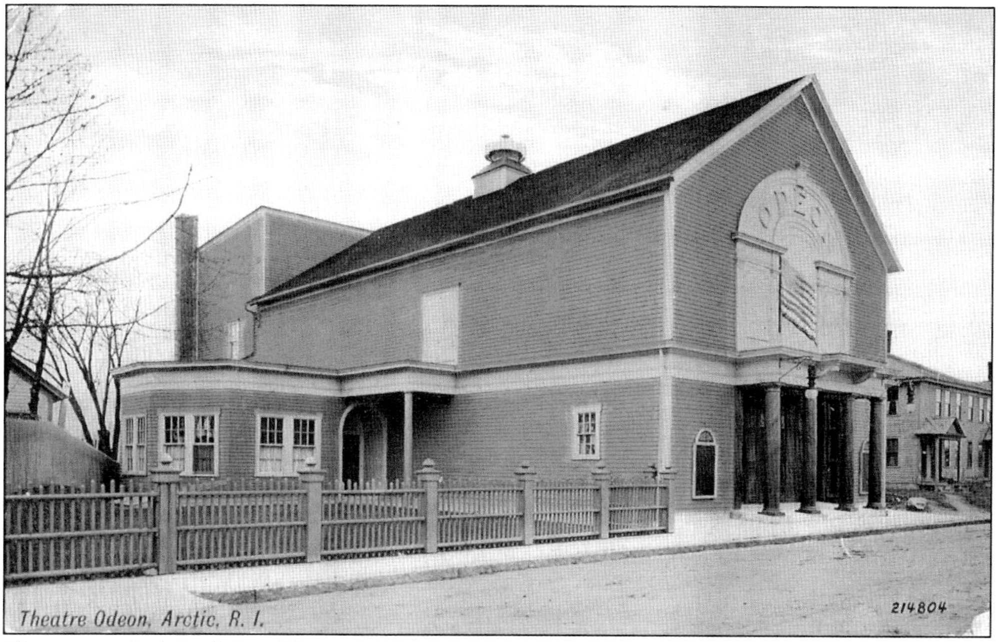

This postcard of the Odeon Theatre was mailed from River Point on August 29, 1912, at 5 p.m. Sent to Frances W. Lawton in Thornton by her cousin, who had arrived in Hope on Saturday morning, the postcard was signed merely, "A.B.L." This building was later used as a furniture store.

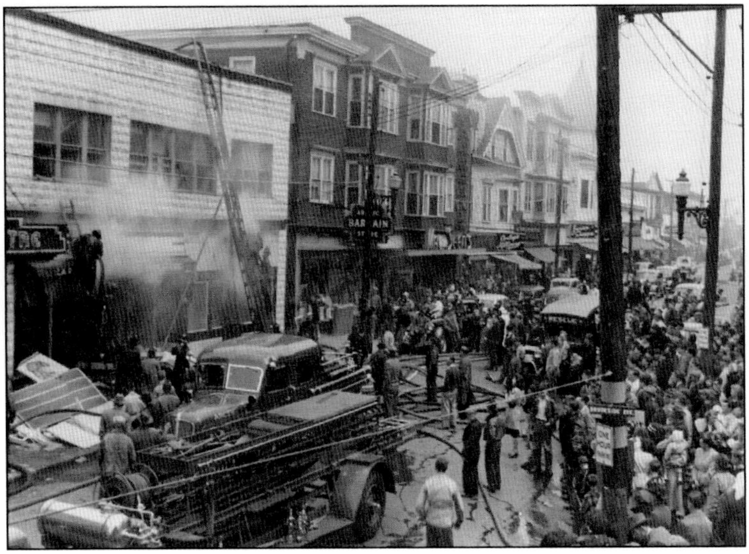

This is a view of the fire at the Brouillard building from the corner of Brookside Avenue. On the left is the Palace Theatre. To the right of the Brouillard, from left to right, are the Arctic Bargain Store, Mac Seen's, Corley's Millinery, Chagnon's Drug, and the Junior Shoppe on Quidneck Street headed towards the square. (Courtesy of Gerard Tellier Jr.)

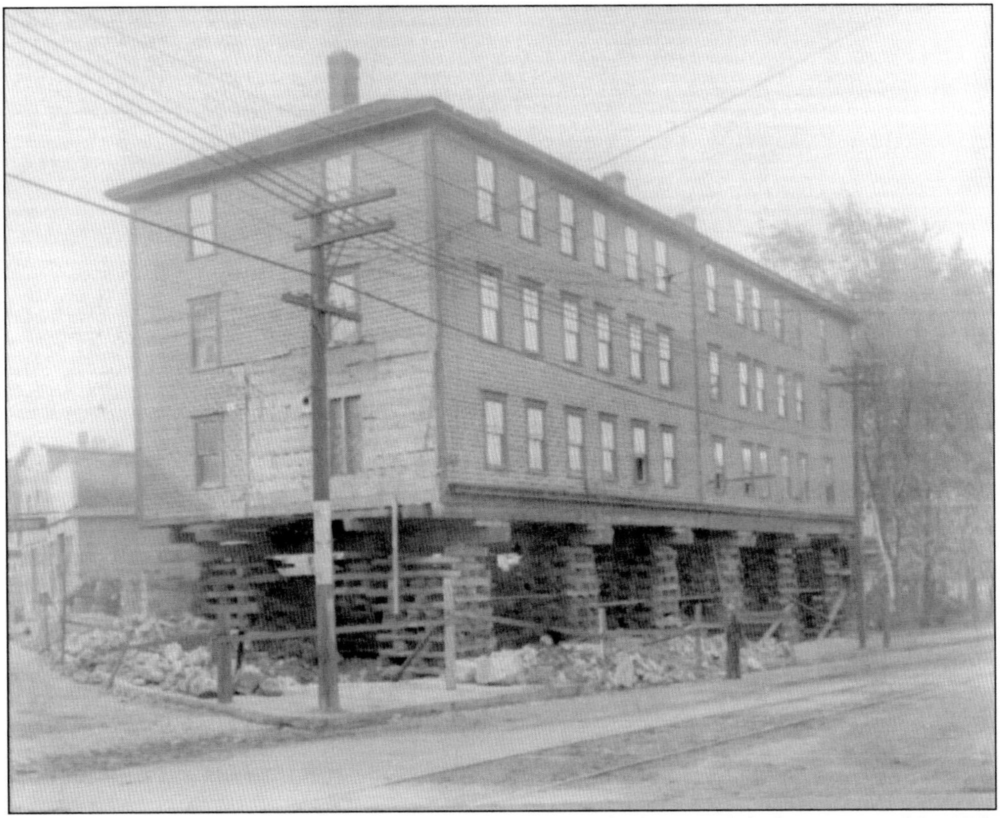

This building on the opposite side of Brookside Avenue was built around the beginning of the 20th century. It was being used as a boardinghouse when Servales "Bob" Archambault purchased it after World War I. This photograph was taken in 1925, when the building was raised to accommodate a pool parlor, a fruit stand, a cleaning business, Kid Blair's Log Cabin, and a Chinese restaurant.

This ad from the *Pawtuxet Valley Daily Times* dated November 18, 1943, will bring back memories for many. It appears this First National store was well stocked for Thanksgiving; bacon cost just 32¢ a pound. The following verses are from "My New Paper Girl" by Helen O. Larson in 1979 at age 68: "I have a new *P.V. Times* carrier, Donnalisa is her name / She is so faithful each day, as she rides her bike up my lane. This little girl is so precious, she means the world to me / For she is my granddaughter, this is the reason you see. She is so energetic, also so saving you know / When the *P.V. Times* man pays her, straight to the bank she does go." (Author's collection.)

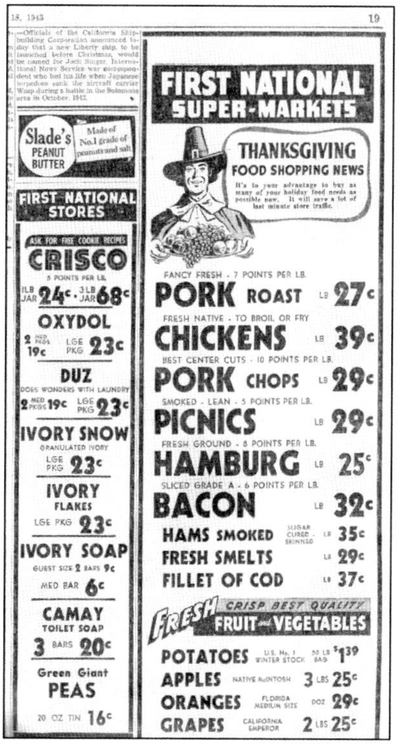
18, 1943 19

—Officials of the California Shipbuilding Corporation announced today that a new Liberty ship, to be launched before Christmas, would be named for Jack Singer, International News Service war correspondent who lost his life when Japanese torpedoes sank the aircraft carrier Wasp during a battle in the Solomons area in October, 1942.

Slade's PEANUT BUTTER
Made of No.1 grade of peanuts and salt

FIRST NATIONAL STORES

ASK FOR FREE COOKIE RECIPES
CRISCO
5 POINTS PER LB.
1 LB JAR 24¢ · 3 LB JAR 68¢

OXYDOL
2 MED PKGS 19¢ LGE PKG 23¢

DUZ
DOES WONDERS WITH LAUNDRY
2 MED PKGS 19¢ LGE PKG 23¢

IVORY SNOW
GRANULATED IVORY
LGE PKG 23¢

IVORY FLAKES
LGE PKG 23¢

IVORY SOAP
GUEST SIZE 2 BARS 9¢
MED BAR 6¢

CAMAY
TOILET SOAP
3 BARS 20¢

Green Giant PEAS
20 OZ TIN 16¢

FIRST NATIONAL SUPER-MARKETS

THANKSGIVING FOOD SHOPPING NEWS
It's to your advantage to buy as many of your holiday food needs as possible now. It will save a lot of last minute store traffic.

FANCY FRESH - 7 POINTS PER LB.
PORK ROAST LB 27¢
FRESH NATIVE - TO BROIL OR FRY
CHICKENS LB 39¢
BEST CENTER CUTS - 10 POINTS PER LB.
PORK CHOPS LB 29¢
SMOKED - LEAN - 5 POINTS PER LB.
PICNICS LB 29¢
FRESH GROUND - 8 POINTS PER LB.
HAMBURG LB 25¢
SLICED GRADE A - 6 POINTS PER LB.
BACON LB 32¢
HAMS SMOKED SUGAR CURED - SKINNED LB 35¢
FRESH SMELTS LB 29¢
FILLET OF COD LB 37¢

FRESH CRISP BEST QUALITY FRUIT and VEGETABLES
POTATOES U.S. No. 1 WINTER STOCK 50 LB BAG $1.39
APPLES NATIVE McINTOSH 3 LBS 25¢
ORANGES FLORIDA MEDIUM SIZE DOZ 29¢
GRAPES CALIFORNIA EMPEROR 2 LBS 25¢

This photograph was taken in April 1948 from the roof of the post office. It looks up Main Street to the building standing majestically at the center of Arctic. The little building at the end of the parking lot before Centreville Bank was the old police station. (Courtesy of Richard Hughes.)

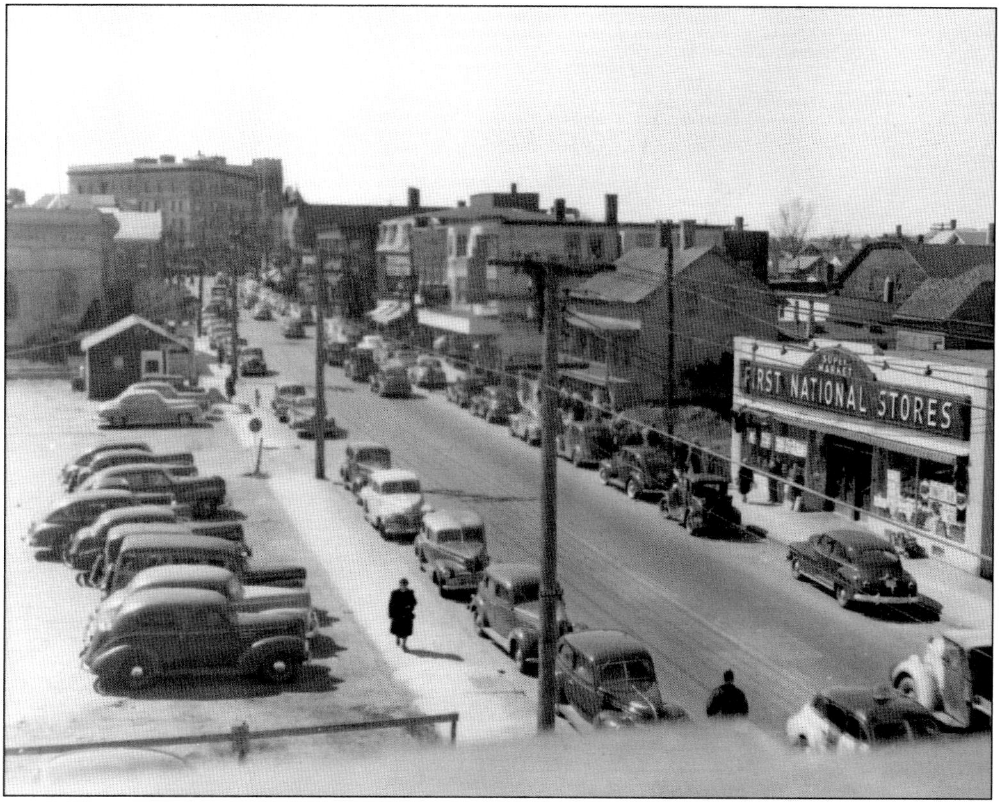

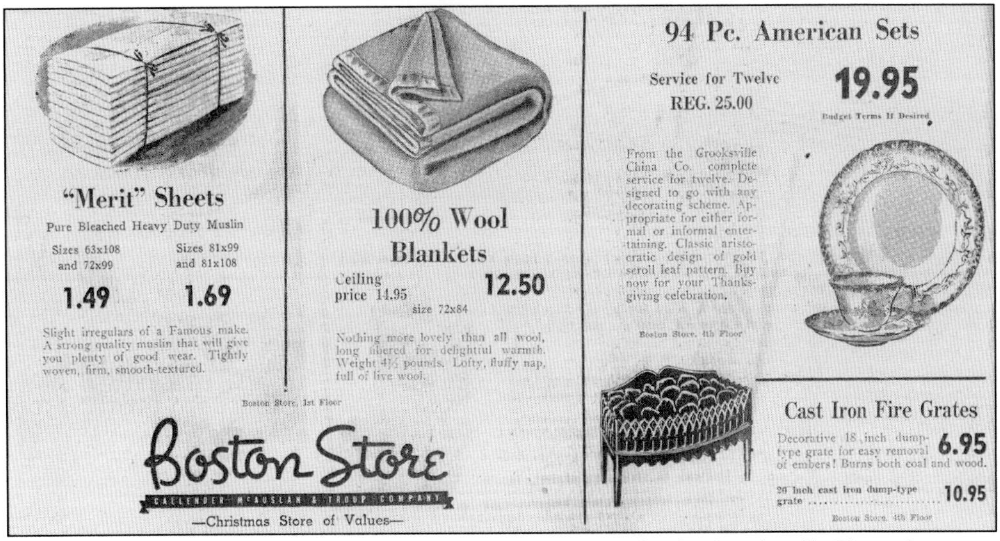

On November 18, 1943, the Boston Store advertised dinnerware by the Grooksville China Company with the classic, aristocratic gold-scroll leaf pattern. It served 12, and the retailer recommended buying now for Thanksgiving celebrations. Lords Jewelers was in the building at the far end of the Boston Store. The following verse is from "Is Arctic Dying" by Helen O. Larson: "I passed Lords Jewelers, and sad memories it did bring / For that is where we bought, our wedding rings." (Author's collection.)

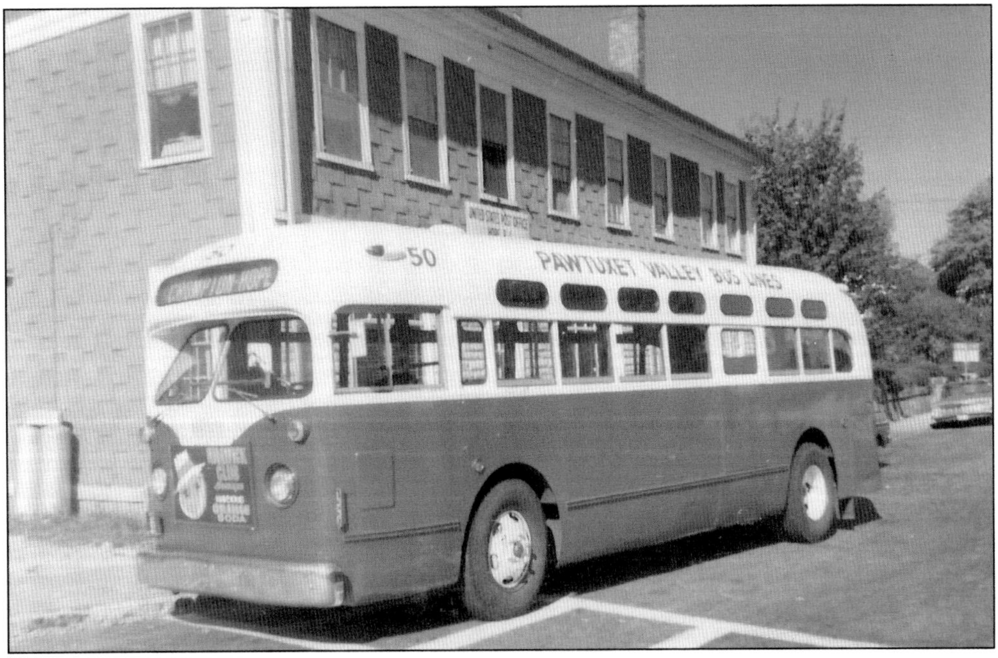

The Pawtuxet Valley Bus Line ran two buses from Hope to Crompton and back. Of course, Arctic was most peoples' destination. The buses would pass each other, and one could be expected every half hour. The following verses are from "My Bus Driver Husband," written by Helen O. Larson on November 1, 1998, at age 88: "I go back in memory, each and every day / To the day I stepped on his bus, early one spring day. The driver I met on the bus, I married one night / And 31 years we had happiness, each and every night." (Author's collection.)

This image dates back to the good old days when a brand-new, 1929 Chevrolet Cabriolet coupe cost just $794. Leo St. Onge Sr. even received $472 for the coupe he traded in, leaving a balance on delivery of $322, which Howard Bell was happy to accept. (Courtesy of Gary St. Onge.)

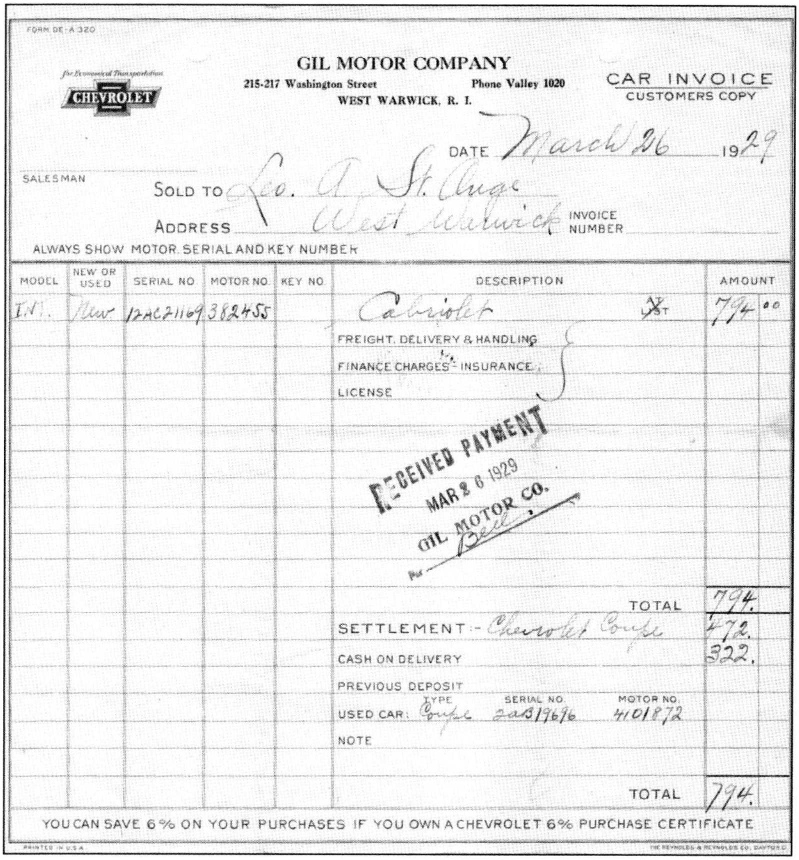
FORM DE-A 320

CHEVROLET

GIL MOTOR COMPANY
215-217 Washington Street Phone Valley 1020
WEST WARWICK, R. I.

CAR INVOICE
CUSTOMERS COPY

DATE March 26 1929

SALESMAN

SOLD TO Leo. A. St. Ange

ADDRESS West Warwick

INVOICE NUMBER

ALWAYS SHOW MOTOR SERIAL AND KEY NUMBER

MODEL	NEW OR USED	SERIAL NO.	MOTOR NO.	KEY NO.	DESCRIPTION	AMOUNT
IN	New	12AC21169	382455		Cabriolet	794.00
					FREIGHT, DELIVERY & HANDLING	
					FINANCE CHARGES - INSURANCE	
					LICENSE	
					TOTAL	794.
					SETTLEMENT :- Chevrolet Coupe	472.
					CASH ON DELIVERY	322.
					PREVIOUS DEPOSIT	
					USED CAR: TYPE Coupe SERIAL NO. 2AB19696 MOTOR NO. 4101872	
					NOTE	
					TOTAL	794.

RECEIVED PAYMENT
MAR 26 1929
GIL MOTOR CO.
Per Bell

YOU CAN SAVE 6% ON YOUR PURCHASES IF YOU OWN A CHEVROLET 6% PURCHASE CERTIFICATE

PRINTED IN U.S.A.

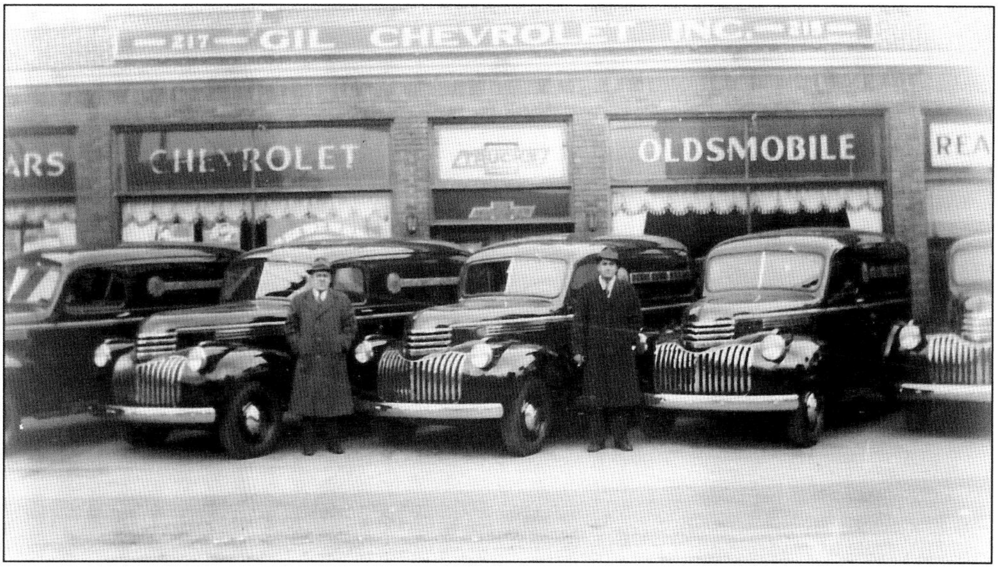

Through the 1920s and 1930s, Gil Motors occupied 215–217 Washington Street. In the 1940s, it became Gil Chevrolet. Later, Marvin Webber took over the Chevrolet franchise. Taken in January 1941, this photograph shows sales manager Armand Soucy (left) and salesman Pete Russo with a lineup of brand-new Chevrolet panel delivery trucks. (Courtesy of Lawrence G. Soucy.)

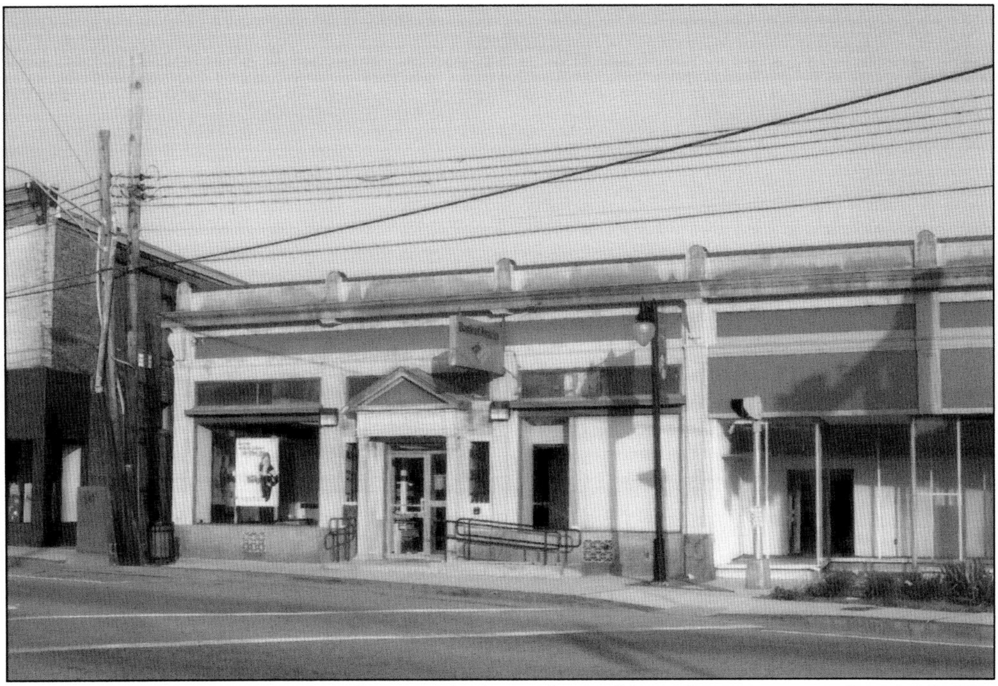

Taken on August 30, 2010, this photograph shows the building that was erected in 1923. The Union Trust Company occupied the left half, and F.W. Woolworth occupied the right half. The following verses are from "The Bench" by Helen O. Larson: "There's a bench on the square, where elderly folks sit each day / Watching traffic go by, living memories of yesterday. Maybe they tell of the old barn dance, where they met the girl of their dreams / The world must have been a better place, to these elderly folks it seems. Someday I may sit on the bench, just to listen to what they say / That they lived in a better world, then we live in today." (Author's collection.)

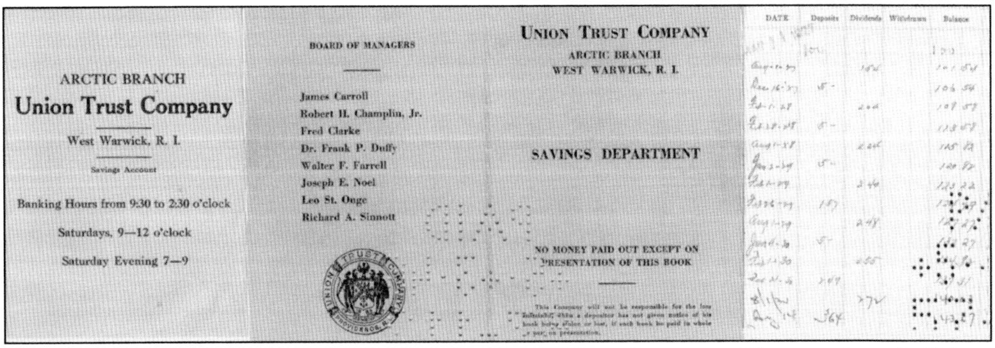

This is an original savings passbook from the Union Trust Company. The envelope (left) lists Saturday hours of 9 a.m.–12 p.m. and Saturday evening hours between 7 p.m. and 9 p.m. The board of managers was listed on the back of the passbook (second from left), and the front stated it was from the Arctic Branch (third from left). The first page shows that Leo St. Onge Sr. opened a savings account for his son Leo Jr. on March 11, 1927, with $100. The ledger is all handwritten. Little did they know that in October 1929, the stock market would crash, triggering the Great Depression. (Courtesy of Leo St. Onge Jr.)

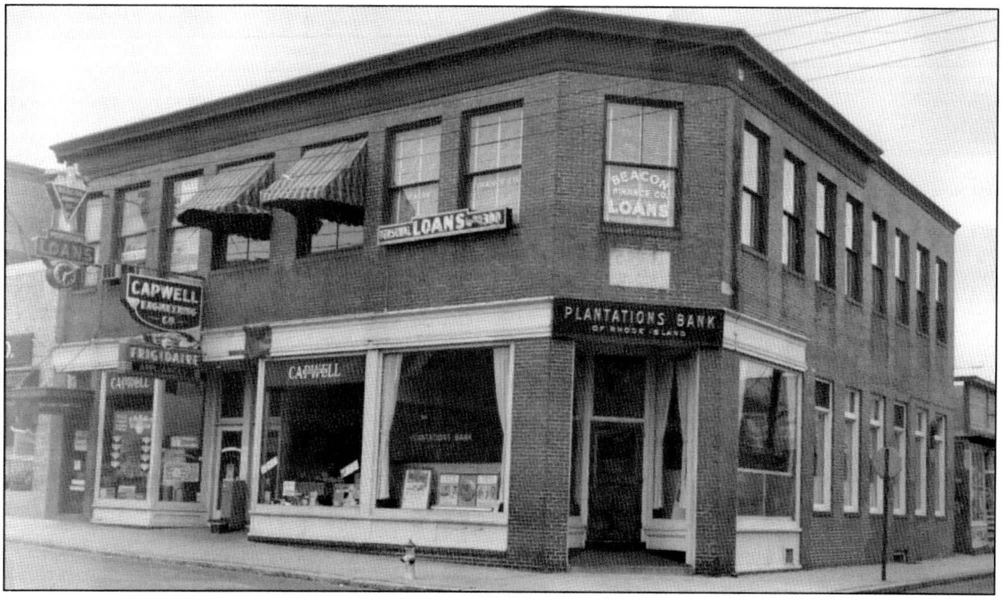

Constructed in 1912, this is how the Curson building looked on June 10, 1951. Businesses have come and gone, but the building is still occupied today. The following verses are from "The Picture Draped in Black," written by Helen O. Larson in November 1964: "From the windows of the stores in Arctic, he smiled as people passed by / It was just a beautiful picture, that's why I saw everyone cry. As I took one final look, at the man that some called Jack [JFK] / My humble heart was breaking as I walked away, from the picture draped in black." (Courtesy of Leo St. Onge Jr.)

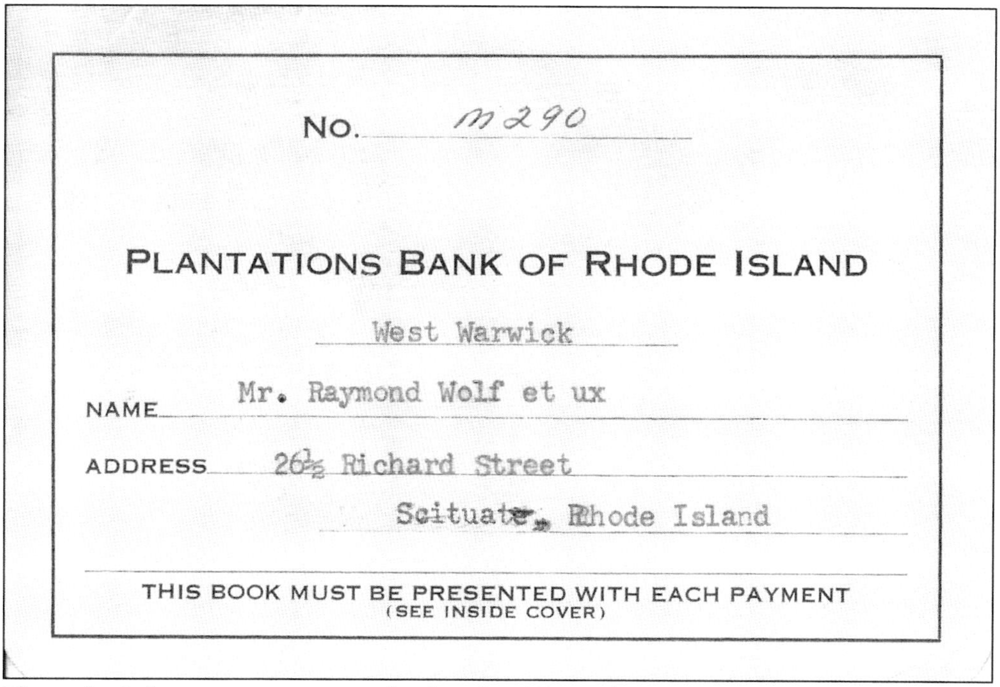

NO. M290

PLANTATIONS BANK OF RHODE ISLAND

West Warwick

NAME Mr. Raymond Wolf et ux

ADDRESS 26½ Richard Street

Scituate, Rhode Island

THIS BOOK MUST BE PRESENTED WITH EACH PAYMENT
(SEE INSIDE COVER)

The author's first mortgage payment book is dated December 15, 1966. This was during a time when residents had to go to the bank each month with their books so the payment could be recorded. (Author's collection.)

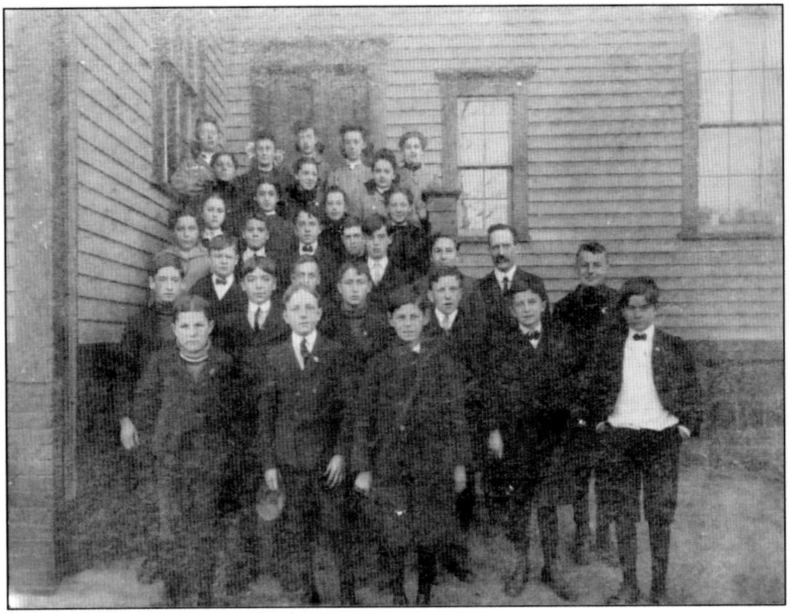

This photograph presents the 1905–1906 eighth and ninth grade classes of Arctic Grammar School. Leo St. Onge Sr. is first on the left in the second row. The school's principal, John F. Deering, is on the right. The boys are lined up in front, and the girls are in back. (Courtesy of Gary St. Onge.)

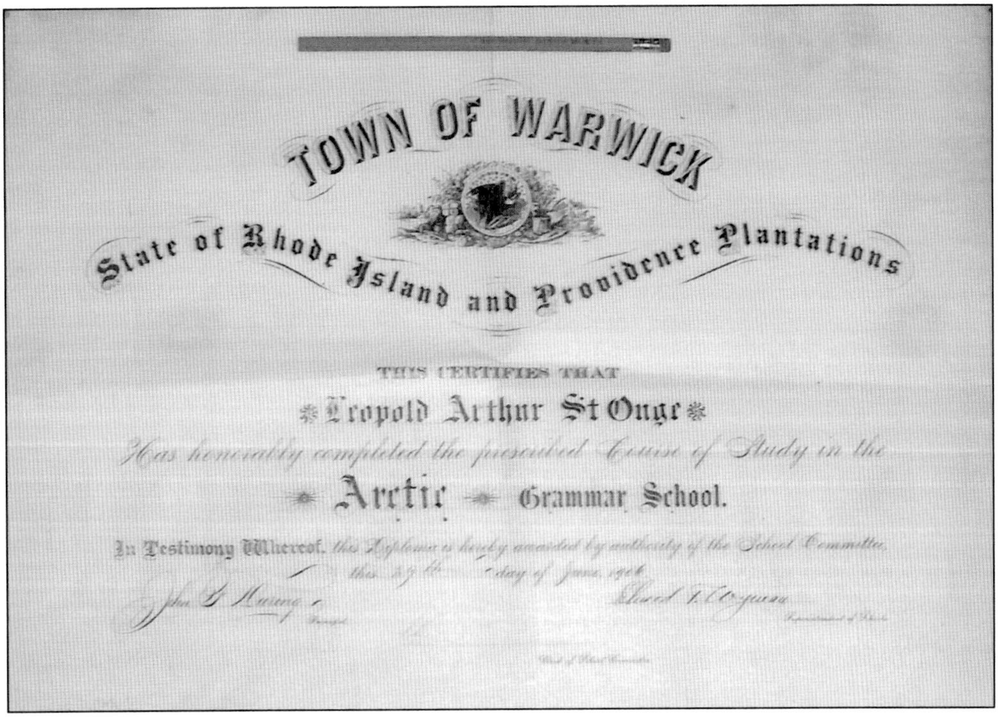

TOWN OF WARWICK

State of Rhode Island and Providence Plantations

THIS CERTIFIES THAT

Leopold Arthur St Onge

Has honorably completed the prescribed Course of Study in the

Arctic Grammar School.

In Testimony Whereof, this Diploma is hereby awarded by authority of the School Committee, this 29th day of June, 1906

The town of Warwick gave this diploma to Leopold Arthur St. Onge on June 29, 1906. It states that he had honorably completed the prescribed course of study in the Arctic Grammar School and is signed by Principal John F. Deering. In 1952, the West Warwick High School became known as the John F. Deering High School. The pencil at the top of the diploma is included for scale. The diploma measures 20 inches by15 inches. (Courtesy of Leo St. Onge Jr.)

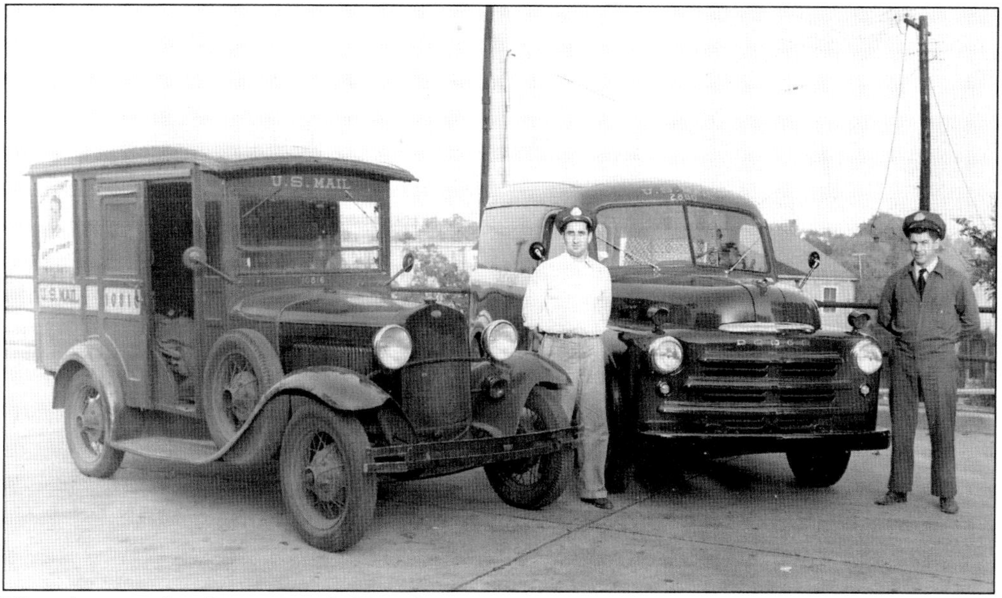

This photograph of Yvon Roy (left) and Norman Anctil was taken in the early 1950s. It shows the post office has bought a new Dodge panel truck to replace its 1930 Ford Model A. The trucks were used to transport carriers to their routes and to drop off bundles of mail, which were known as relays. Relays were deposited in the mailboxes along the route so the carrier would not have to carry all the mail at once. As the carrier passed a mailbox, he would unlock it and retrieve the relay bundle to continue on his route. (Courtesy of Richard Hughes.)

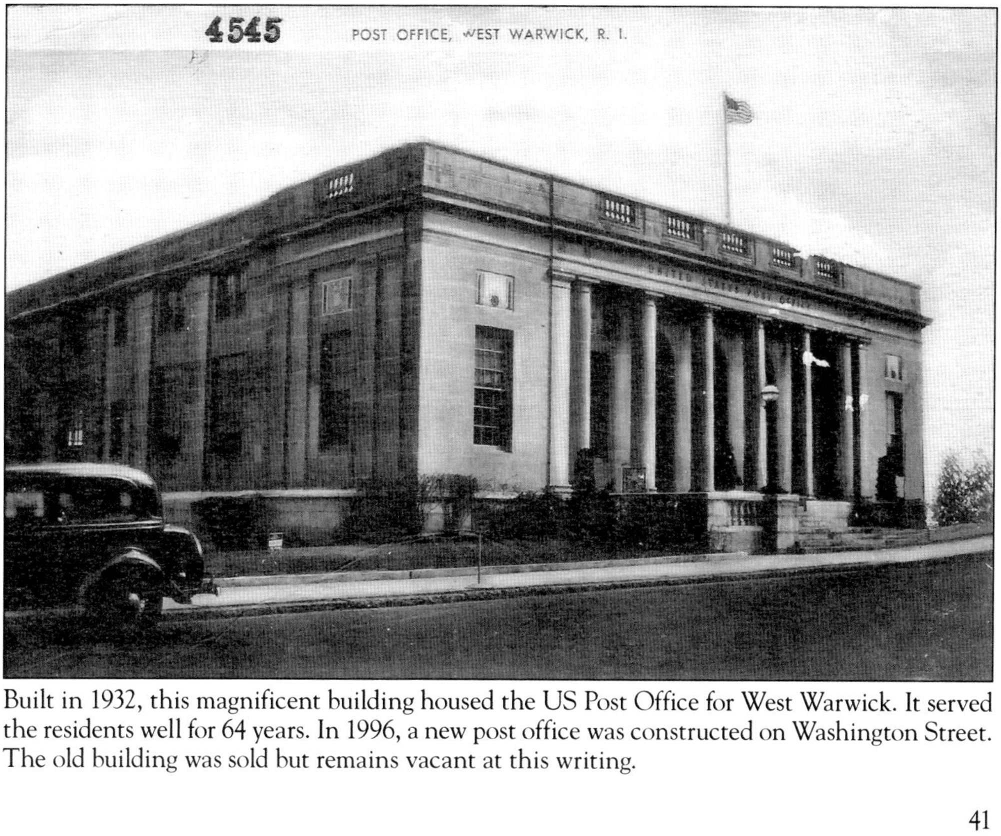

Built in 1932, this magnificent building housed the US Post Office for West Warwick. It served the residents well for 64 years. In 1996, a new post office was constructed on Washington Street. The old building was sold but remains vacant at this writing.

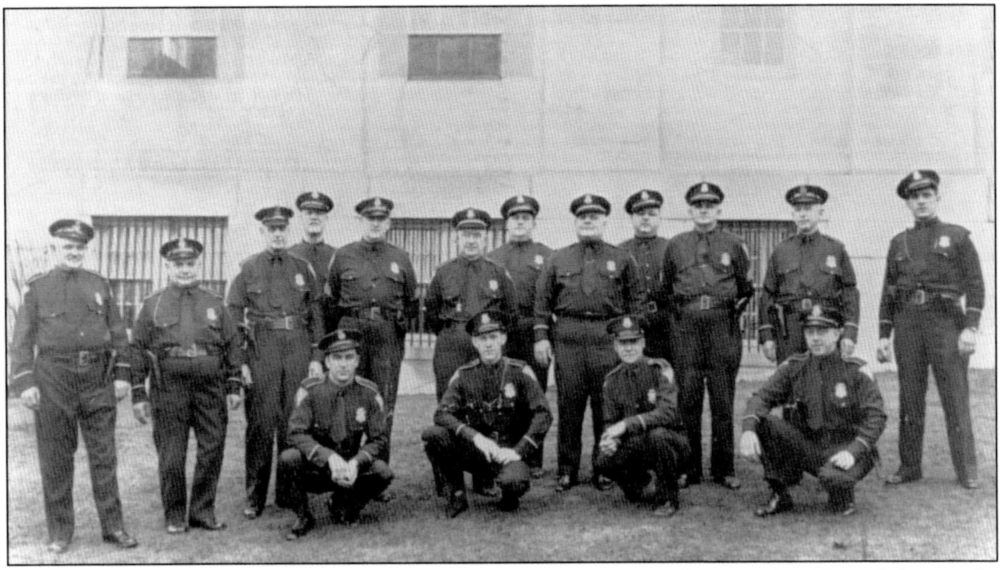

This photograph of the West Warwick Police Department was taken in 1941. From left to right are (first row) Rocco Lombardi, Philip Eldridge, Victor Grandchamp, and Clarence Matteson; (second row) James Lamb, Benjamin Lautieri, Wallace Greene, Edward Asselin, Chief Louis Peltier, William Mailloux, Wallace Jalbert, Edward Lamb, and Ovila Ratte; (third row) John Holmes, Harry Miller, and Louis Boudreau. The following verses are from "The Brave Policeman," written by Helen O. Larson in September 1989 at age 78: "How must his wife feel, when the phone rings at night / She wonders if it's a message of doom, is her husband all right. So please respect them, and the uniform they wear, For soon after your call comes in, the police will be there."

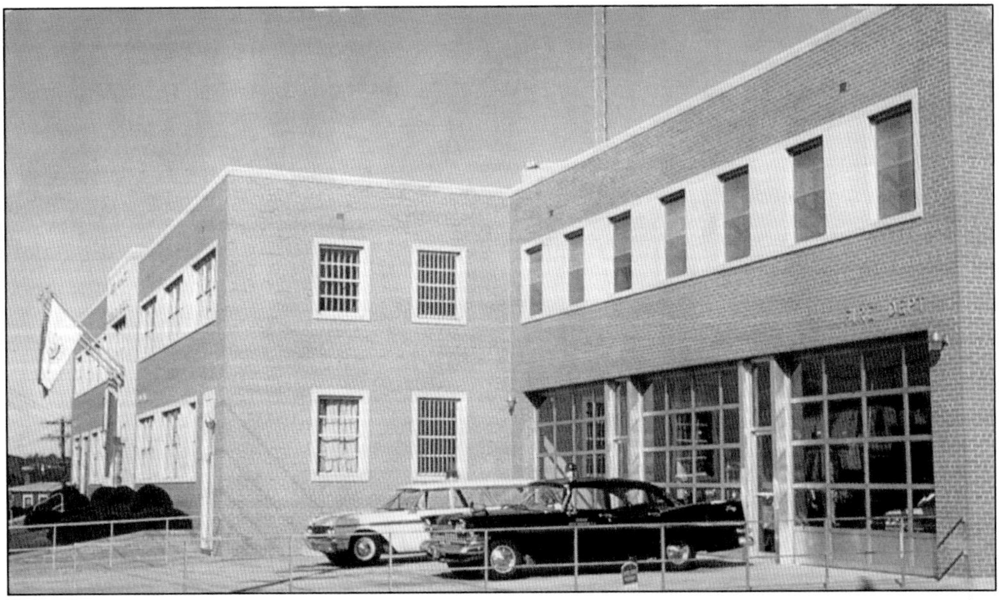

The new West Warwick Veterans Memorial Building was dedicated on November 11, 1959. This postcard, mailed 10 years later on December 17, 1969, shows the town hall in the center with the police station on the left and the fire department on the right. The black 1959 Plymouth Savoy and the white 1961 Ford Station Wagon will bring back memories for some. (Courtesy of Donald Carpenter.)

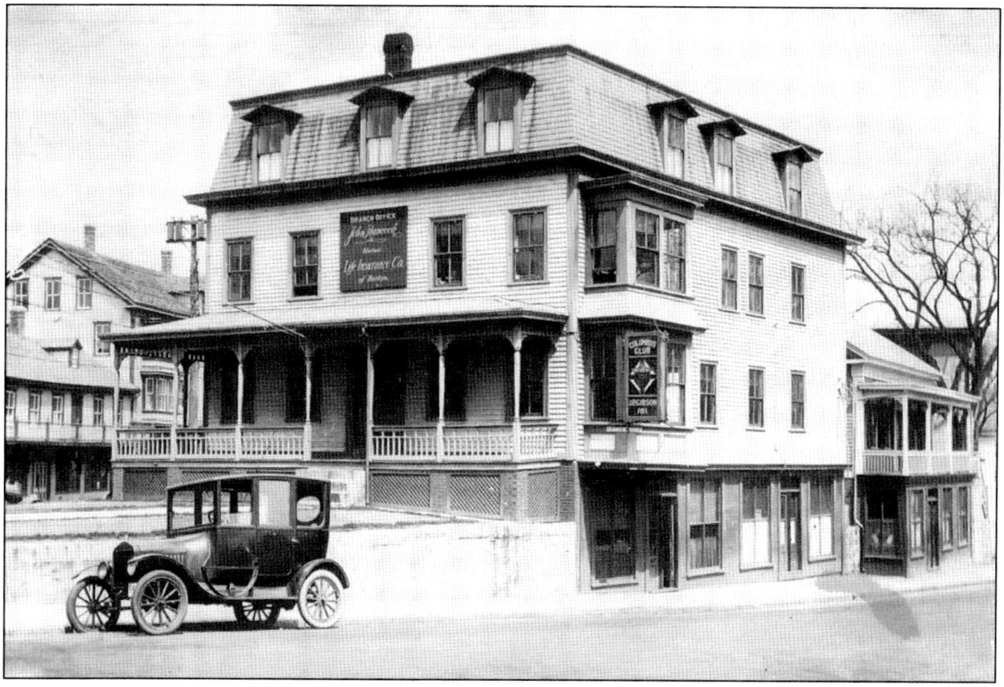

Today, a Shell gas station occupies this location. The CVS drugstore is to the left across Main Street. The sign on the right of the building announces, "Columbus Club K of C J.P. Gibson 181." The windowsill under the sign denotes Columbus Square. On the lower level, Oliver Desmarais maintained a store. John Hancock Insurance proudly displays their sign in the front.

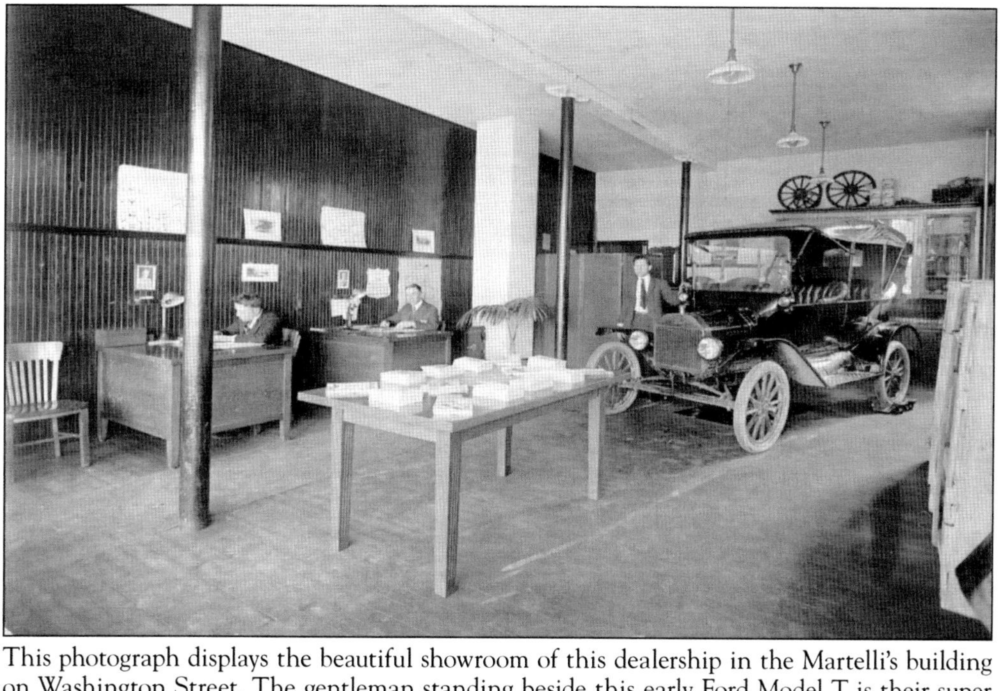

This photograph displays the beautiful showroom of this dealership in the Martelli's building on Washington Street. The gentleman standing beside this early Ford Model T is their super salesman, Charles H. Andrews.

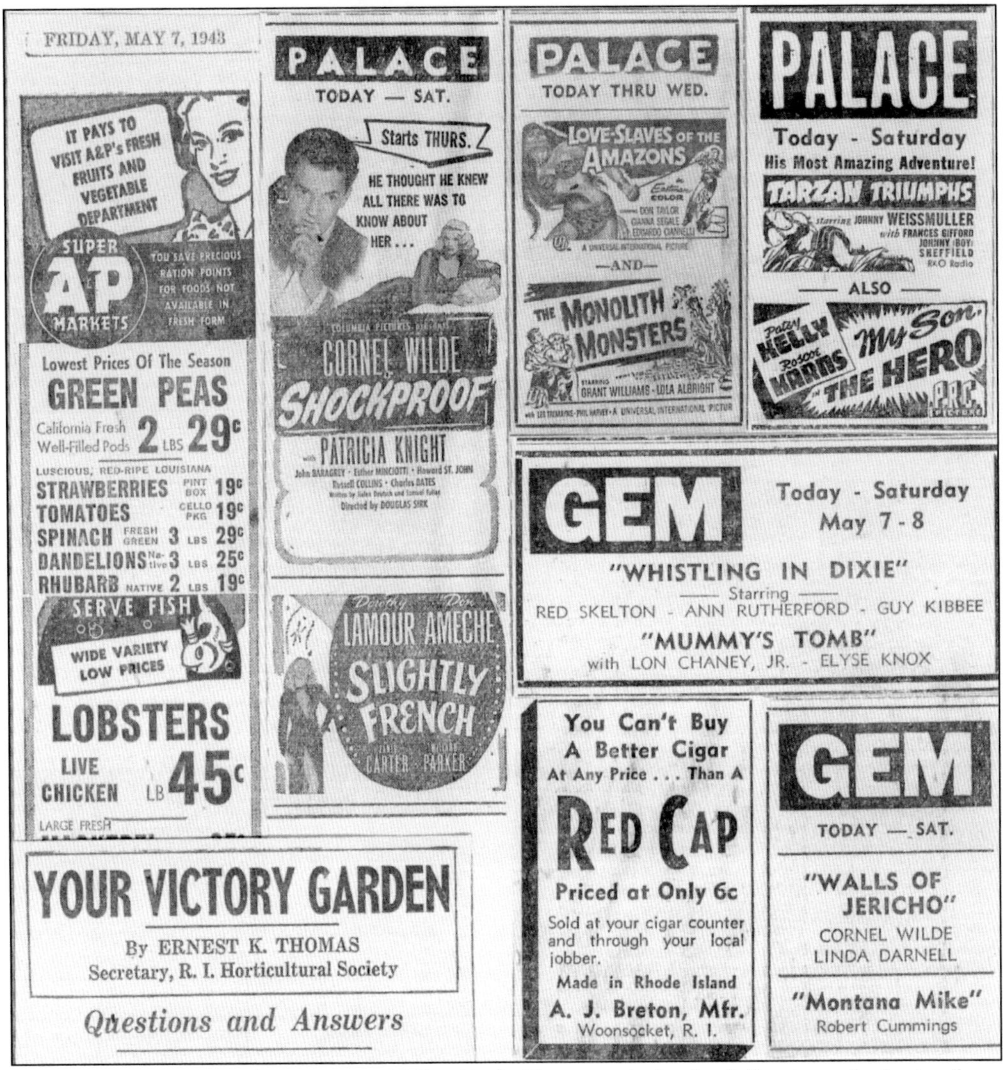

Advertisements from the *Pawtuxet Valley Daily Times* include the following, clockwise from the top left: On Friday, May 7, 1943, A&P Super Markets advertised, "You save precious ration points for food not available in fresh form;" on February 11, 1949, the Palace Theatre was showing *Shockproof* and *Slightly French*, starring Dorothy Lamour and Don Ameche; on January 14, 1958, the Palace was showing *Love Slaves of the Amazon* and *The Monolith Monsters*; on May 7, 1943, the Palace was showing *Tarzan Triumphs* and *My Son the Hero*; on May 7, 1943, the Gem was showing *Whistling In Dixie*, starring Red Skelton, and *Mummy's Tomb* with Lon Chaney Jr.; on February 11, 1949, the Gem was showing *Walls of Jericho* (Jericho was Arctic's original name) and *Montana Mike*, starring Robert Cummings; Red Cap cigars cost 6¢ and were made in Woonsocket, Rhode Island; and the Horticultural Society offered information on Victory Gardens. During the war, many folks planted Victory Gardens because they could not afford the 19¢ the A&P was asking for a pound of tomatoes.

Two

CENTREVILLE VILLAGE

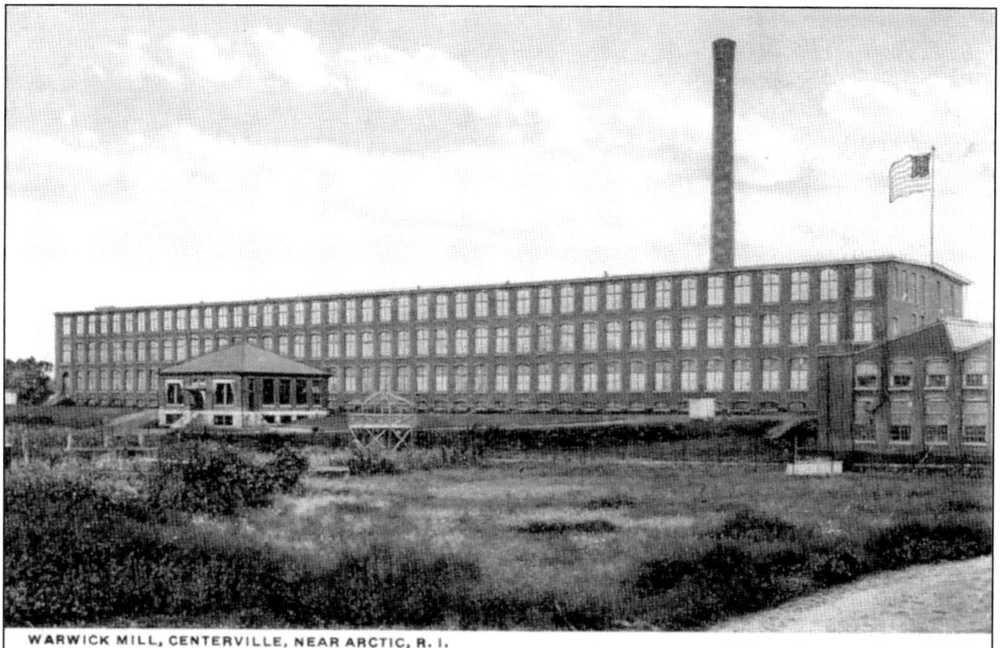

Warwick Mill was founded in New Ipswich, New Hampshire, in 1870. It incorporated in 1888 and had several locations: Jaffrey, Greenville, and New Ipswich, New Hampshire, and one in Maine. This postcard shows a fifth mill located in the Centreville area of Warwick, Rhode Island. Buildings were constructed in 1873, 1896, and in 1907 to create the Warwick Mill complex.

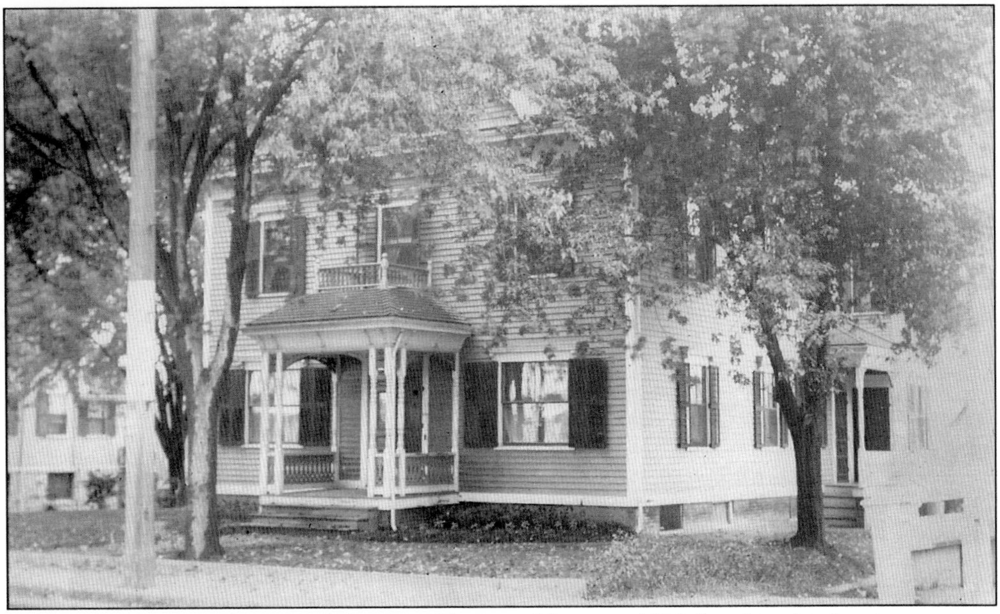

Stanislas St. Onge, who started the Star Clothing House in 1894, lived in this lovely two-story house at 1447 Main Street in Centreville in 1918. This house still stands beside Pat's Garage today. (Courtesy of Gary St. Onge.)

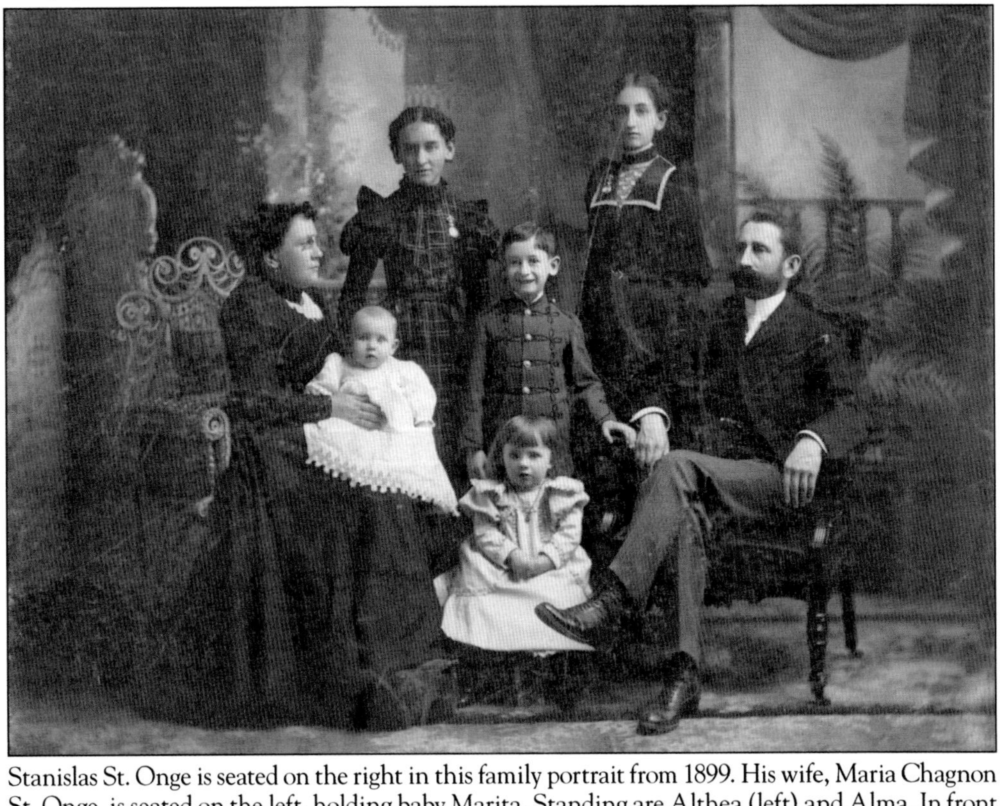

Stanislas St. Onge is seated on the right in this family portrait from 1899. His wife, Maria Chagnon St. Onge, is seated on the left, holding baby Marita. Standing are Althea (left) and Alma. In front of them is Leo Sr. with sister Violette in front of him. (Courtesy of Leo St. Onge Jr.)

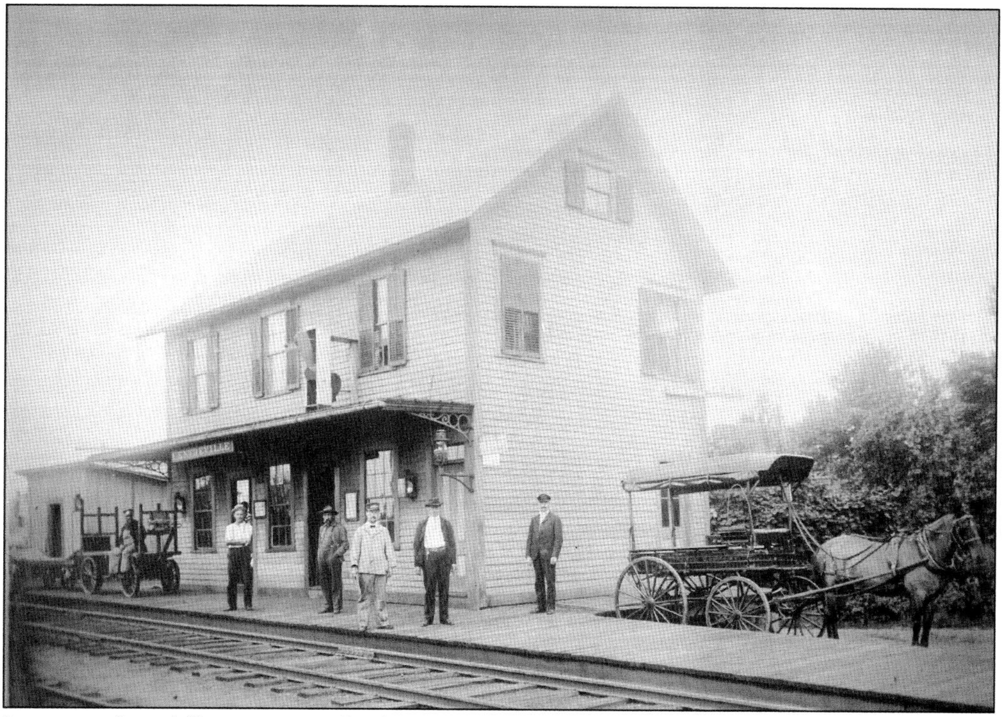

It appears these folks are waiting for the train to arrive. A horse and carriage are standing by with the driver on the platform. The ticket master in the white coat watches the cameraman while the porter rests on his wagon. (Courtesy of Donald Carpenter.)

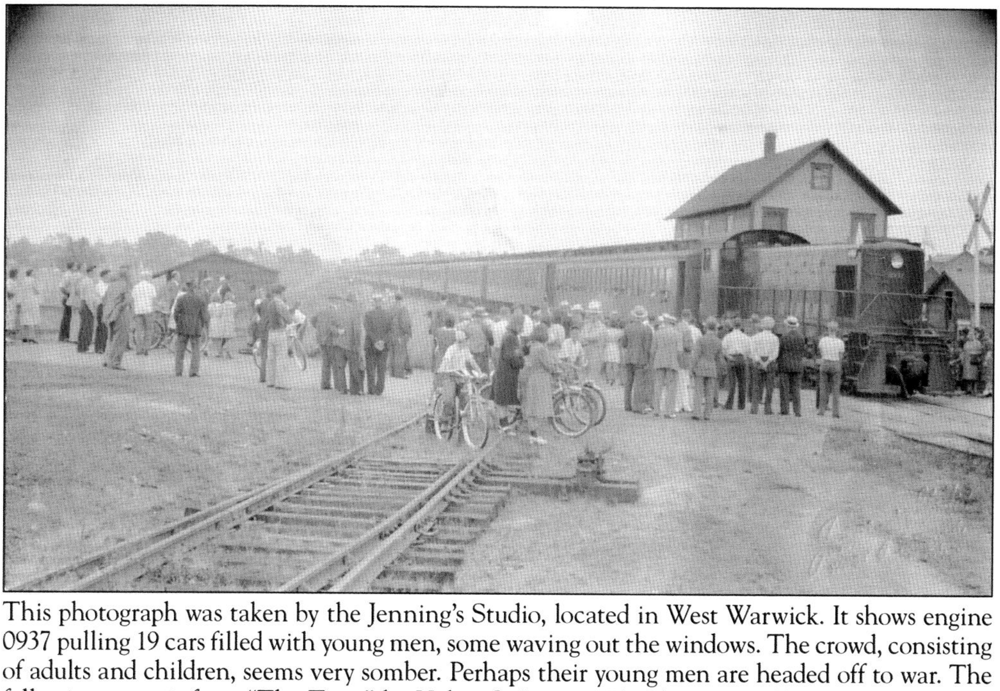

This photograph was taken by the Jenning's Studio, located in West Warwick. It shows engine 0937 pulling 19 cars filled with young men, some waving out the windows. The crowd, consisting of adults and children, seems very somber. Perhaps their young men are headed off to war. The following verse is from "The Train" by Helen O. Larson: "As the train rolled along, it blew its whistle loud / And soon people gathered, a weeping mournful crowd."

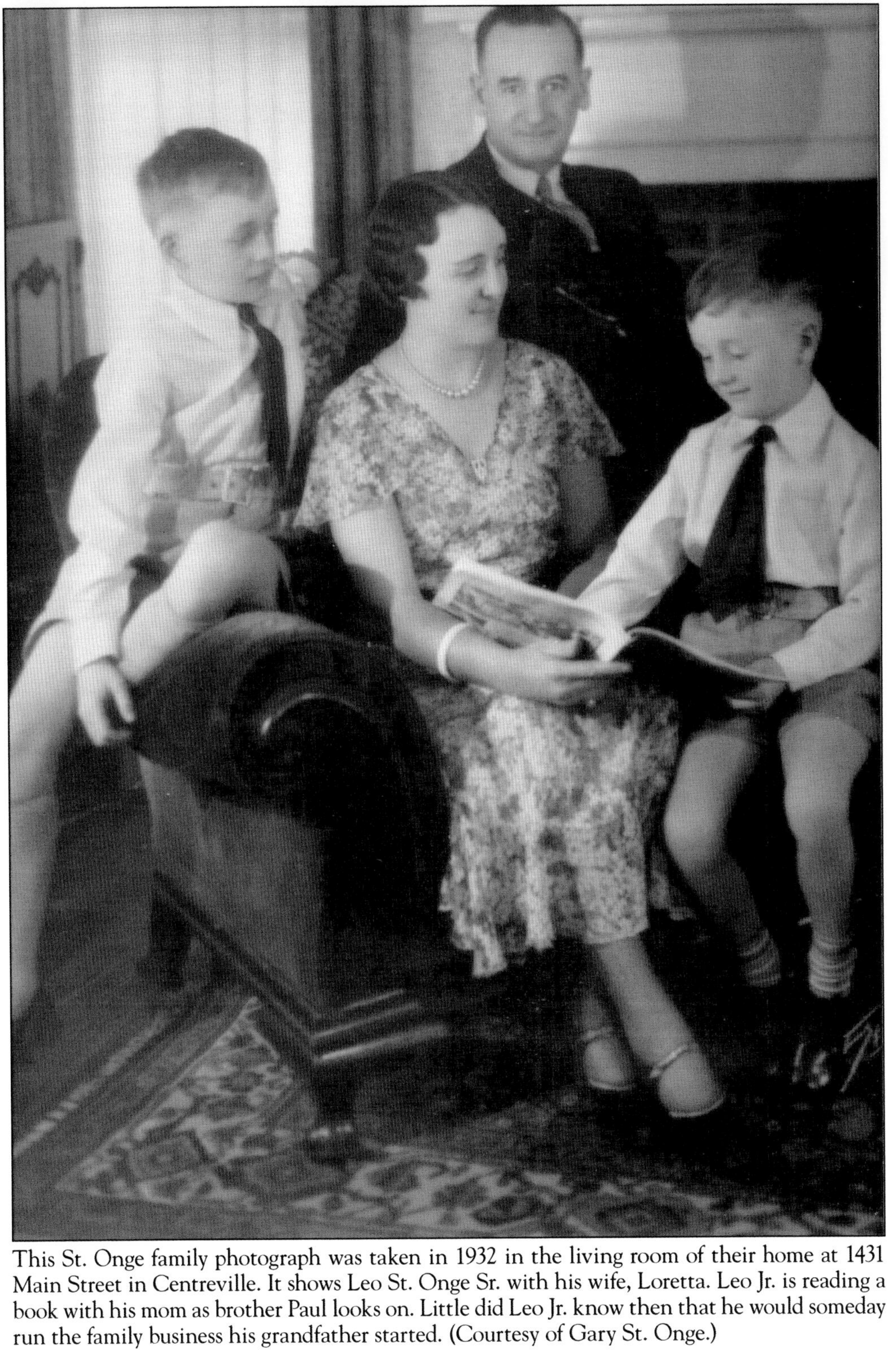

This St. Onge family photograph was taken in 1932 in the living room of their home at 1431 Main Street in Centreville. It shows Leo St. Onge Sr. with his wife, Loretta. Leo Jr. is reading a book with his mom as brother Paul looks on. Little did Leo Jr. know then that he would someday run the family business his grandfather started. (Courtesy of Gary St. Onge.)

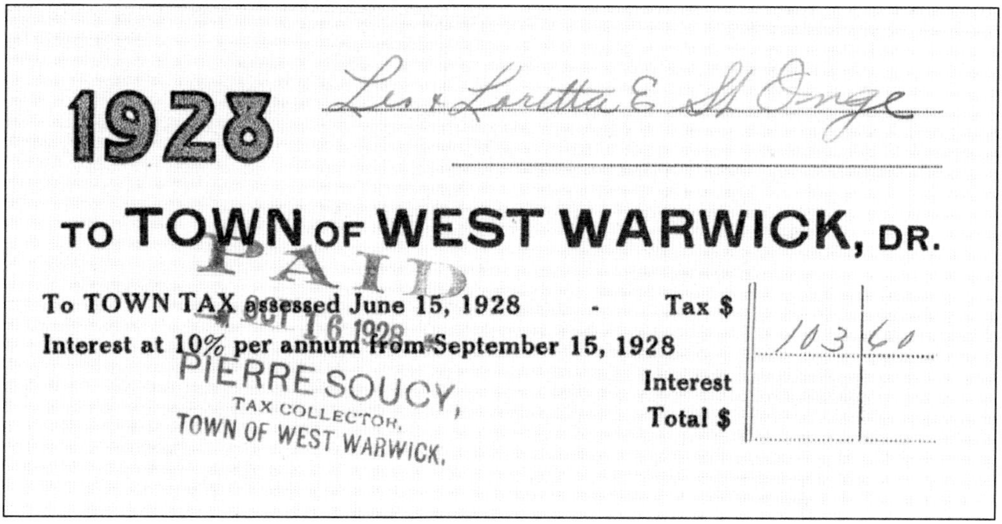

1928 Leo & Loretta E. St Onge

TO TOWN OF WEST WARWICK, DR.

PAID

To TOWN TAX assessed June 15, 1928 - Tax $ 103 60

Interest at 10% per annum from September 15, 1928

OCT 16 1928

PIERRE SOUCY, TAX COLLECTOR, TOWN OF WEST WARWICK.

Interest

Total $

Leo St. Onge Sr. and his wife, Loretta, lived at 1431 Main Street in Centreville, close to where his dad had lived. It is interesting that this 1928 tax bill from West Warwick was handwritten and does not give a value for the property. Taxes that year were $103.60. (Courtesy of Leo St. Onge Jr.)

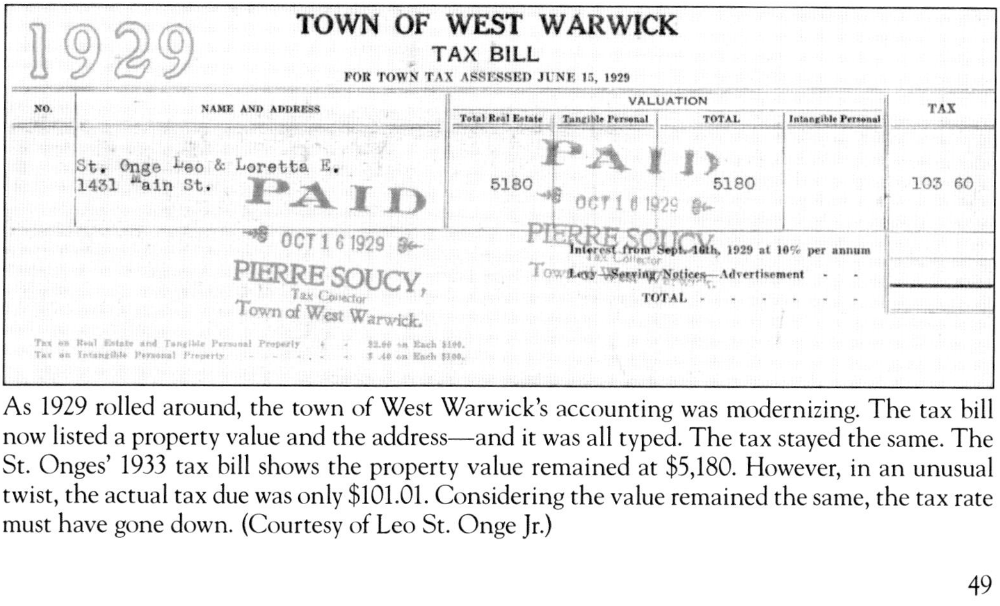

1929

TOWN OF WEST WARWICK

TAX BILL

FOR TOWN TAX ASSESSED JUNE 15, 1929

NO.	NAME AND ADDRESS	Total Real Estate	Tangible Personal	TOTAL	Intangible Personal	TAX
	St. Onge Leo & Loretta E. 1431 Main St.	5180		5180		103 60

PAID

OCT 16 1929

PIERRE SOUCY, Tax Collector, Town of West Warwick.

Interest from Sept. 16th, 1929 at 10% per annum

Levy—Serving Notices—Advertisement

TOTAL

Tax on Real Estate and Tangible Personal Property $2.00 on Each $100.

Tax on Intangible Personal Property $ .40 on Each $100.

As 1929 rolled around, the town of West Warwick's accounting was modernizing. The tax bill now listed a property value and the address—and it was all typed. The tax stayed the same. The St. Onges' 1933 tax bill shows the property value remained at $5,180. However, in an unusual twist, the actual tax due was only $101.01. Considering the value remained the same, the tax rate must have gone down. (Courtesy of Leo St. Onge Jr.)

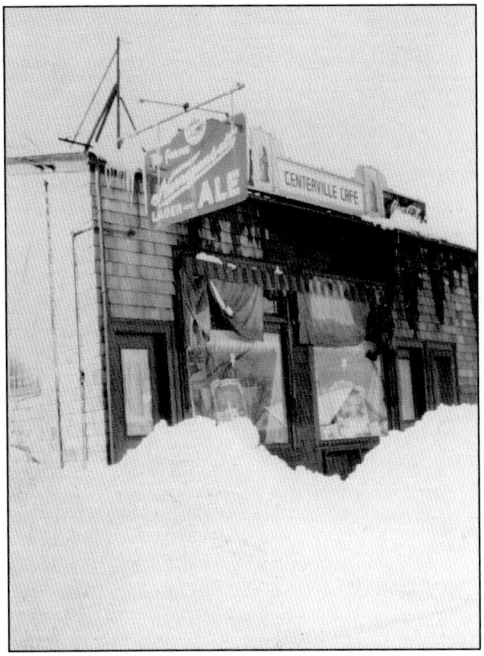

This photograph of the Centreville Café was taken in 1944. It is occupying the building where Treffle Boucher established his variety store in the 1930s. Coca-Cola is advertised on the roof, and Narragansett beer is advertised over an entrance. A separate ladies' entrance was located at the rear of the establishment. (Courtesy of Armand Boucher.)

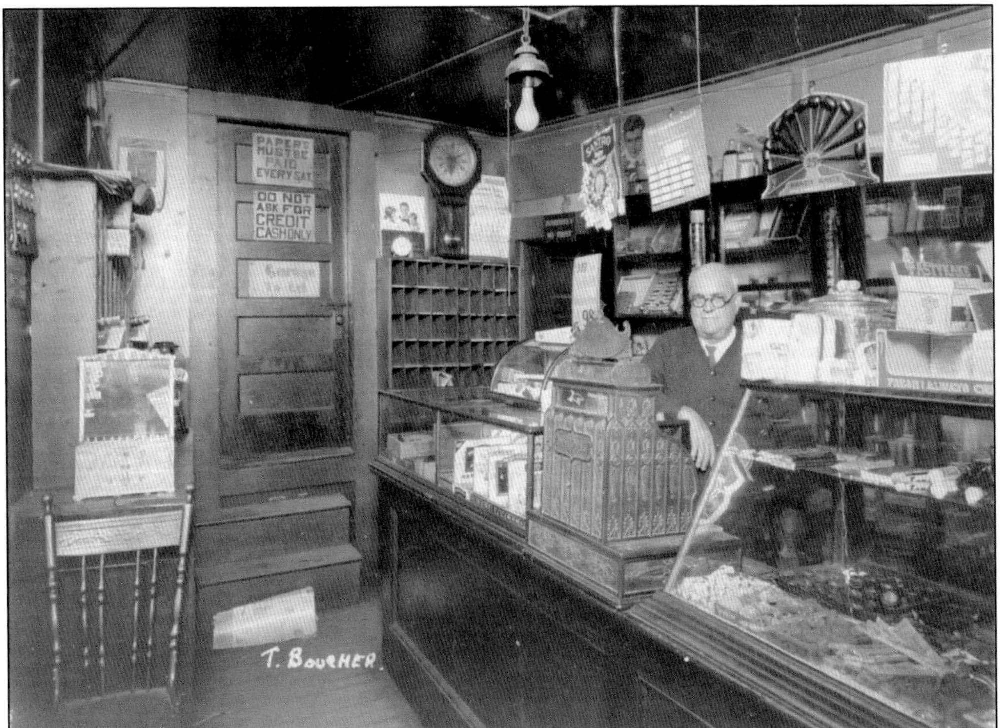

Treffle Boucher is leaning on his National cash register in his store on the corner of New London Turnpike and Centreville Road in this photograph from the 1930s. A candy case with Hershey bars on the top shelf is to the right, and a case displaying cigars is on the left. Behind Boucher is a fan of Handy Andy pipes selling for 25¢ each. The signs on the door advertise a garage for rent. Boucher only took cash, and papers had to be paid for on Saturday. (Courtesy of Armand Boucher.)

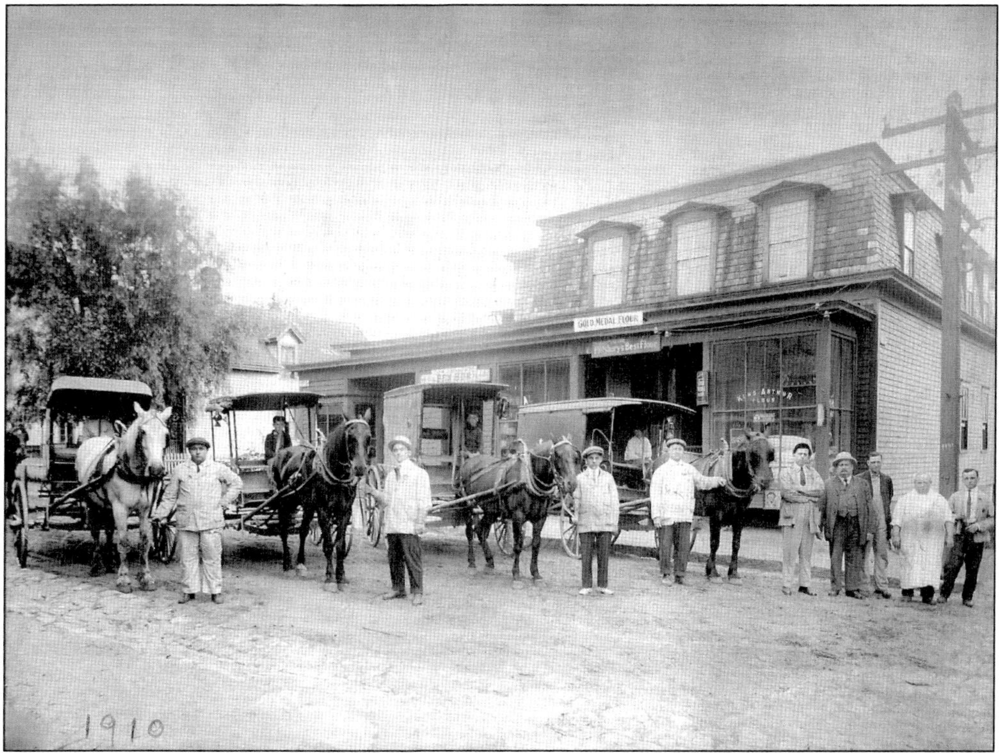

Above the third delivery carriage from the left, a sign on the building reads, "J.B. Tellier We Sell Ben Hur Flour." Gold Medal Flour, Pillsbury's Best Flour, and King Arthur Flour were also advertised. It appears the Centreville Market had a thriving business when this photograph was taken in 1910. (Courtesy of Lawrence G. Soucy.)

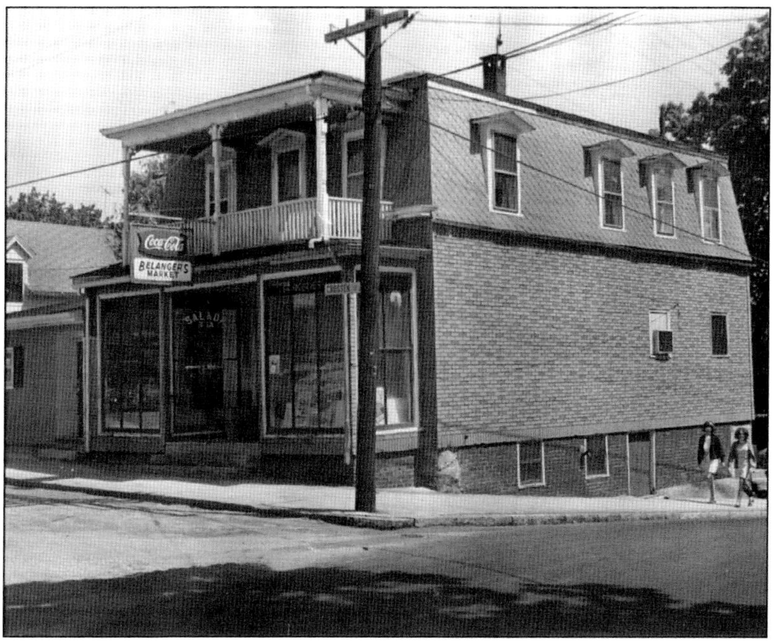

Taken in 1968, this photograph shows that the store on the corner of Crossen Street and Brookside Avenue became Belanger's Market. A covered porch has been added along with new siding. Perhaps the two girls are going to the market for their mother. (Courtesy of Lawrence G. Soucy.)

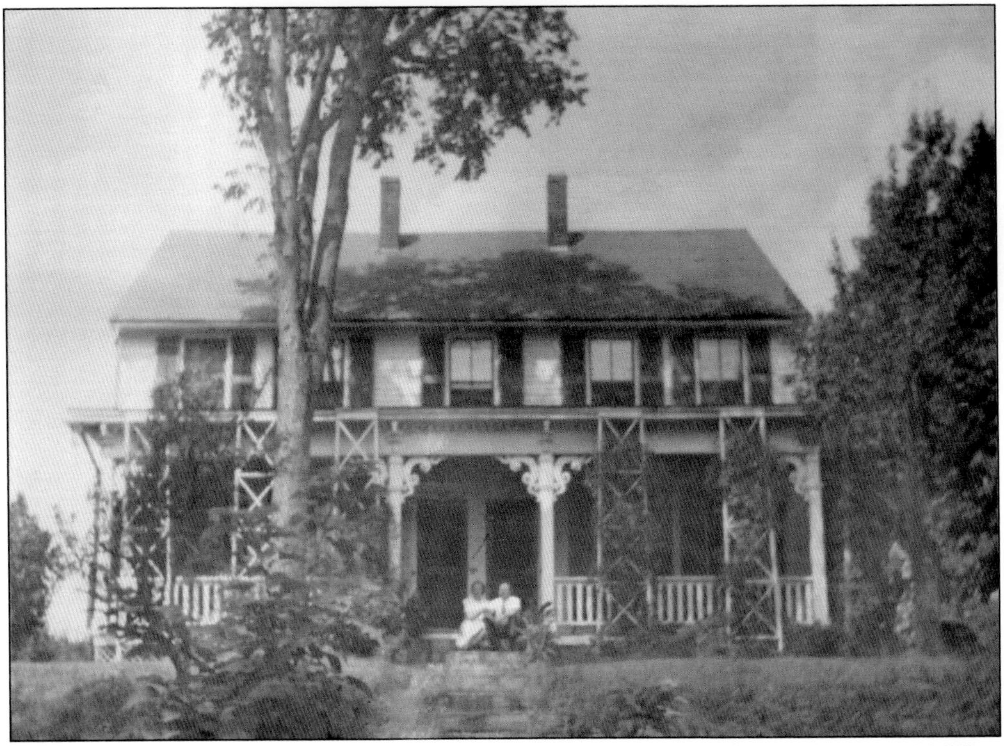

This beautiful house was prominently set back from the corner of Main Street at 92 West Warwick Avenue. It was known as the Powell House in 1947 when this photograph was taken. The family on the front steps seems to be watching the photographer. Pat's 24-Hour Towing and Recovery Service (below) resides there now. The corner has been rounded off to give a turn lane, and a traffic light has been added. This photograph was taken on August 30, 2010. (Below, author's collection.)

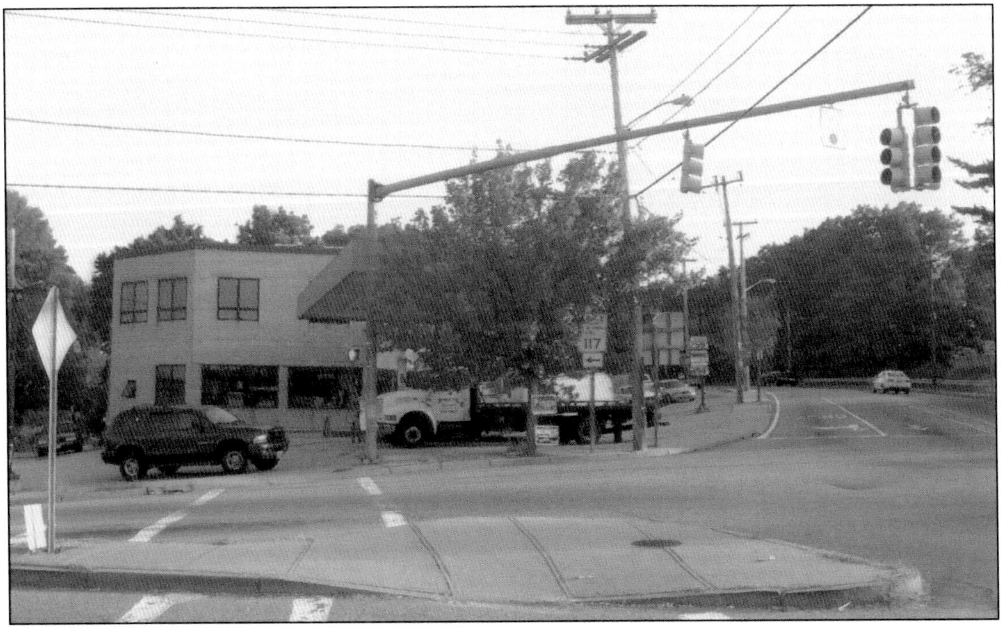

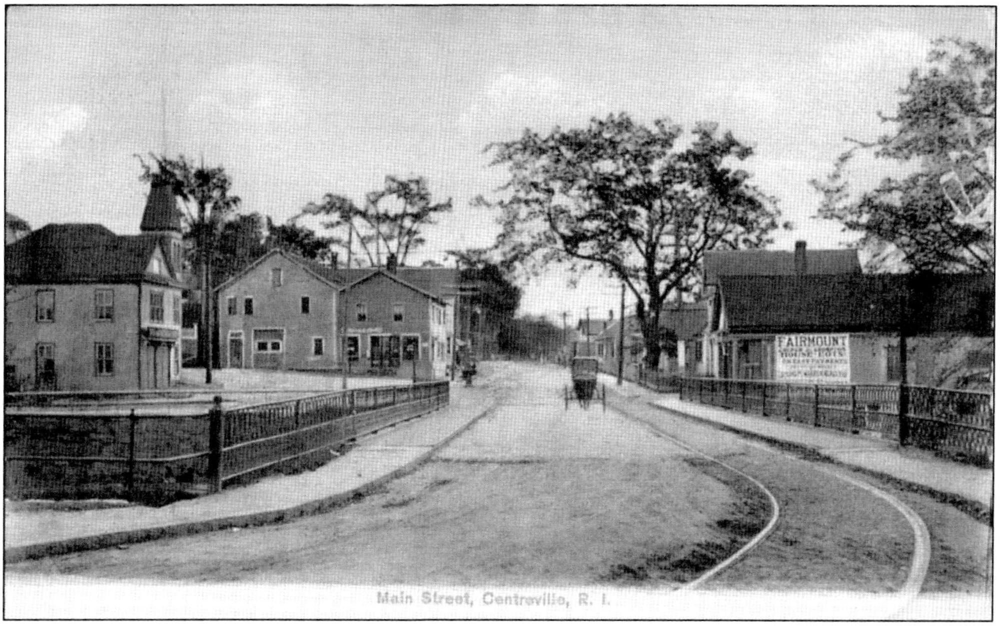

This is a postcard view of Main Street crossing the Centreville Bridge. At the end of the bridge is a sharp left turn on Bridal Avenue. It follows the fence on top of the wall, past the fire station, leading to the Centreville Mill complex. The sign on the building to the right reads: "FAIRMOUNT CHURCH ST. CROMPTON HOUSE LOTS ON EASY PAYMENTS 75¢ DOWN $1.50 WEEKLY EDMUND M. WARREN REALTY."

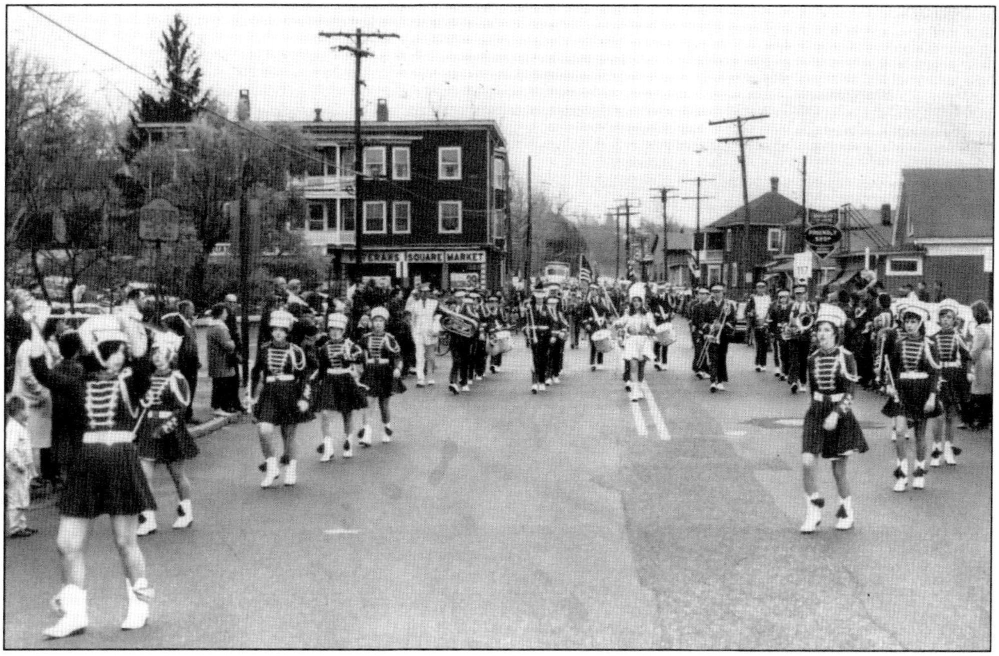

The Coventry High School band performs in a parade in 1947. In this image, they are marching across a new bridge on their way to Arctic. They have already passed the Veteran's Square Market, which replaced the two small buildings in the photograph above. The Veteran's Square Diner was on the right, just out of the picture.

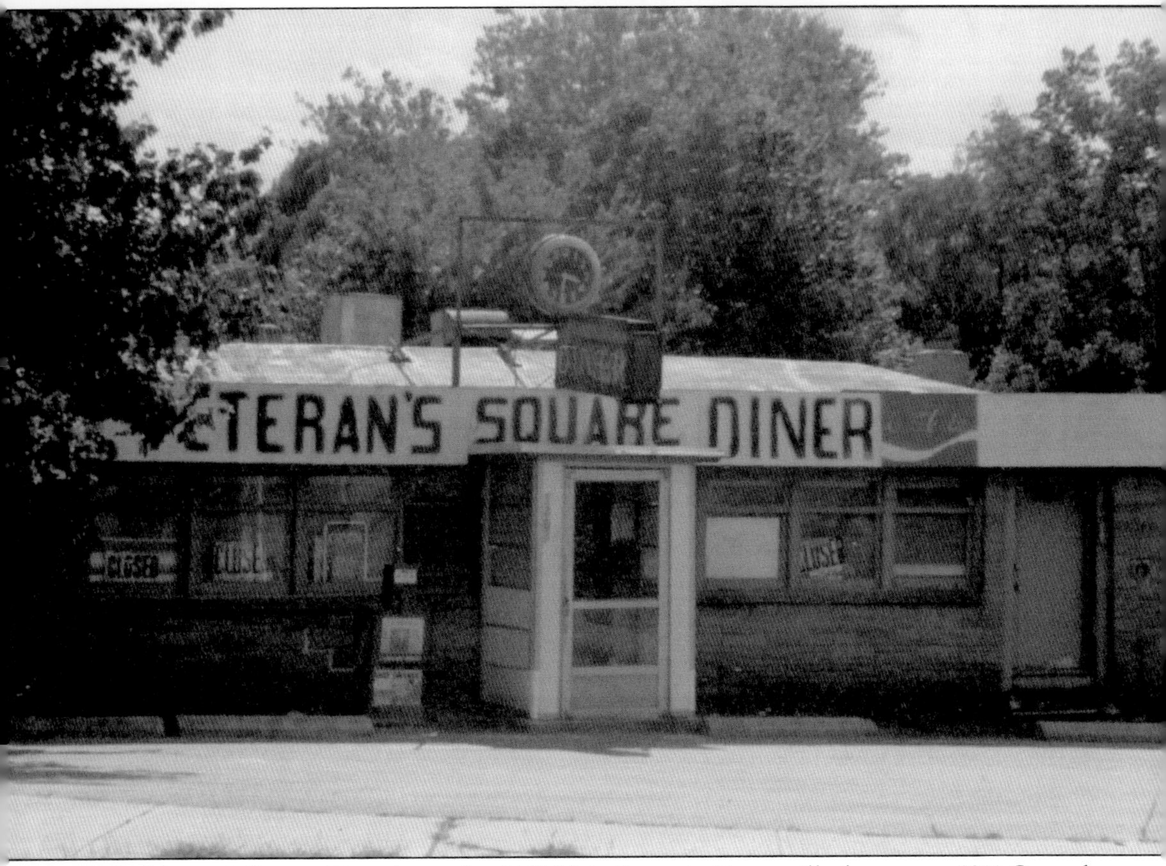

The Veteran's Square Diner, located at 1461 Main Street in Centerville, began as a 1911 Osgood Bradley electric trolley car, no. 1068. In 1912, the City of Providence, Rhode Island, bought 32 cars numbered 1068 to 1099 to run on the Broad Street Line. They were operated by the United Electric Railway (UER) until 1939. By then, buses run by United Transit Company (UTC) were taking over. In 1940, Leo Levallee bought trolley car no. 1068 from the City of Providence. Then, in 1941, he moved it to Veteran's Square, remodeled it, and opened a diner that only sat 10 customers. Samuel Richer took over ownership in 1956 and ran the diner into the 1990s. After the diner was hit by an automobile in 2000, the town considered it an eyesore, and it was set to be demolished. Richard Shappy decided to save it and bought the diner trolley from the Town of West Warwick on August 28, 2002. He was given two weeks to move it. It took one week to brace the inside so it could be transported to his place of business in Providence.

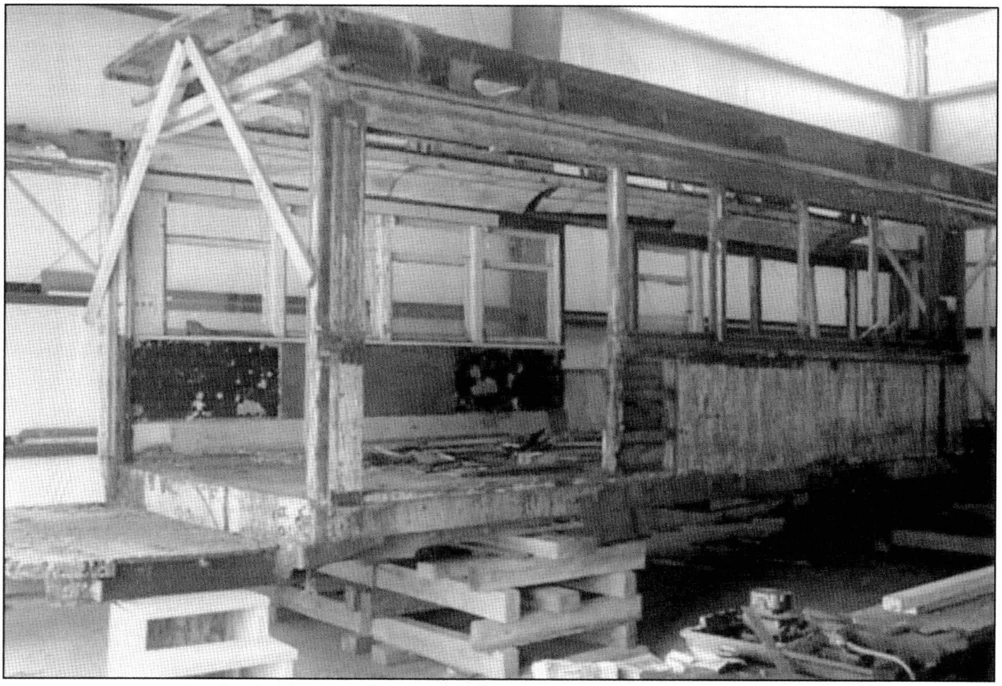

After arriving at Richard Shappy's business, the trolley sat in the parking lot for a year. Above, the trolley is in a building erected for it, where a complete restoration would take place. As the restoration began, it was discovered that the areas for the motorman on both ends had been cut off. Fortunately, the platforms were not disturbed. Shappy's son Brandon worked diligently to strip off 90 years of paint buildup. The photograph below shows his progress. (Both, courtesy of Richard Shappy.)

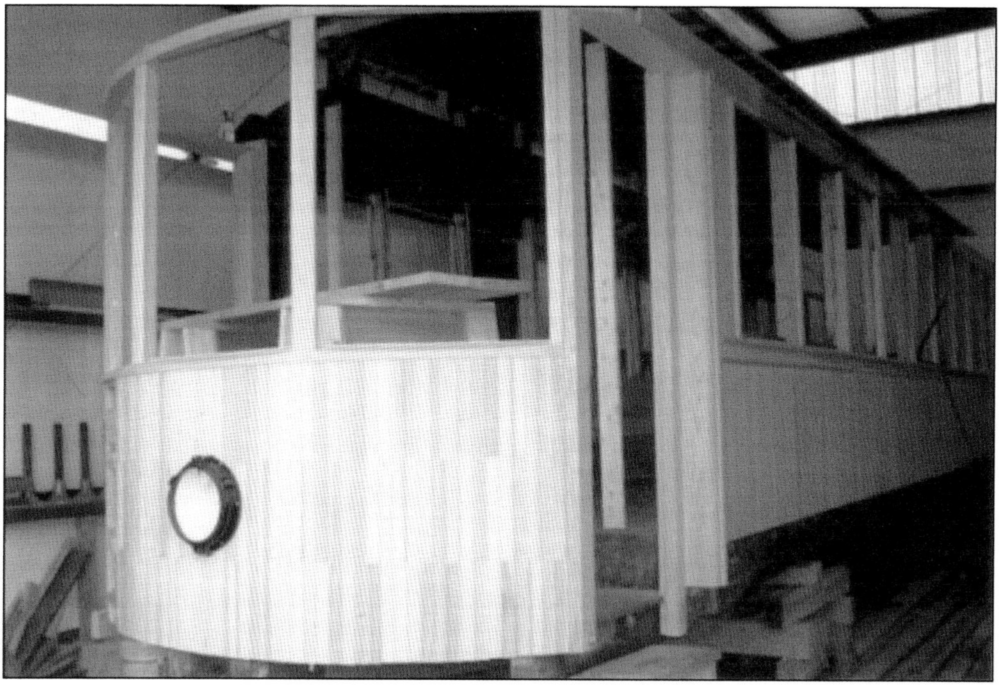

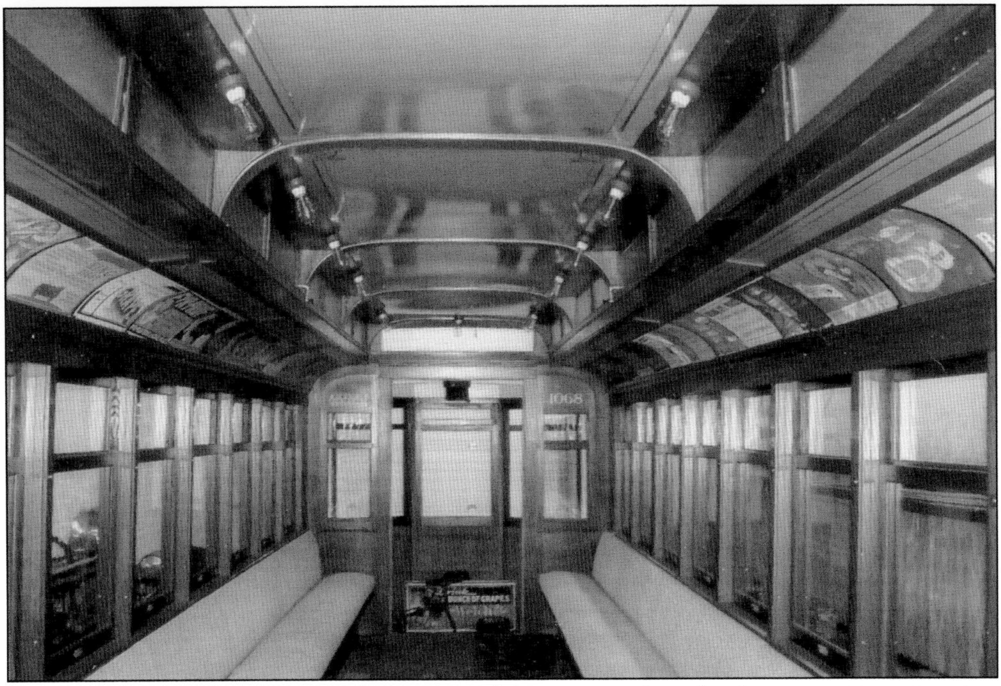

The completed trolley interior is the result of three years work under the supervision of project foreman Chris Brayton. Many of the parts seen needed to be reproduced and 80 windows replaced. All the advertising signs pictured are original. The small sign to the left of the door reads: "Spitting on the floor of this car is forbidden." Osgood Bradley Trolley 1068 was the first built in the series. Now, thanks to Richard Shappy, it is the last one to survive. Shappy (below) is standing in the entrance to the trolley he brought back to life from near-extinction. Keeping it company is a 6-cylinder, 90-horsepower, Model JS 4 Ahrens-Fox pumper from 1925. It was originally built in Cincinnati, Ohio, and bought new by the Washington, Ohio, Fire District on July 17, 1925. These photographs were taken on February 10, 2011. (Both, author's collection.)

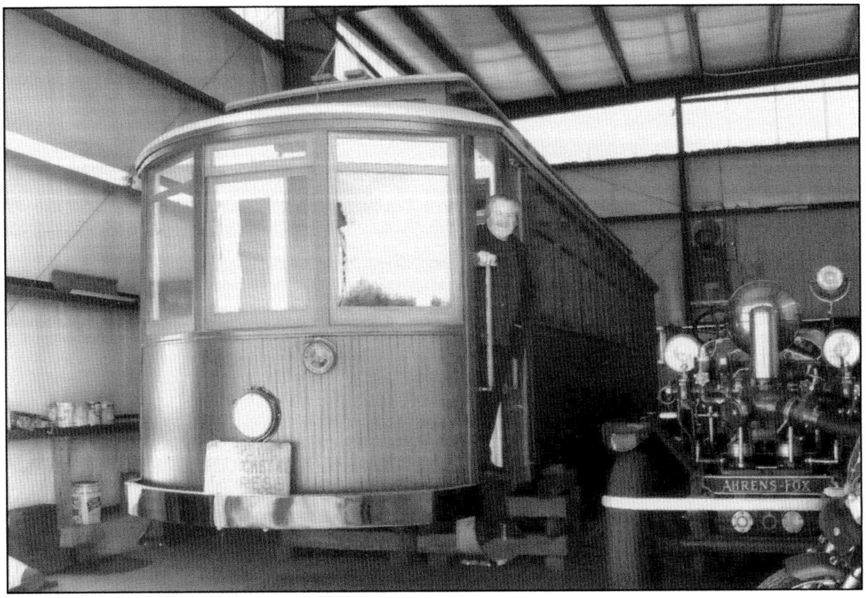

Three

Clyde Village

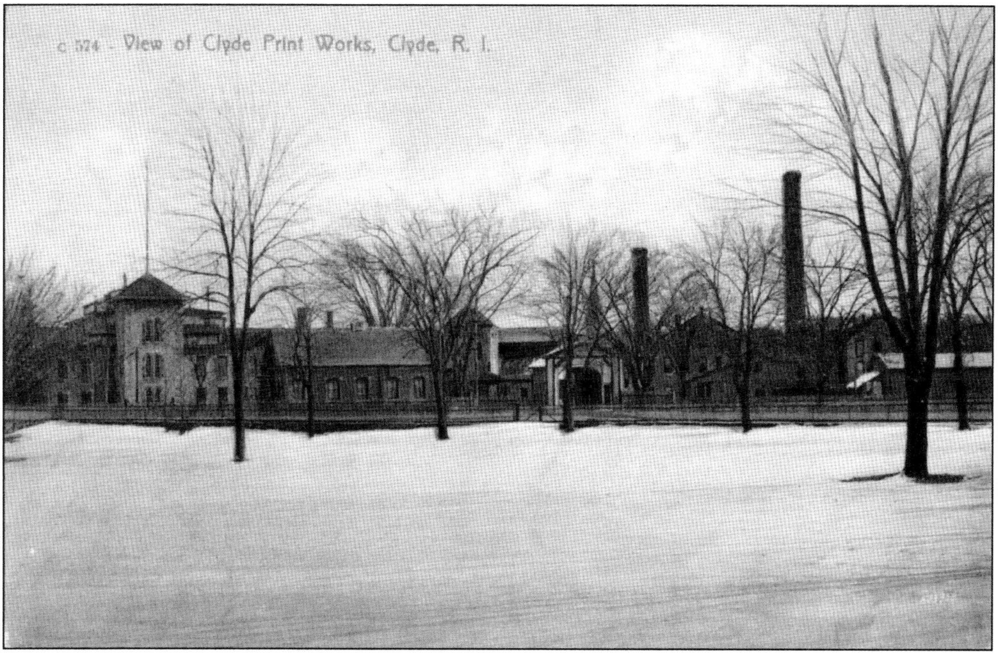

Clyde Bleachery and Print Works was founded in 1828 by Simon H. Greene and Edward Pike. Greene bought out Pike's heirs when he died in 1842. In 1865, Greene formed S.H. Greene and Sons. In 1899, he incorporated as S.H. Greene and Sons Corporation. By 1908, when the photograph for this postcard was taken, the company was printing 1.25 million yards of cloth per week. The business was placed in receivership in 1925, and four generations of Greene family ownership ended at a public auction in 1926. The complex has since been used by Almacs Supermarket, the Pawtuxet Valley Bus Line (presently Academy Bus), and C.J. Coutu Lumber Company.

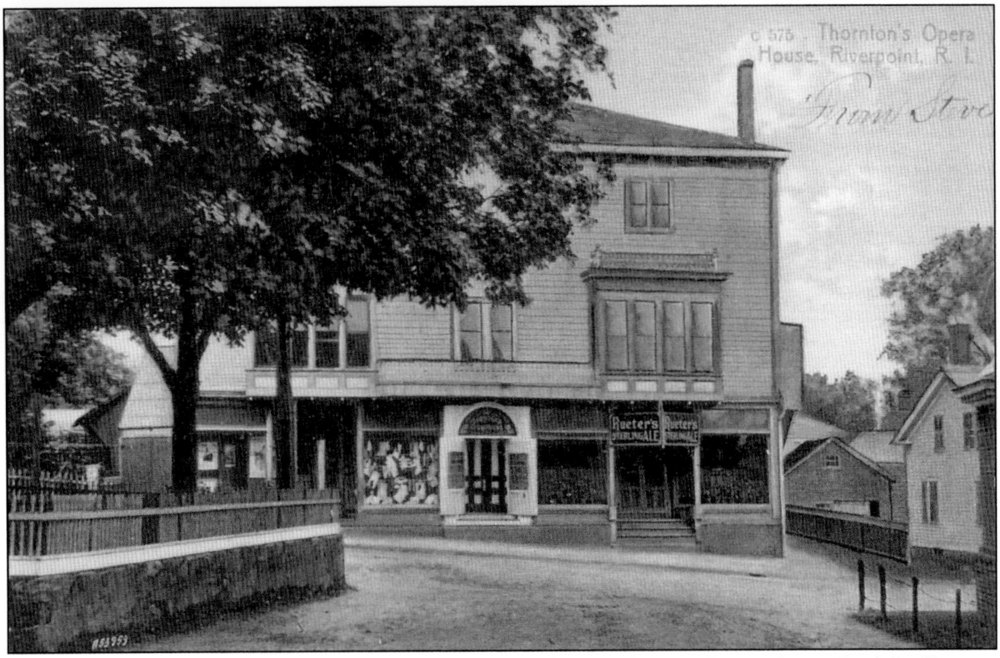

This postcard shows Thornton's Opera House, located at 1005 Main Street. It was built by Eugene Baxter in 1896 for brothers John, James, and Owen Thornton. In December 1929, talkie movies made their initial appearance. At one time, the building's basement included 10 bowling lanes. Owen Thornton set a world record in duckpin bowling there. (Courtesy of Lawrence G. Soucy.)

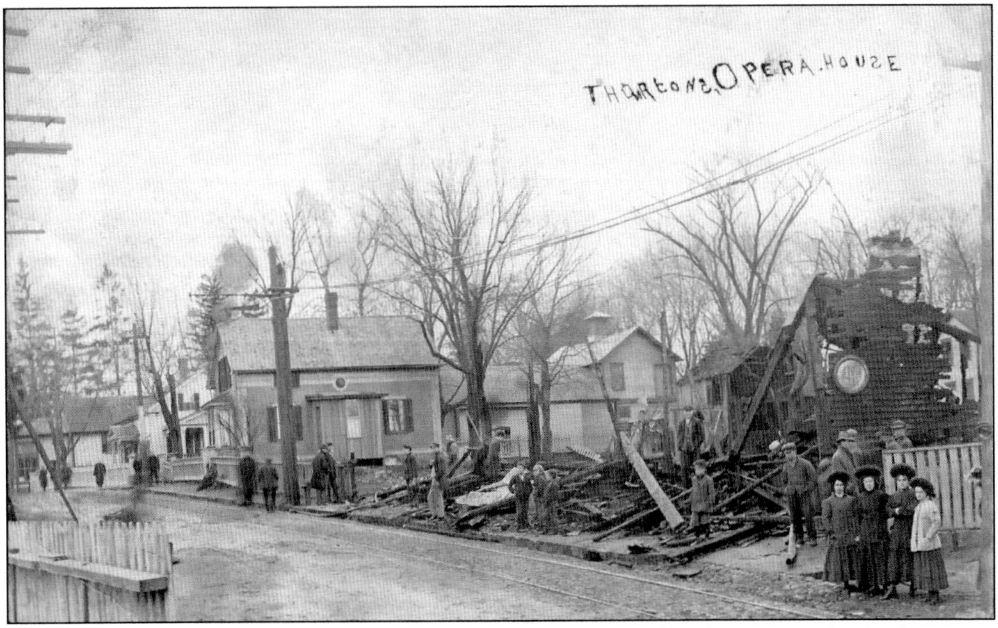

This postcard shows the remains of Thornton's Opera House. This devastating fire broke out on Thanksgiving night in 1910. The new Thornton's Theatre opened to the public on Labor Day in 1911. The following verse is from "Dedicated to Firemen," written by Helen O. Larson in 1980 at age 70: "When the siren starts screeching, they're once more on the go / They jump on the trucks, there's another fire we know." (Courtesy of Lawrence G. Soucy.)

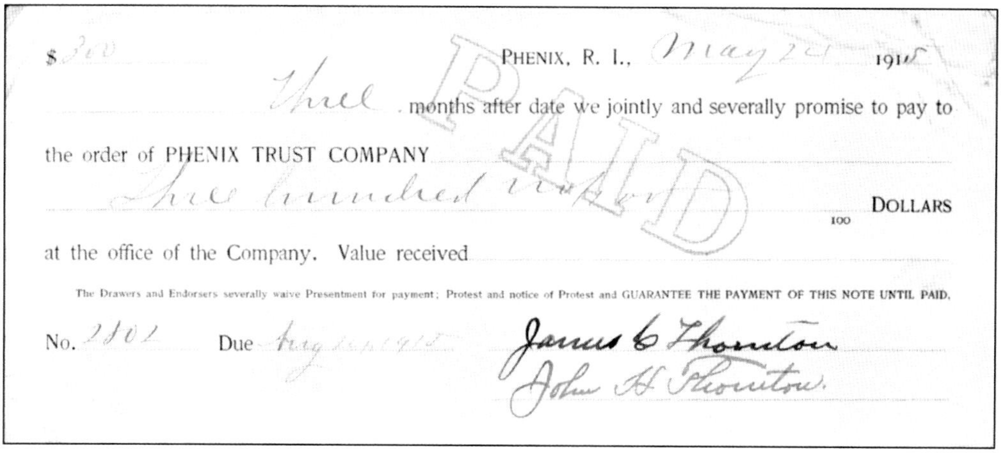
$300 PHENIX, R. I., May 24 1915

three months after date we jointly and severally promise to pay to

the order of PHENIX TRUST COMPANY

Three hundred no/100 DOLLARS

at the office of the Company. Value received

The Drawers and Endorsers severally waive Presentment for payment; Protest and notice of Protest and GUARANTEE THE PAYMENT OF THIS NOTE UNTIL PAID.

No. 2101 Due Aug 24 1915

James C Thornton

John H Thornton

PAID

On May 24, 1915, John and James Thornton borrowed $300 from the Phenix Trust Company. It was a three-month note and was paid off on August 24, 1915, as promised. The author spent many a Saturday afternoon at their new Thornton's Theatre as a young boy, watching two Westerns, cartoons, and a newsreel—all for just 25¢. To obtain fee admission, he would collect empty soda bottles around the village of Hope and bring them to D. Noel's Service Station to collect 2¢ each. An insurance agency was to the right of Thornton's and Berman's Variety Store was to the left in the same building. Berman's carried Tip Top bread and, of course, good old comic books. In fact, they used to hang a few in the window to tempt children to spend their money within. (Courtesy of Lawrence G. Soucy.)

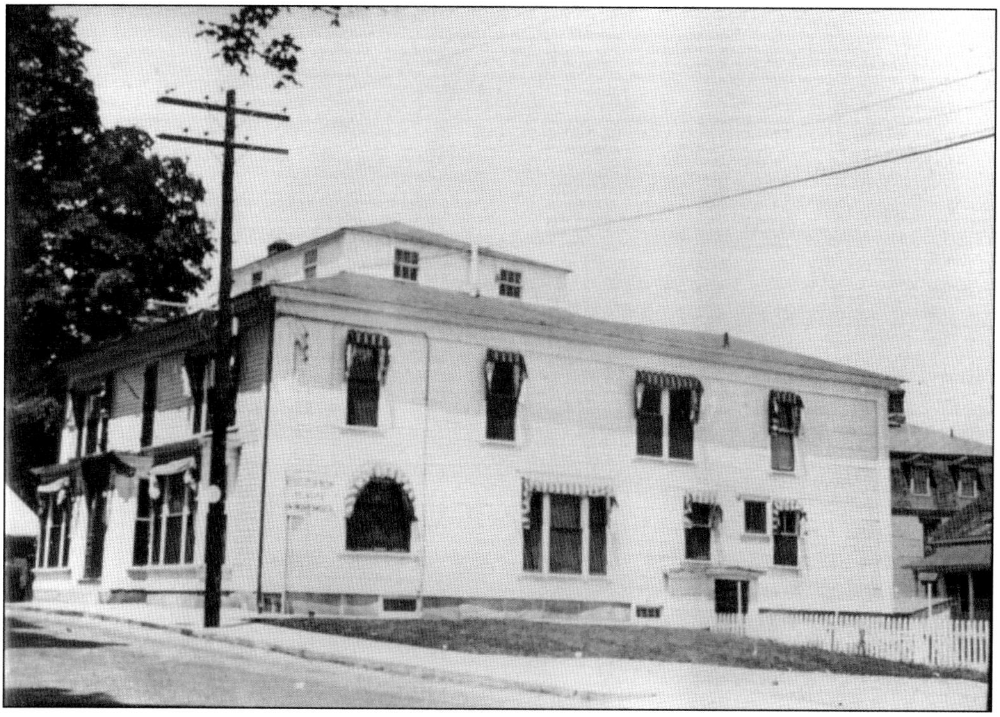

George Kenyon constructed this building in 1839. It was once the residence of Edward Pike, co-owner of Clyde Print Works. Located at 20 Pike Street, it is still referred to as the Pike House. In 1913, the new town of West Warwick chose the building for its first town hall. The town moved to its present building on Main Street in Arctic in November 1959 (seen on page 42).

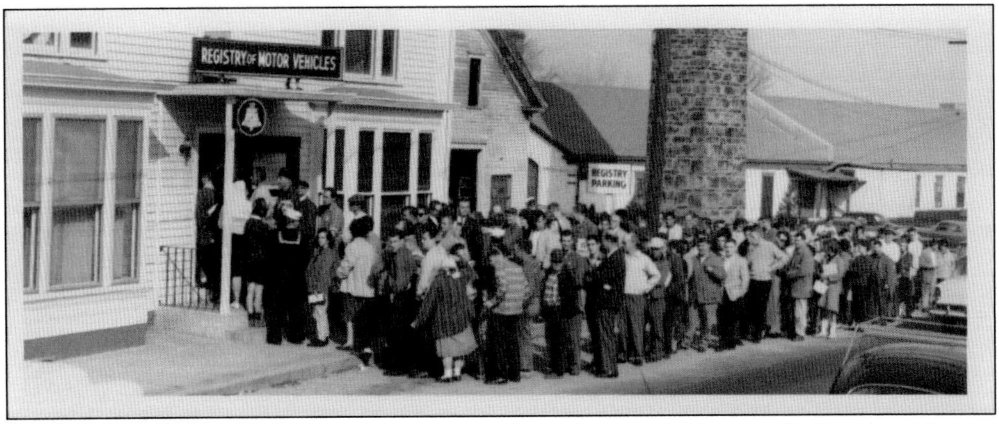

The Registry of Motor Vehicles also occupied the Pike House with the town hall in the 1950s. As this photograph records, some things change, and others never change. Comparing the shadows in this photograph with the one below tells that it must be about 4 p.m. in the afternoon, as the sun is coming around in the west.

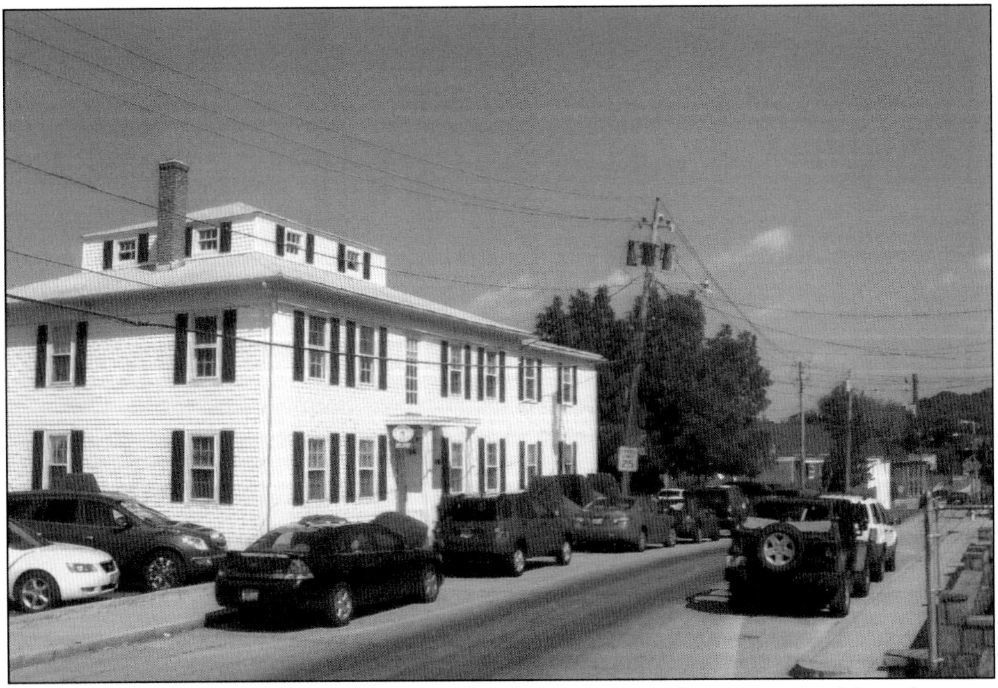

Today, Guill Tool uses the Pike House as its headquarters. Pike Street is situated directly across from where Thornton's Opera House was located on Main Street (seen on the top of page 58). This photograph was taken at 3:30 p.m. on August 31, 2010. (Author's collection.)

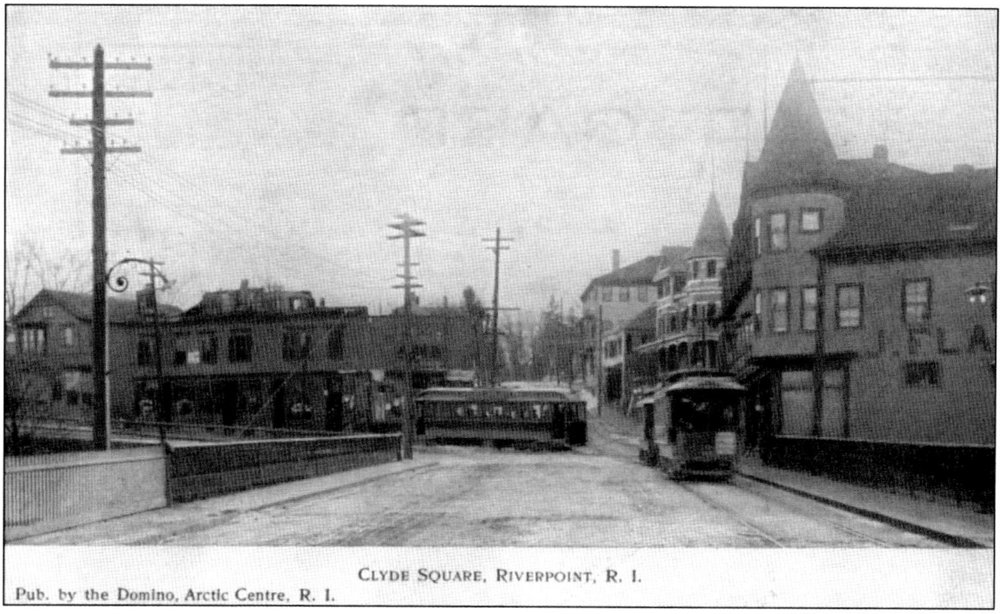

This postcard shows a view of Clyde Square, which was part of River Point at the time. It was mailed to Connecticut on December 1, 1905. Edward Cassidy owned the building on the corner of East Main and Main Streets, known as the Cassidy Block. It is being razed after a fire destroyed it around 1890. The Flanagan building is on the right just after the bridge, followed by the Clyde Hotel, and ending with Thornton's Theatre at the top of the hill. (Courtesy of Richard Hughes.)

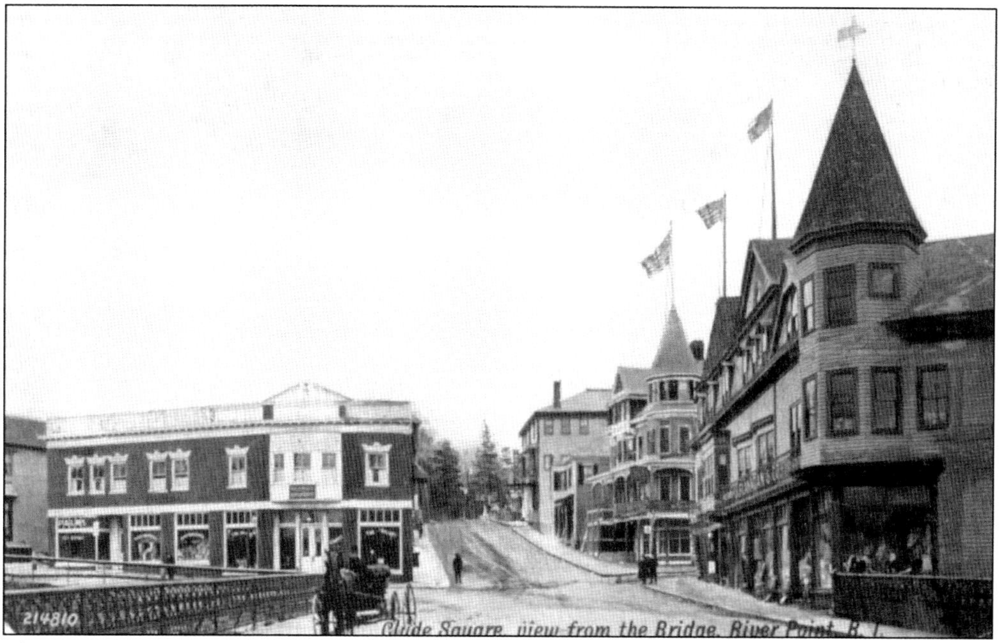

This postcard photograph was taken from almost the same location as the one above. The newly rebuilt Palm's Cassidy Block is prominent on the corner of East Main Street. Raymond Page ran the Hobbyhorse hobby shop, located on the ground floor of the Flanagan building. The author could never resist the temptation of stopping in on his walks home on Saturday afternoons after watching Westerns at Thornton's Theatre. The unemployment office also occupied space there.

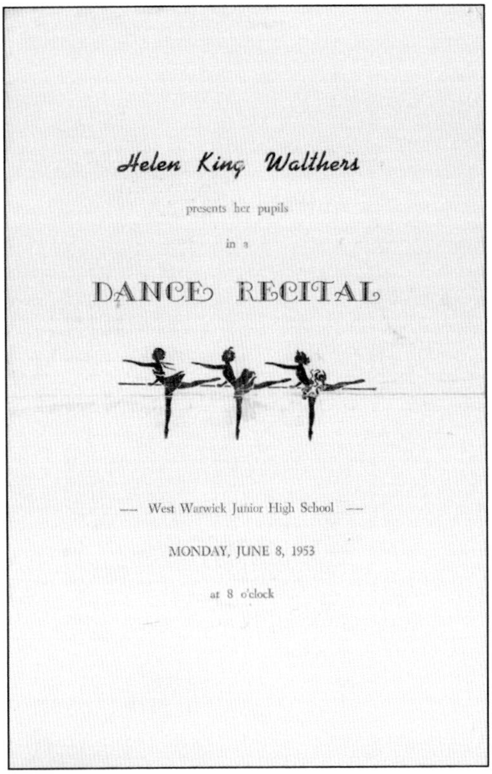

Helen King Walthers

presents her pupils

in a

DANCE RECITAL

— West Warwick Junior High School —

MONDAY, JUNE 8, 1953

at 8 o'clock

Helen King Walthers ran a dance studio on the third floor of the J. Flanagan building, pictured on the left of the photograph below. At left is the program from Marcia Carpenter's recital on June 8, 1953, at the West Warwick Junior High School. (Courtesy of Marcia Carpenter.)

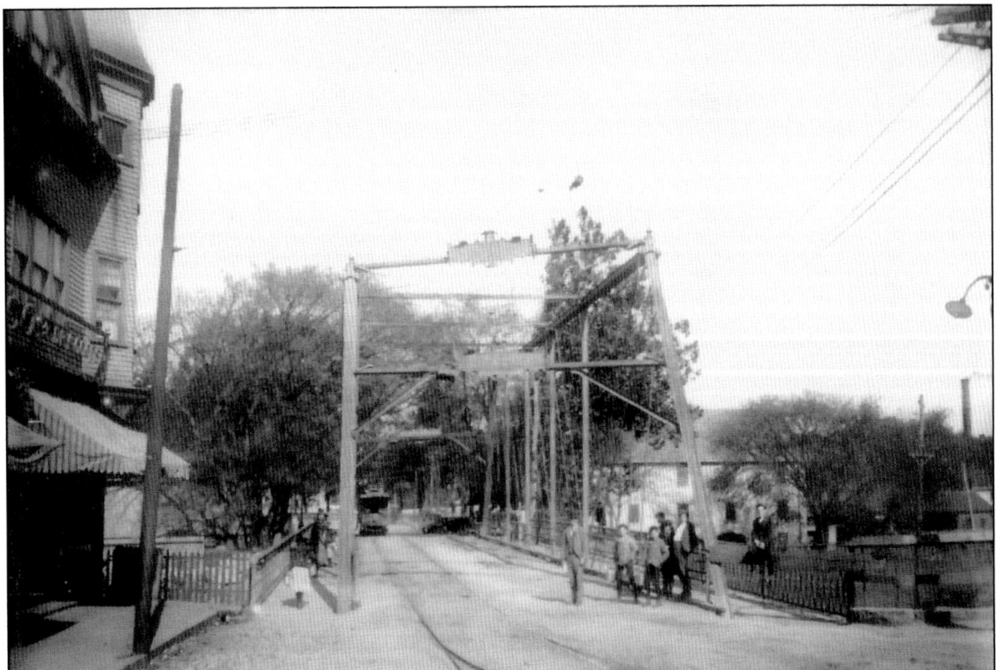

The original Clyde Bridge was washed away during the freshet of February 1886. This photograph, taken about 1900, shows the truss bridge that replaced it. The trolley is approaching from Lippitt as the group of boys watches the cameraman. (Courtesy of Lawrence G. Soucy.)

This advertisement is from the *Pawtuxet Valley Daily Times* dated Wednesday July 20, 1892. It is noteworthy that this newspaper edition is number one of the first volume. The advertisement states the retailer has a complete line of dry goods and clothing. The following verses are from "My New Paper Girl" by Helen O. Larson: "She always closes my door, after she places the paper inside / Then she jumps on her bike, to take another short ride. To the next house she goes, and leaves the *P.V. Times* there / Again she jumps on her bike, to leave the *Times* elsewhere." (Courtesy of Gary St. Onge.)

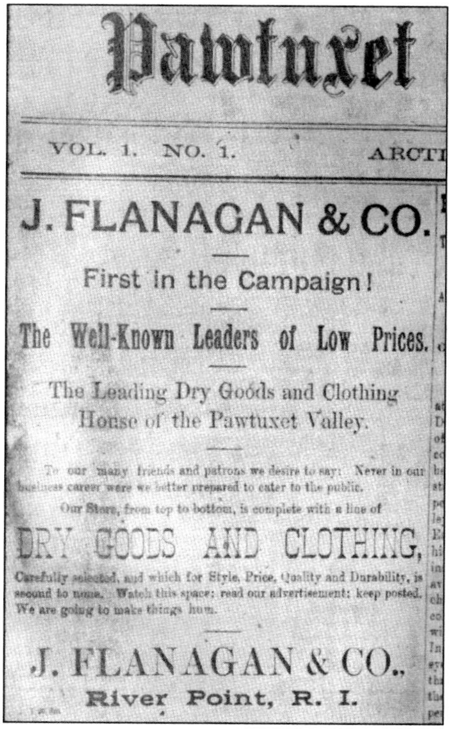

Pawtuxet

VOL. 1. NO. 1.

J. FLANAGAN & CO.

First in the Campaign!

The Well-Known Leaders of Low Prices.

The Leading Dry Goods and Clothing House of the Pawtuxet Valley.

To our many friends and patrons we desire to say: Never in our business career were we better prepared to cater to the public.

Our Store, from top to bottom, is complete with a line of

DRY GOODS AND CLOTHING,

Carefully selected, and which for Style, Price, Quality and Durability, is second to none. Watch this space: read our advertisement: keep posted. We are going to make things hum.

J. FLANAGAN & CO.,

River Point, R. I.

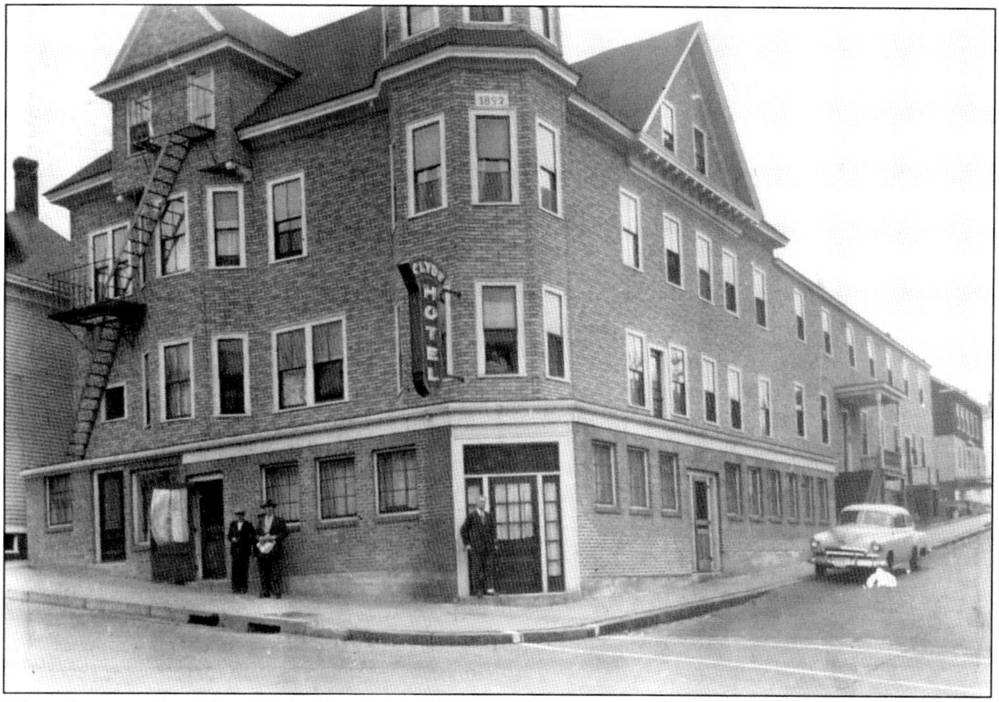

This photograph of the Clyde Hotel was taken in the 1950s. It was located on Main Street across from the Palm's building. It was also on Maple Avenue across from the J. Flanagan building. A block set in the bricks, which can be seen above the third-story window, recorded it was built in 1892.

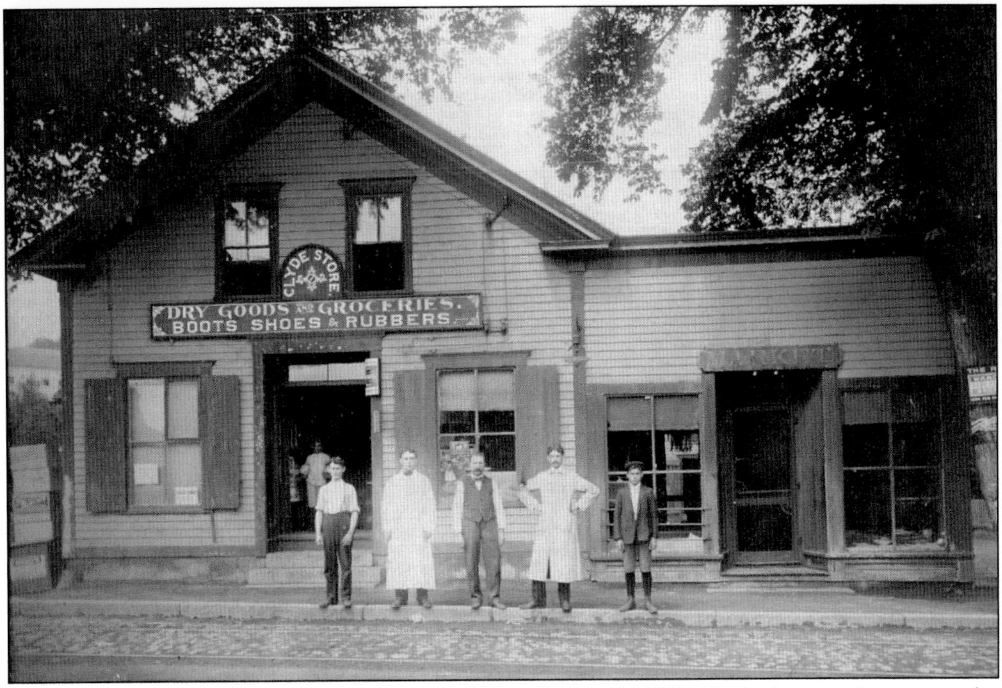

The Clyde Store was located on the corner of Main Street and Woodside Avenue. It appears the workers are taking a break to pose for a photograph. The sign in the window is advertising Rocky Point Amusement Park. This building, minus the addition on the right, can also be seen behind the telephone pole in the picture at the bottom of page 58. (Courtesy of Larry G. Soucy.)

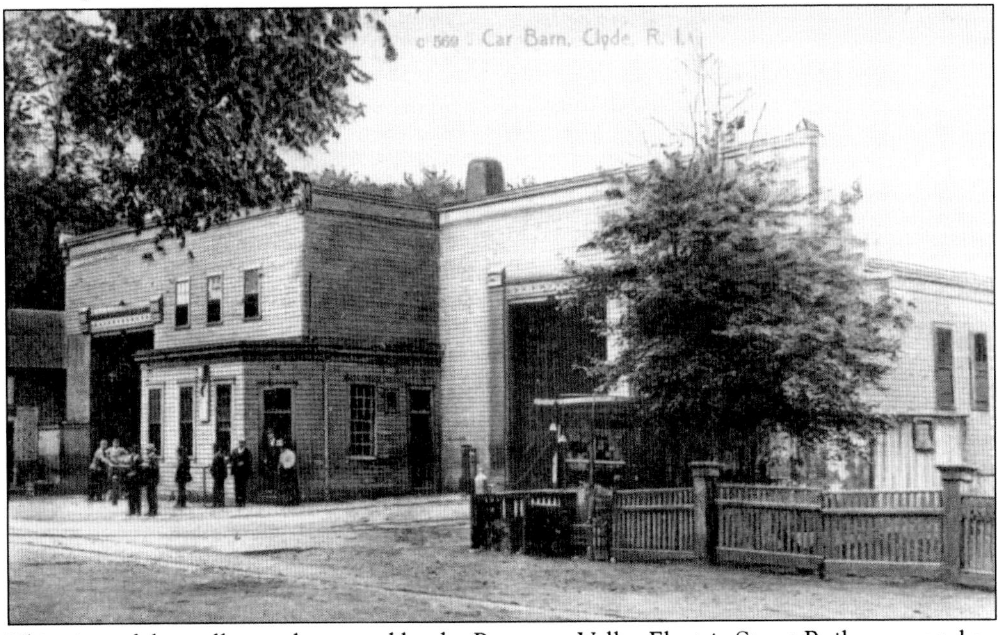

This view of the trolley car barn used by the Pawtuxet Valley Electric Street Railway was taken in 1908. It was built in the 1890s as a place where repairs and maintenance could be done on the trolleys. The small area in the front of the building was where tickets could also be bought. Today, this building would be located approximately where the Sweet November's parking lot is.

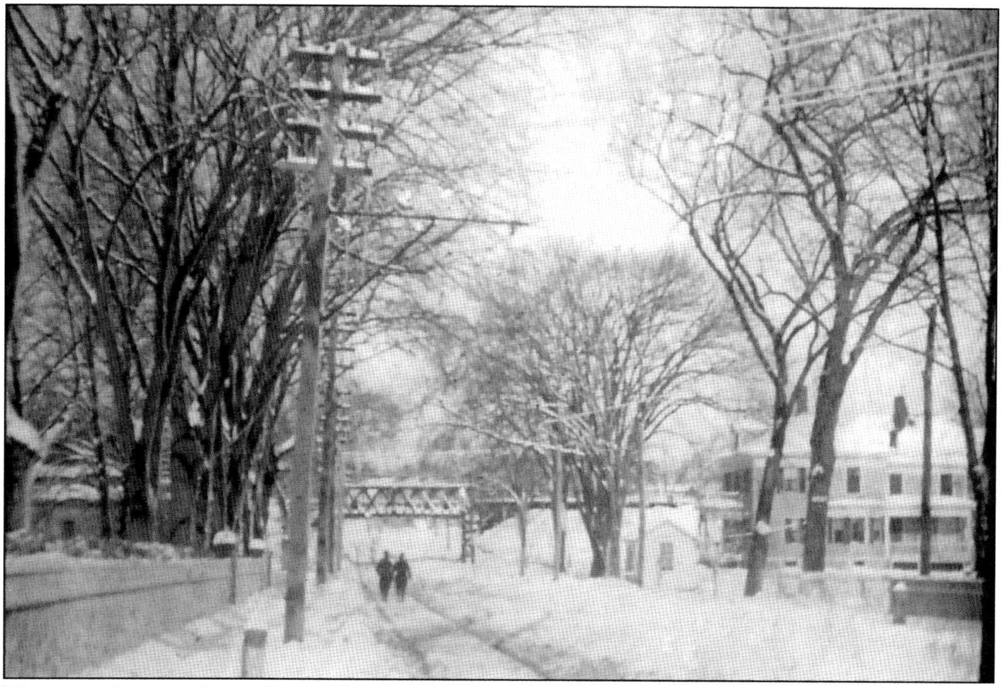

These two boys are headed toward Lippitt on Main Street. They are passing the large house on the right where Phillip Duffy lived. Today, across the street is Sweet November's Bakery, near where the trolley car barn was located. The following verse is from "Winter Wonderland," written by Helen O. Larson on January 16, 1978, at age 77: "I was looking out my window, and as I looked around / I could see a blanket of white, it covered all the ground." (Courtesy of Lawrence Soucy.)

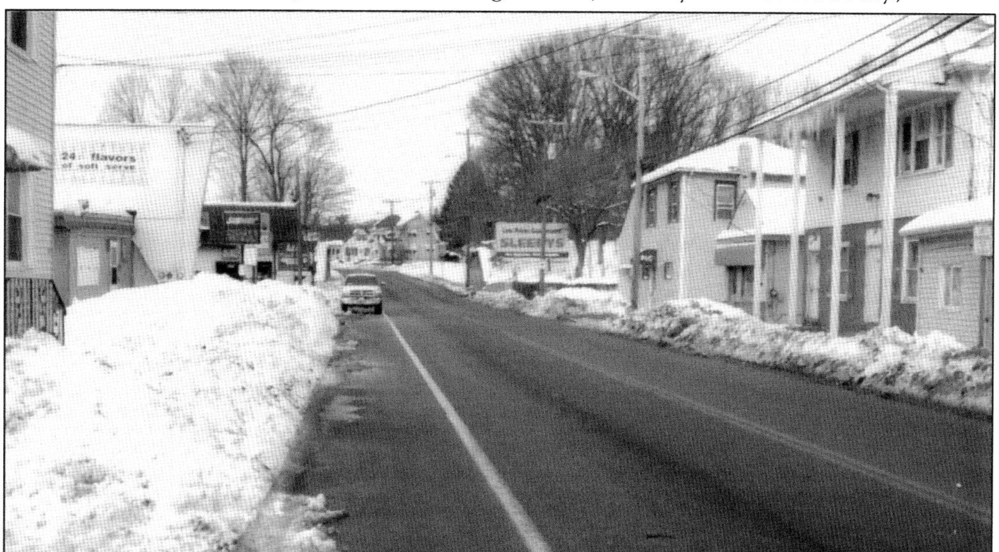

This photograph was taken on January 28, 2011, from about the same location as above. The bridge of the Pawtuxet Valley Railroad, built in 1874, is gone. The railroad was a three-mile-long spur that traveled from River Point to Hope. In 1875, it was leased to the trustees of the Hartford, Providence & Fishkill Railroad. (Author's collection.)

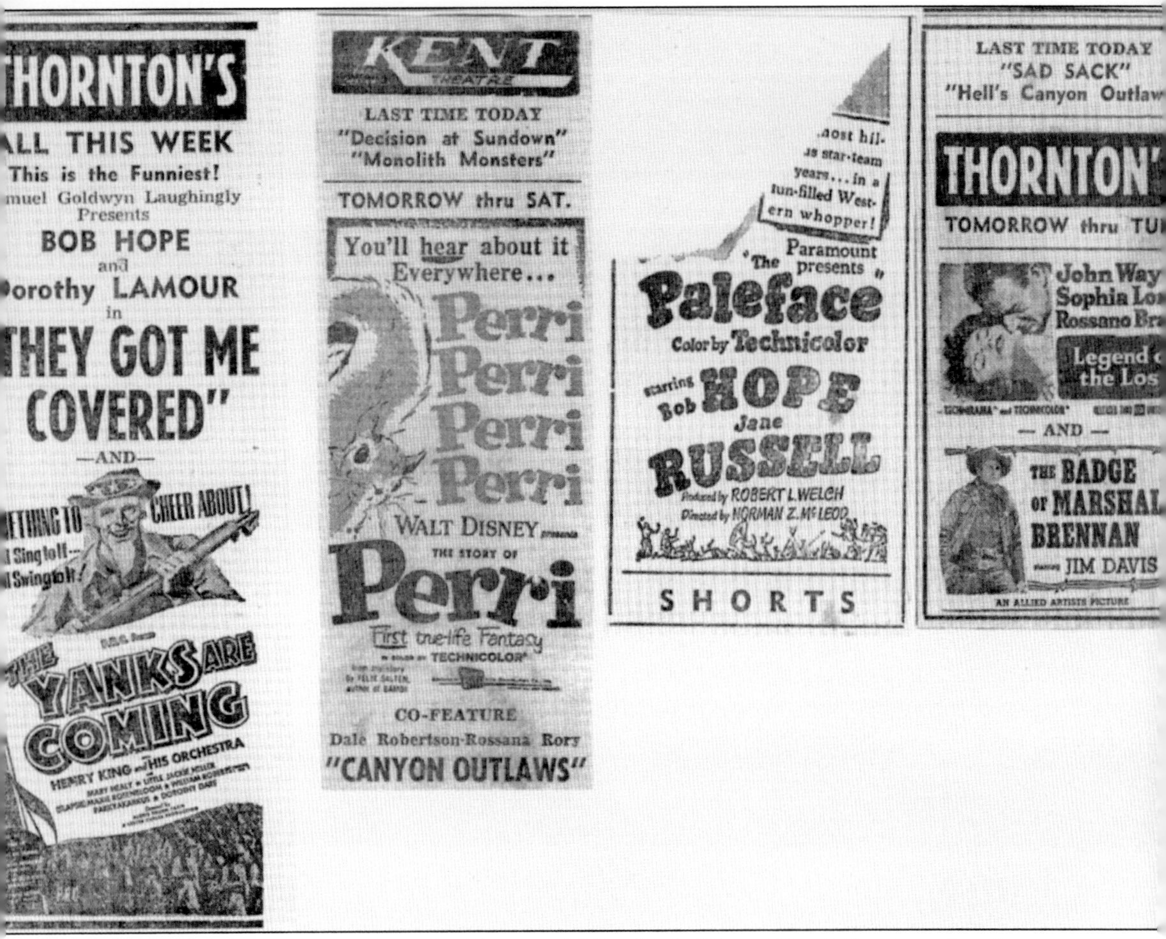

These advertisements are from the *Pawtuxet Valley Daily Times*. The following advertisements appear from left to right: Thornton's advertised the movie *The Yanks Are Coming* in the Friday edition on May 7, 1943; the Kent Theatre advertised Walt Disney's story of *Perri* in the Tuesday edition on January 14, 1958, and the second feature was, of course, a Western, *Canyon Outlaws*, starring Dale Robertson of the television series *Wells Fargo*; Thornton's advertised *Paleface*, featuring Bob Hope and Jane Russell, on Friday, February 11, 1949; and Thornton's advertised *Legend of the Lost*, starring John Wayne and Sophia Loren, on Wednesday, January 15, 1958. Henry and Irene Erinakes of Lachance Street in West Warwick owned several theaters, including the Palace and Thornton's, plus the Hilltop and Lonsdale Drive-Ins. Brother George and his wife, Blanche, owned the Kent and East Greenwich Theatres. (Author's collection.)

Four

CROMPTON VILLAGE

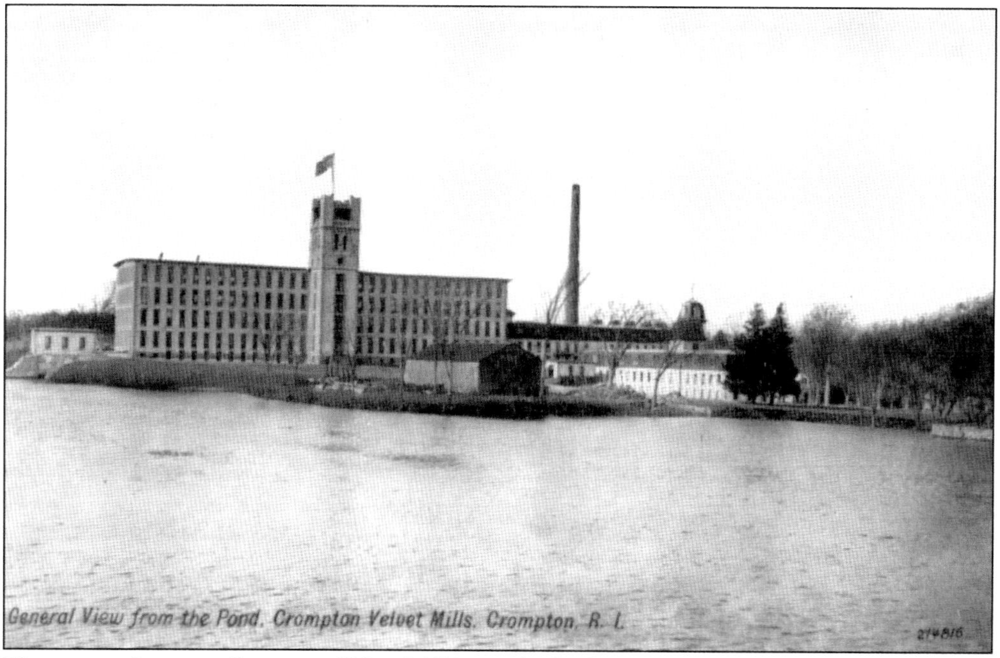

This postcard pictures Crompton Velvet Mill No. 4, built of granite in 1882 by Stone and Carpenter. Corduroy was produced at the mill. The small building to the left was the mill's hydropower plant. The original mill was the Stone Jug Mill, built in 1807. The village was officially named Crompton in honor of Samuel Crompton, inventor of the spinning mule. In 1885, it started making velvet and became the first mill in the United States to make both corduroy and velvet. Crompton was nicknamed the "Velvet Village."

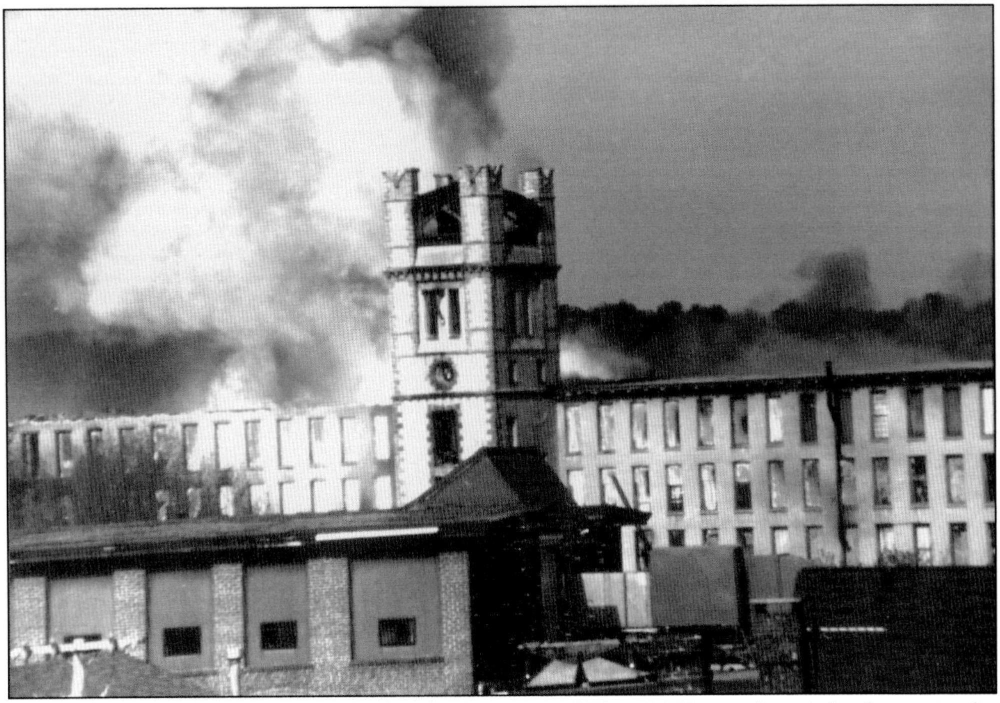

May 15, 1992, was a devastating day for the Crompton Velvet Mill complex. A fire began in the south end of the building and quickly spread throughout the structure. For 185 years, the mill was a landmark in the village that proudly carries its name. After the blaze was extinguished, the only remains of the four-story building were the skeleton granite walls as pictured below. A crane had already been brought to the site to complete the demolition job the fire began.

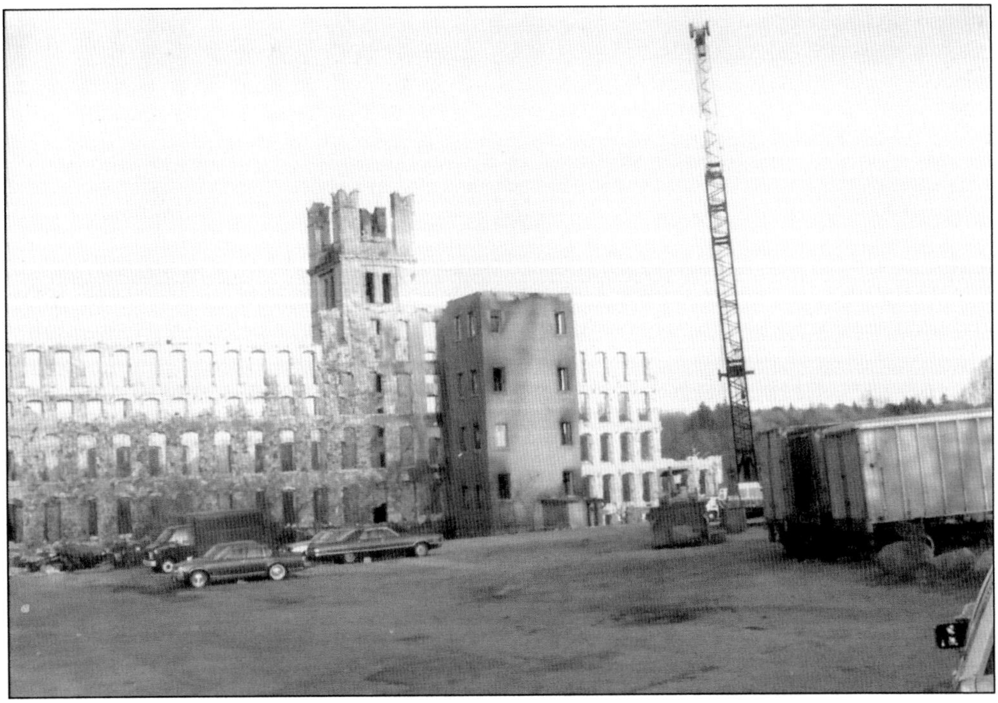

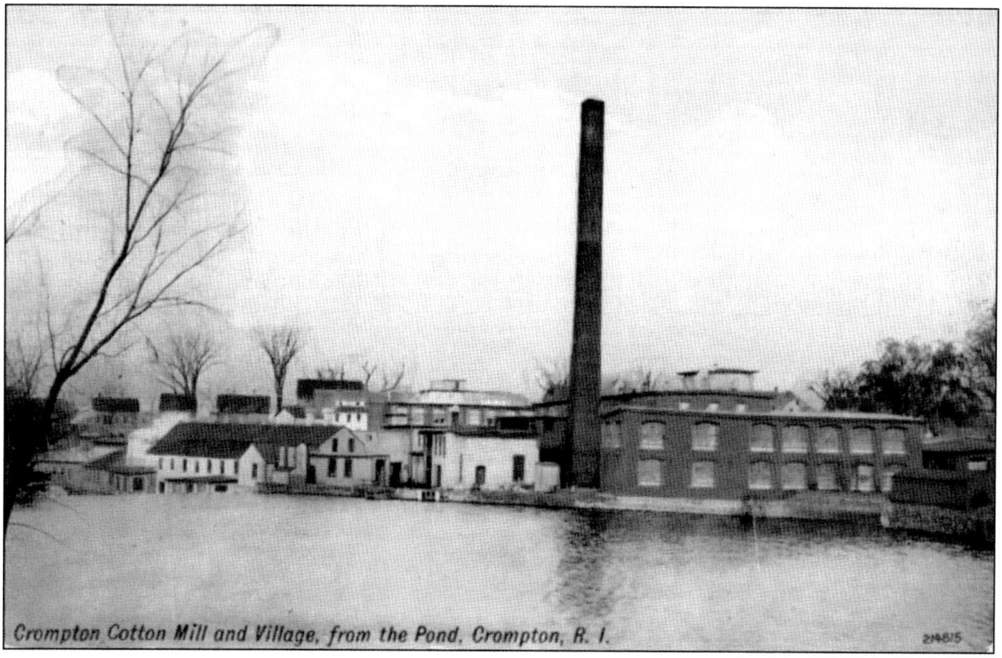

This postcard of Crompton Mill and village was taken from the west side of the millpond looking east. It was sent to Mrs. Pierce Tuckerman of 51 Harrison Street in Providence, Rhode Island, on July 18, 1911. The postcard was signed, "Love to all, Grace." Below, another photograph of the same mill was taken from Pulaski Street. Mrs. Tuckerman's sister writes that Myrtle and she are coming up on Wednesday and staying all night if convenient, but not to put herself out. It was mailed August 17, 1910, from Anthony and signed, "Your sister, Jennie." (Both, courtesy of Richard Hughes.)

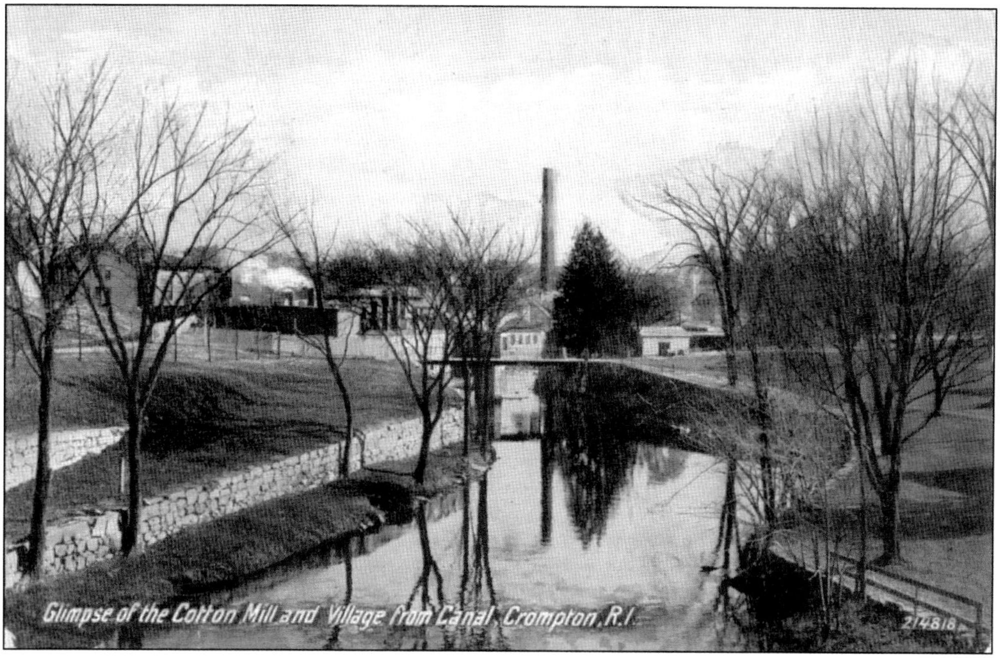

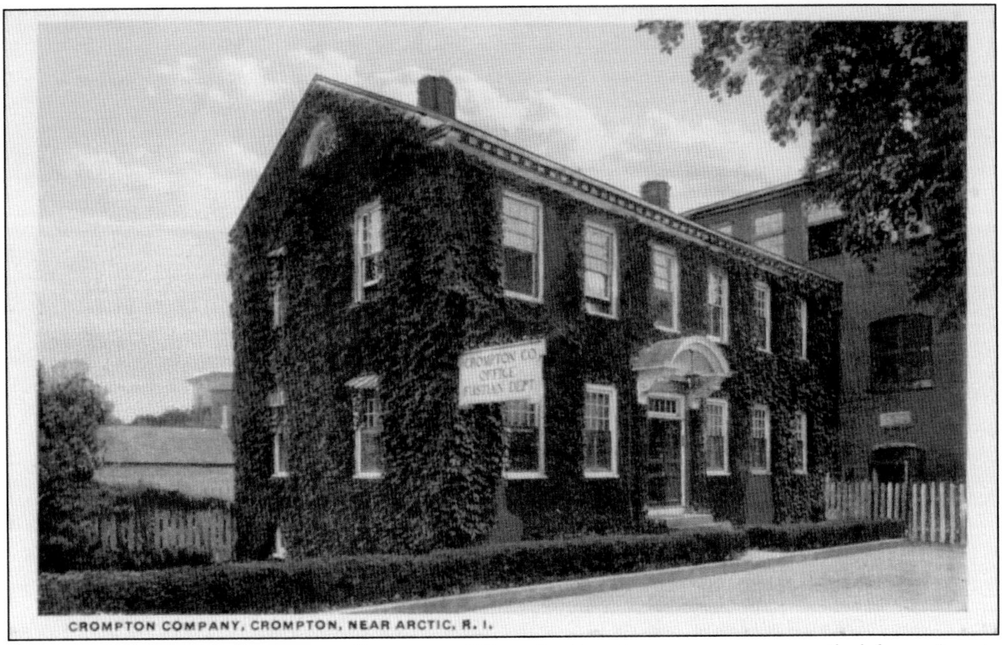

This postcard of the Crompton Company Office fustian department was mailed from Arctic to Highland Falls, New York. This two-story brick building still exists at 20 Remington Street. (Courtesy of Donald Carpenter.)

Ye Olde
Crompton Remnant Room
at
Crompton, R. I.

Open Daily Except Saturday
7.30 A. M. to 12 M., 1 to 5 P. M.
Open Saturdays
7.30 A. M. to 11 A. M.

SHORT LENGTHS AT ATTRACTIVE PRICES

VELVETEENS
For Coats, Suits, Dresses, Jackets, Hats, Trimmings, Children's Dresses, Children's Coats.

VELVET CORDUROYS
For Negligees, Tea Gowns, Kimonas, Sport Coats, Children's Coats and Dresses.

CORDUROYS
For Boys' Suits, Knee Pants and Rompers.
Men's Riding Breeches, Trousers, Hunting Coats.
Baby Carriage Covers and Robes, Upholstery, Cushions and Slip Covers.

Silk Duvetyns and Cotton Duvetyns
For Hats, Dresses, Trimmings, Coat Linings, Waists.

CHENILLES
For Dresses, Tunics, Blouses, Wraps, Trimmings.

SATEENS AND JEANS
For Linings, Aprons and House Dresses.

DRILLS
For Overalls and Boys' Rompers.

CHEAP COTTON GOODS
In Fancy Colors, Useful for Many Purposes.

DIRECTIONS
to
Ye Olde
Crompton Remnant Room

BY BUS FROM PROVIDENCE
Busses leave at 10 past and 40 past the hour from Eddy Street, opposite the Biltmore. Change at Arctic (end of line) for trolly to Crompton.

BY AUTOMOBILE FROM PROVIDENCE
Elmwood Avenue, to Reservoir Avenue, Reservoir Avenue direct to Arctic Centre. At Arctic Centre take left fork to Crompton Village. Total distance Twelve Miles.

CROMPTON CO.
WEST WARWICK, R. I.

The Crompton Company maintained the Ye Olde Crompton Remnant Room. As this foldout card advertises, it sold short lengths of material at attractive prices. The store sold velveteen remnants, velvet corduroys, regular corduroys, silks, chenille, sateen, jeans, drills, and cheap cotton goods. On the back of the card are bus and automobile directions to the store from Providence. (Courtesy of Donald Carpenter.)

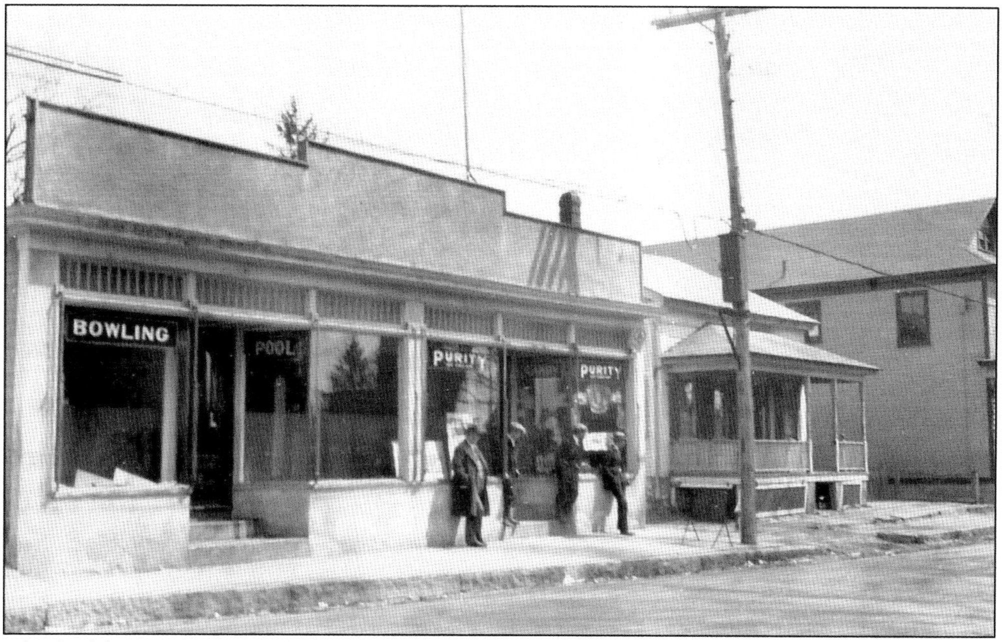

This building on New London Turnpike was used as a bowling alley and pool parlor at one time. It later became a restaurant. This was a time when homes mingled between businesses, as the little cottage shows. The next building is the Family Company Store.

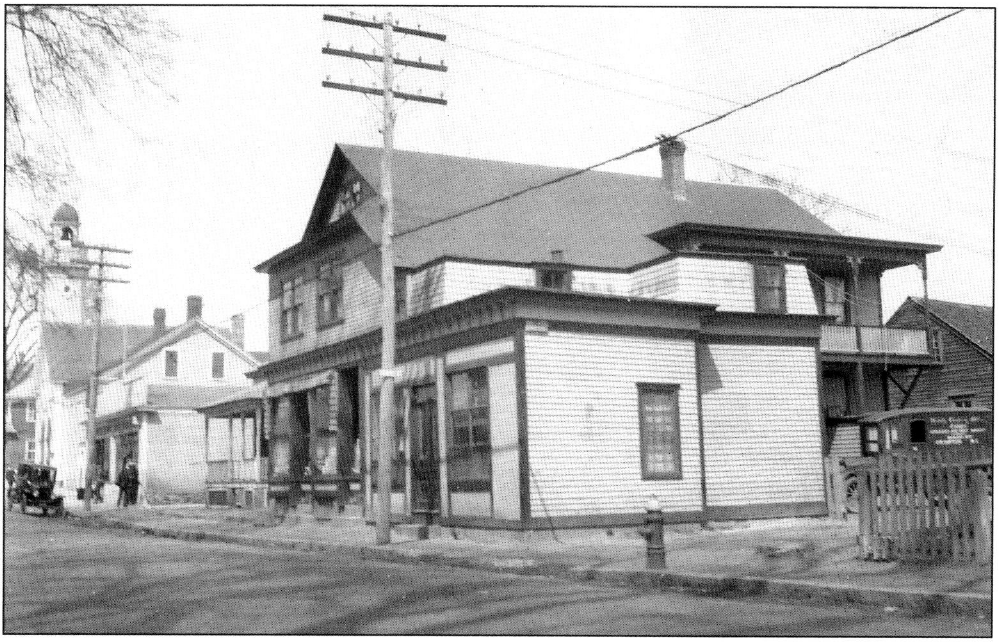

This postcard pictures the Family Company Store, established in 1923 by Luke Moskalyk in partnership with Michael Szelest. Moskalyk's daughter, Ann Moskalyk Tucker, lived above the store for 69 years. The delivery truck parked in the rear advertises, "Groceries and Meat Market."

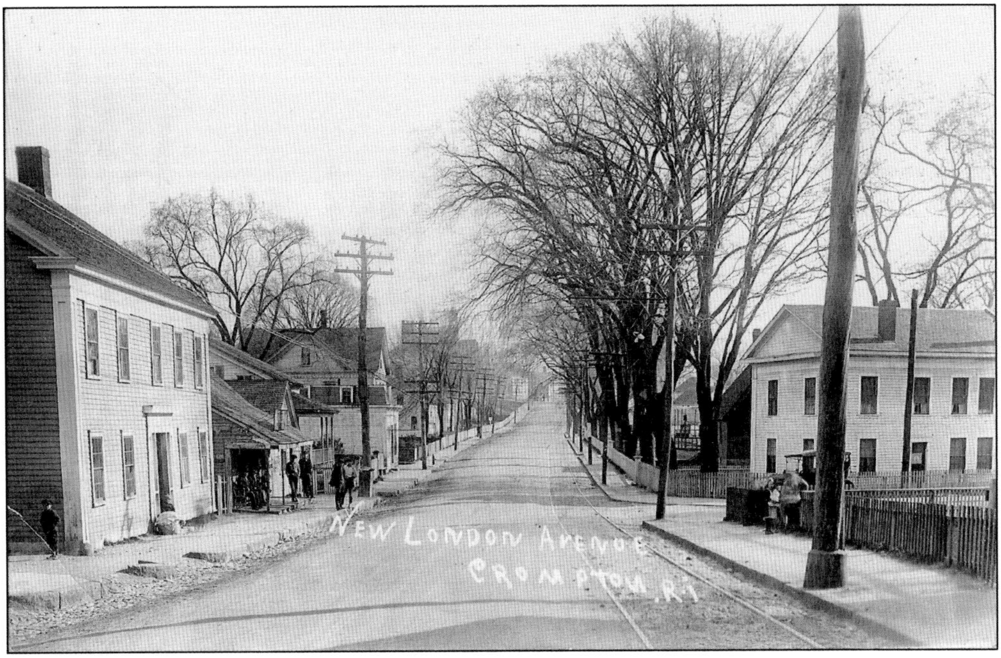

New London Turnpike, completed in 1820, is also Main Street in Crompton. The Crompton Free Library, shown on the opposite page, was located on the right, just after the large white house on the corner of Remington Street. This small, freestanding building (below) was on the corner of School Street. It can be seen in the photograph above on the left, across from the library.

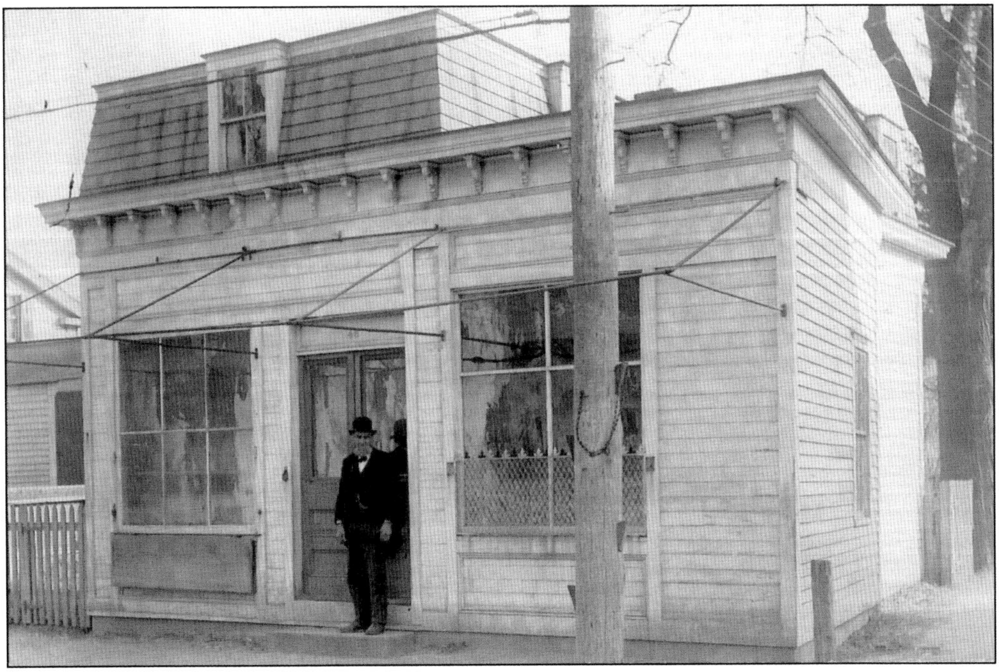

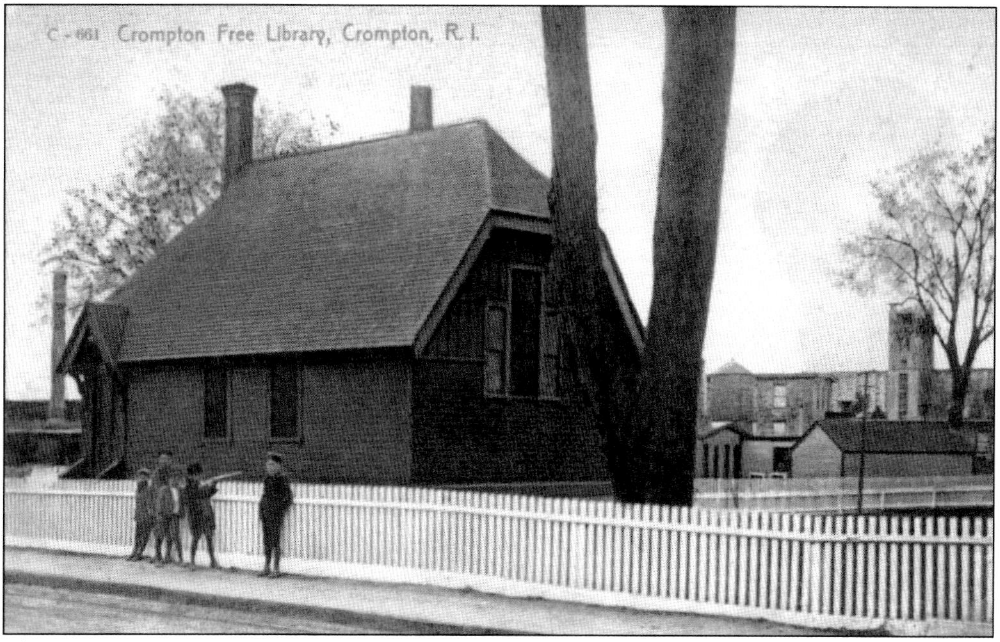

The Crompton Company, seen to the right in the distance, built the Crompton Free Library in 1876 for its workers. Stone and Carpenter of Providence were the builders. This postcard was mailed on May 24, 1913. (Courtesy of Lawrence G. Soucy.)

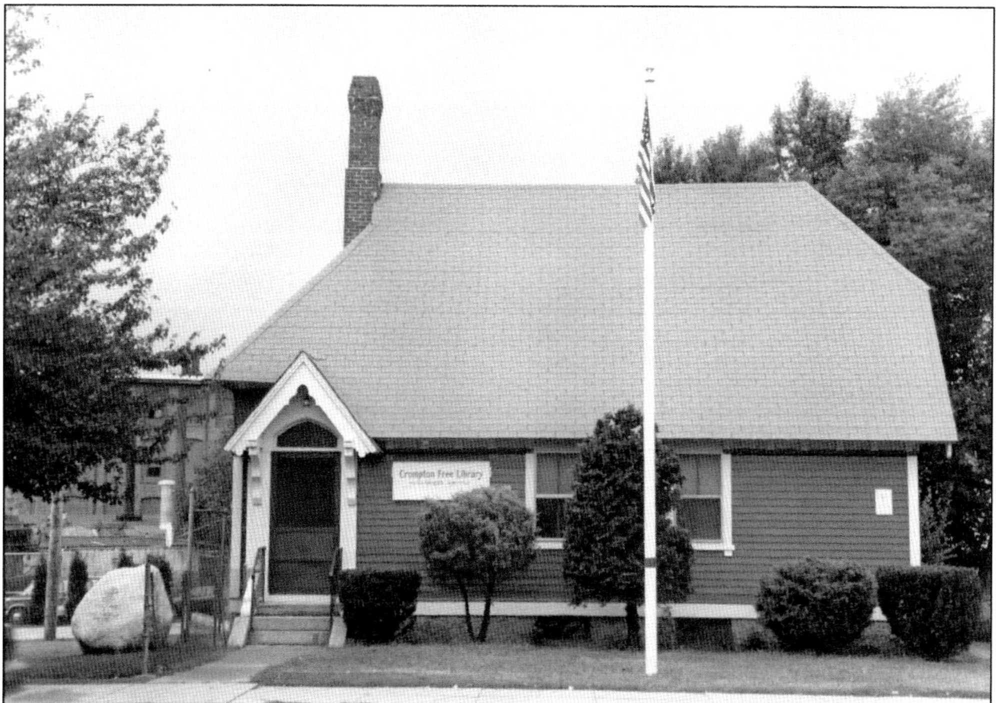

The library shown is located at 1679 Main Street and is now occupied by the Pawtuxet Valley Preservation and Historical Society. It opens every Saturday from 9 a.m. to 2 p.m. All are invited to stop in and view the extensive collection of literature and artifacts of the valley.

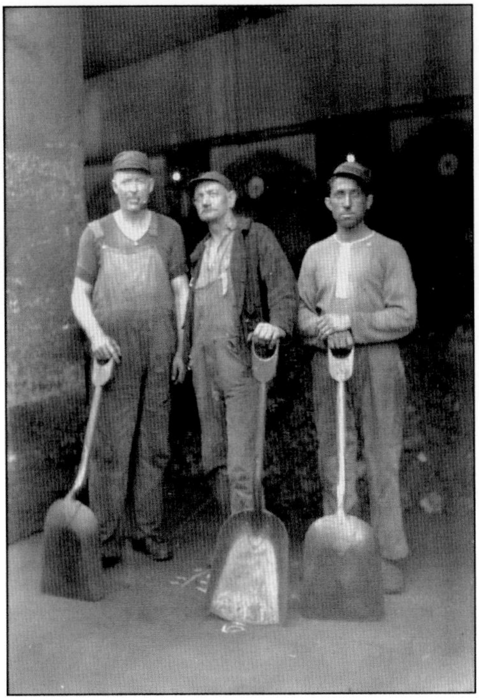

These three men shoveled about 15 tons of coal per day at the Crompton Mill plant. They are head day fireman G. Goulet (left); Eldridge Carr (center), who kept coal handy for the firemen and prepared wood for the boilers; and second fireman Leon Picard.

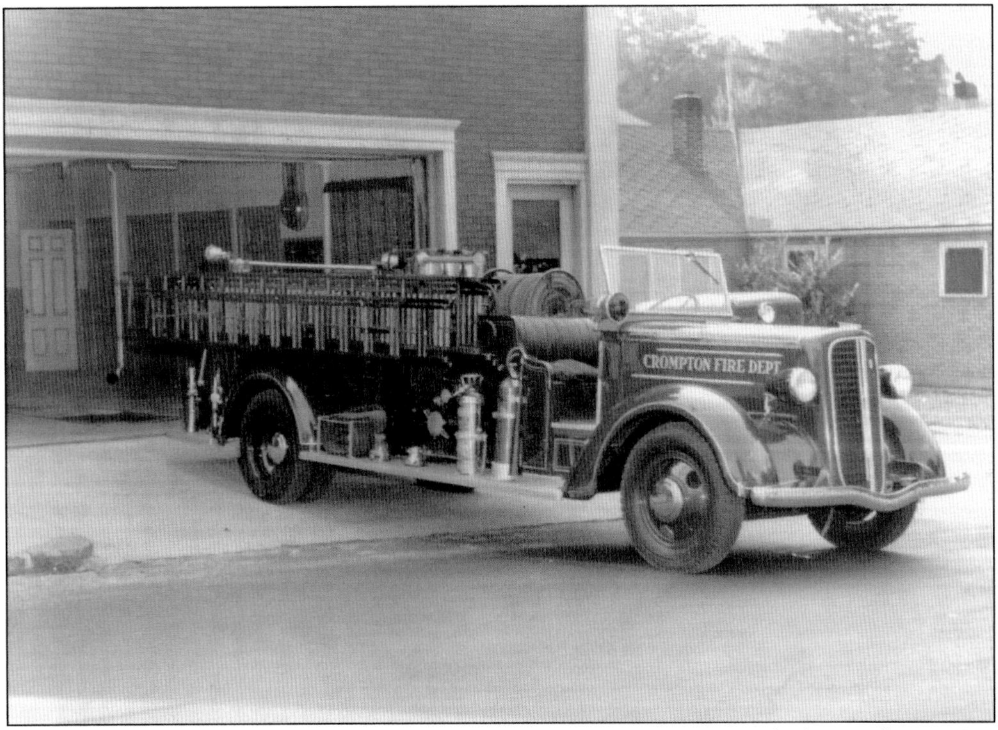

This photograph displays Crompton Fire Department's engine No. 4 parked partially on New London Turnpike. The following verse is from "Dedicated to Firemen," written by Helen O. Larson in 1980 at age 70: "They climb ladders to the roof, with axes they break through it / And some get smoke inhalation, before they have time to sit." (Courtesy of Gerard Tellier Jr.)

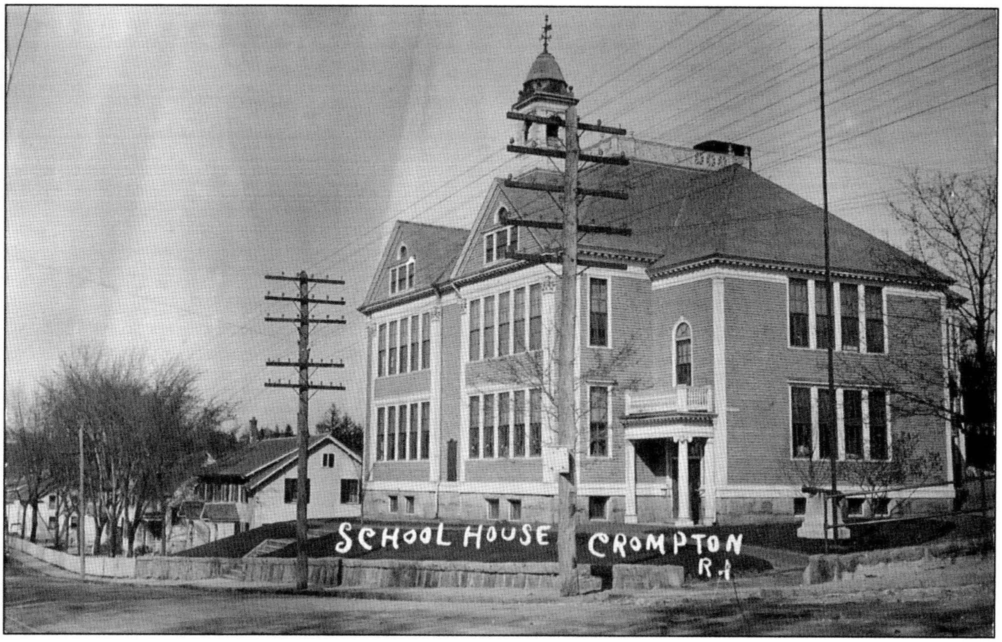

This postcard pictures the Crompton School. It was located on Main Street at the intersection with Cowesett Avenue. The cannon on the right side of the building was forged at the Hope Furnace in the village of Hope. It now resides in front of the Hope Library.

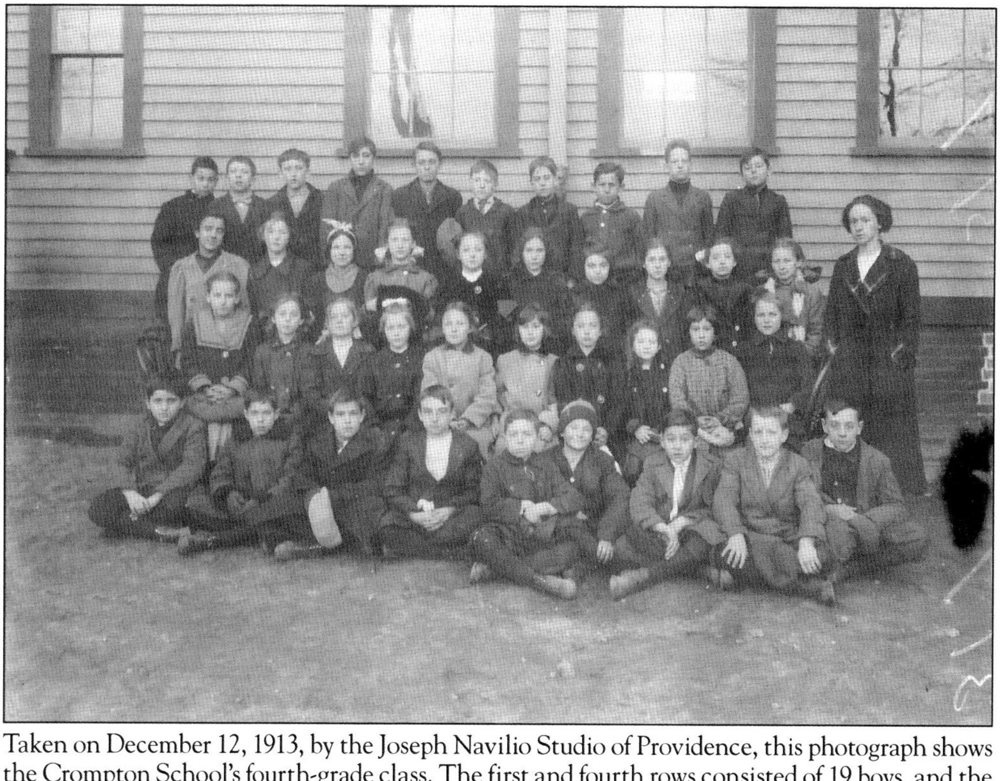

Taken on December 12, 1913, by the Joseph Navilio Studio of Providence, this photograph shows the Crompton School's fourth-grade class. The first and fourth rows consisted of 19 boys, and the second and third rows included 20 girls and the teacher. (Courtesy of Lawrence G. Soucy.)

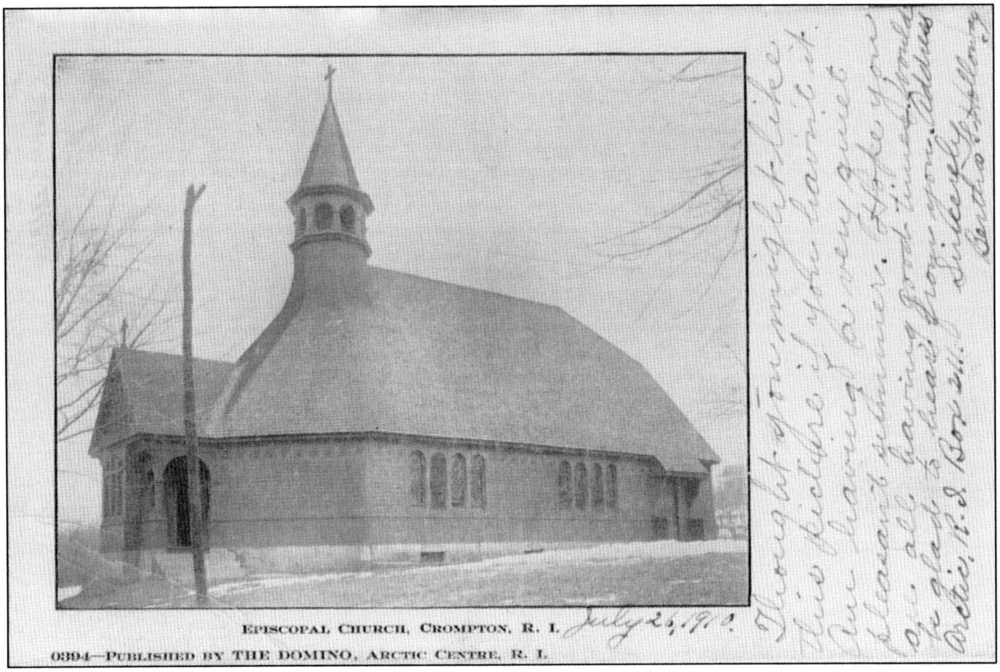

This postcard was mailed on July 26, 1910. Bertha Holloway of Arctic sent it to Lily Walton of Providence. It shows the St. Phillips Episcopal Church that replaced the first one, which was razed in a fire. The area on the right of the card—instead of the back—was reserved for messages. The postcard below was mailed from Centreville on September 5, 1907, to Fall River, Massachusetts. It beautifully displays the church interior. The church was torn down in the early 1970s. (Both, courtesy of Donald Carpenter.)

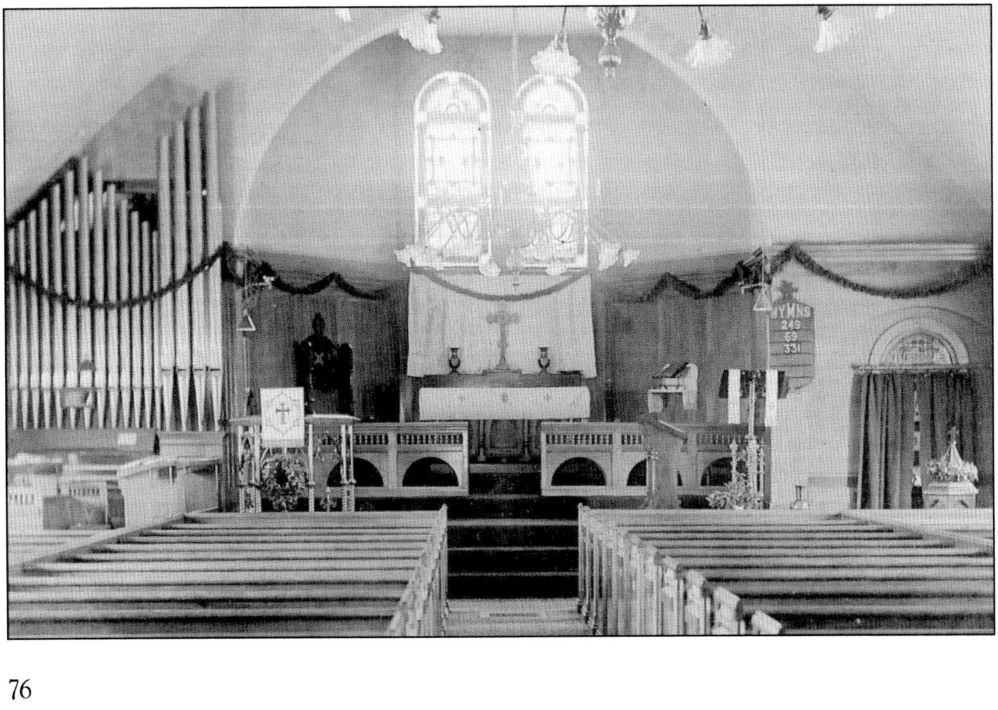

Five

Lippitt Village

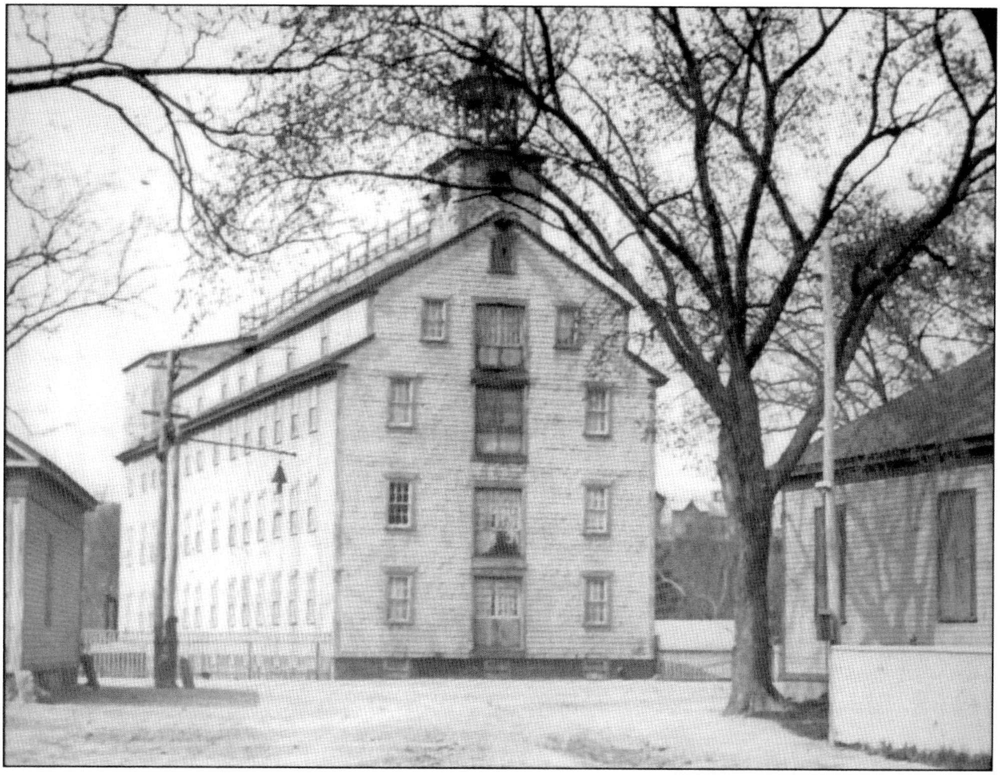

The Lippitt Mill was built in 1809 by Christopher Lippitt, Charles Lippitt, Benjamin Aborn, and George Jackson. It was sold on July 19, 1889, to Benjamin Brayton and Robert Knight and again in 1925 to Joseph Hayes, the owner of River Point Lace Works. The mill again exchanged hands in 2008 but remains the oldest continuously operating lace works in the United States. The building on the right is the fire station, and on the left is the company store, which can be seen on page 80. This photograph was taken from Wakefield Street. (Courtesy of Lawrence G. Soucy.)

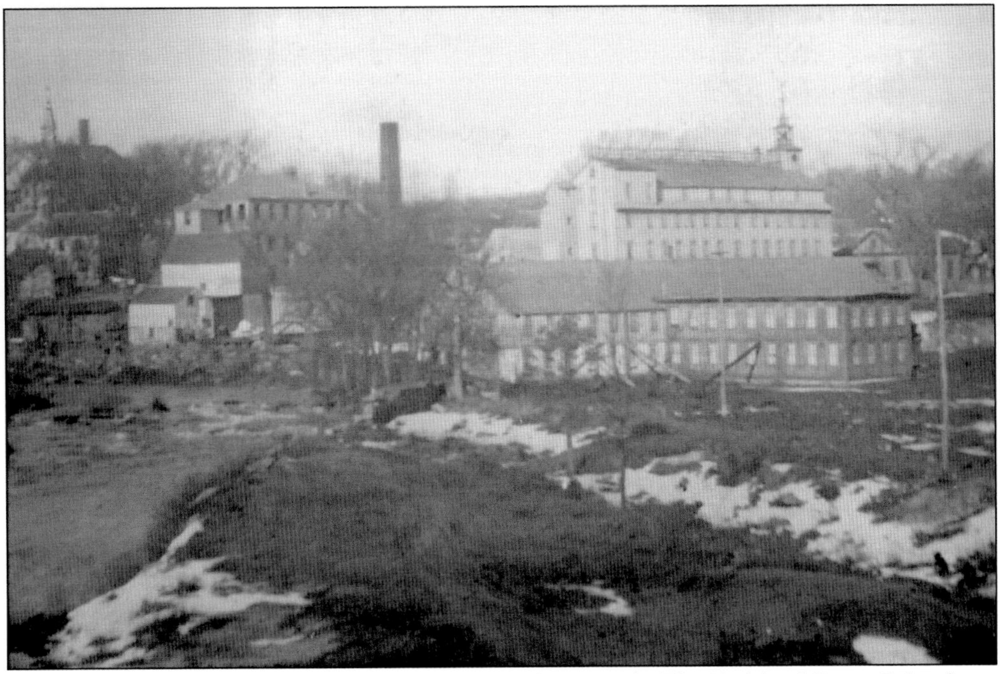

This is the rear view of the Lippitt Mill complex looking north. The Highland Street School can be seen in the top left corner. Below it is part of the Phenix Mill complex. The Pawtuxet River is flowing in the lower left corner. (Courtesy of Lawrence Soucy.)

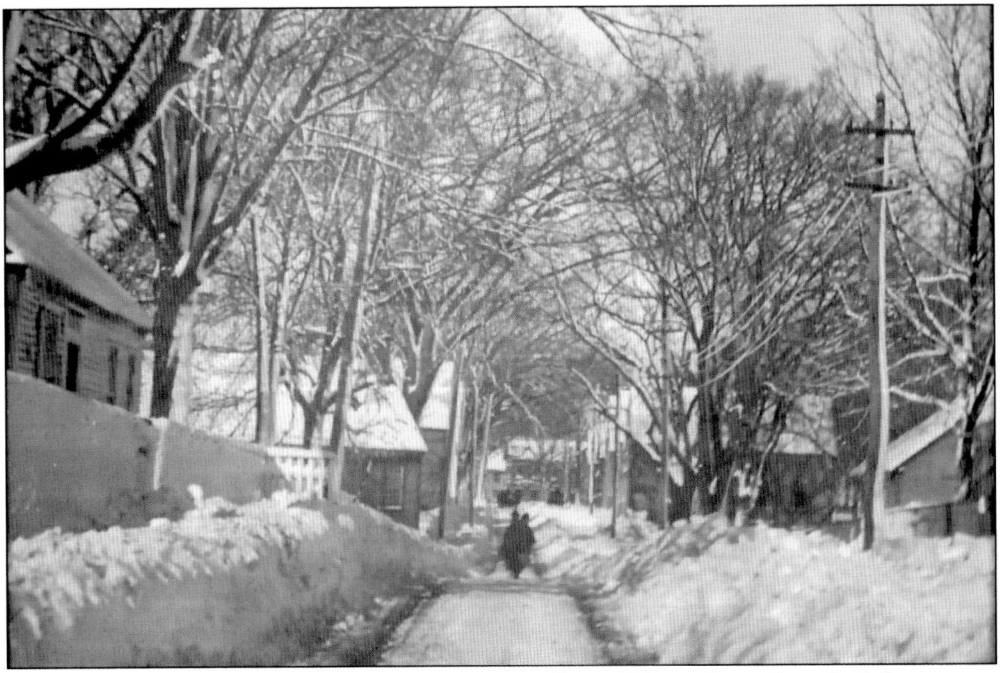

This view is looking west on Main Street. Lippitt Mill would be at the end on the left, opposite from Wakefield Street. The following verse is from "Winter Wonderland," written by Helen O. Larson on January 16, 1978, at age 77: "The Sun was shining, there was a gentle breeze / The ice on the branches was sparkling, like diamonds on the trees." (Courtesy of Lawrence G. Soucy.)

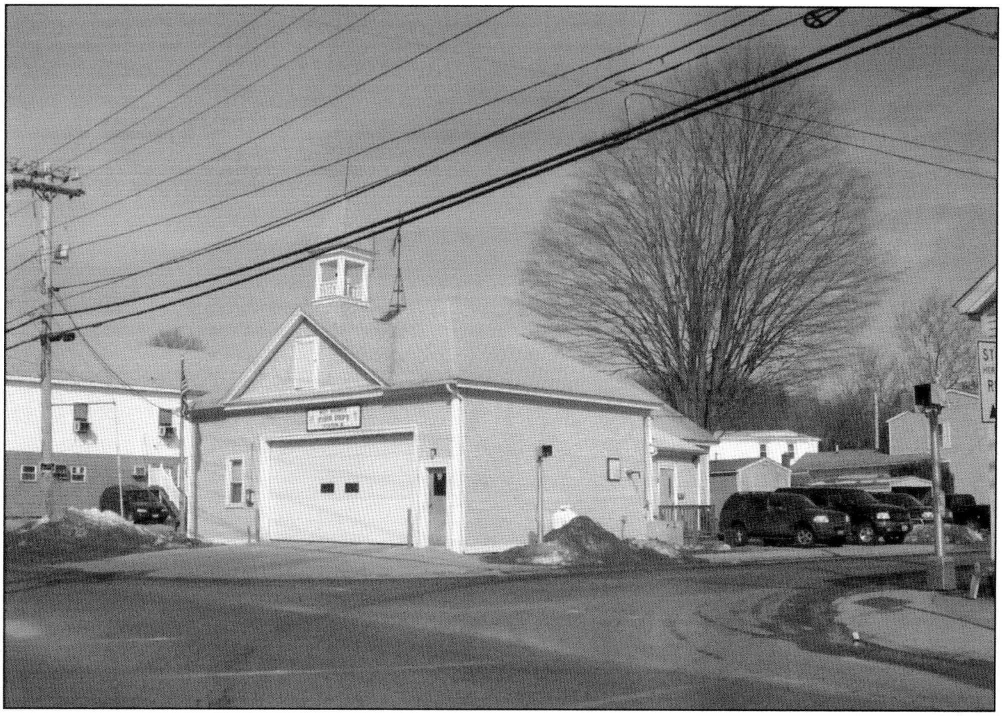

The West Warwick Fire Station No. 2 was built in the late 1800s. The bell tower is on the front of the gable-roofed building. It was used as a voting place in its early days. This photograph was taken on February 17, 2011, on the corner of Wakefield Street. (Author's collection.)

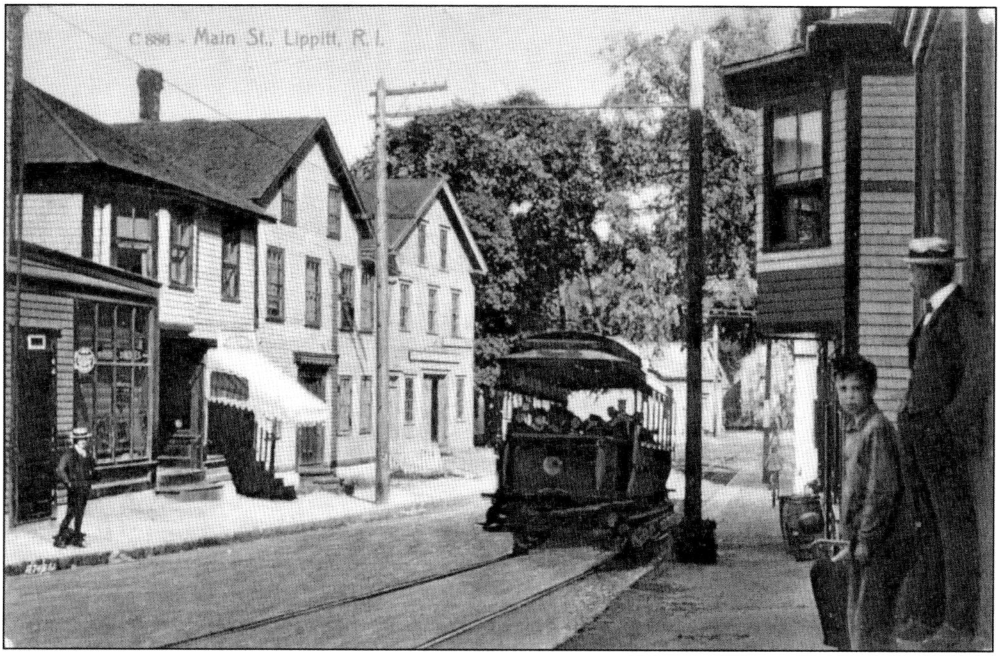

This postcard of Lippitt's Main Street was mailed at Phenix on June 8, 1909. The trolley traveling towards Clyde seems to be full. It appears the boy on the right has a shoe shine kit in his hands. (Courtesy of Donald Carpenter.)

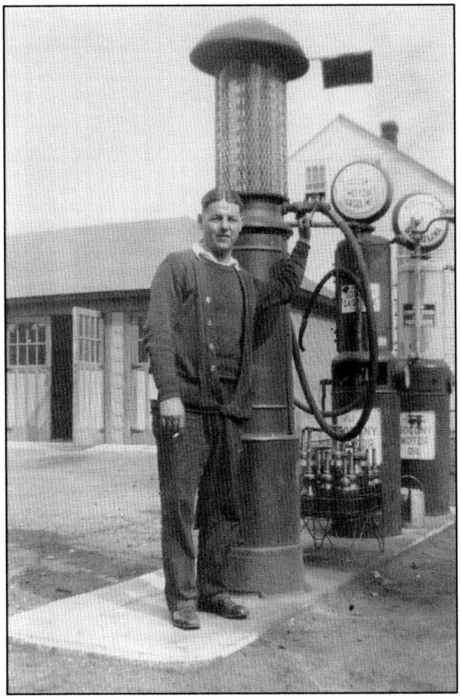

This photograph of Rudy Bettez was taken in 1920. He is ready to pump Socony Motor Gasoline for a customer. He also has a rack of one-quart jars of Socony Motor Oil in case motorists are low when he checks their oil. If a motorist's radiator is low, a bucket of water is handy, and Bettez may have even given the windows a wipe. This all took place where Deanco's is today. The house can also be seen in the picture below. (Courtesy of Dean Cook.)

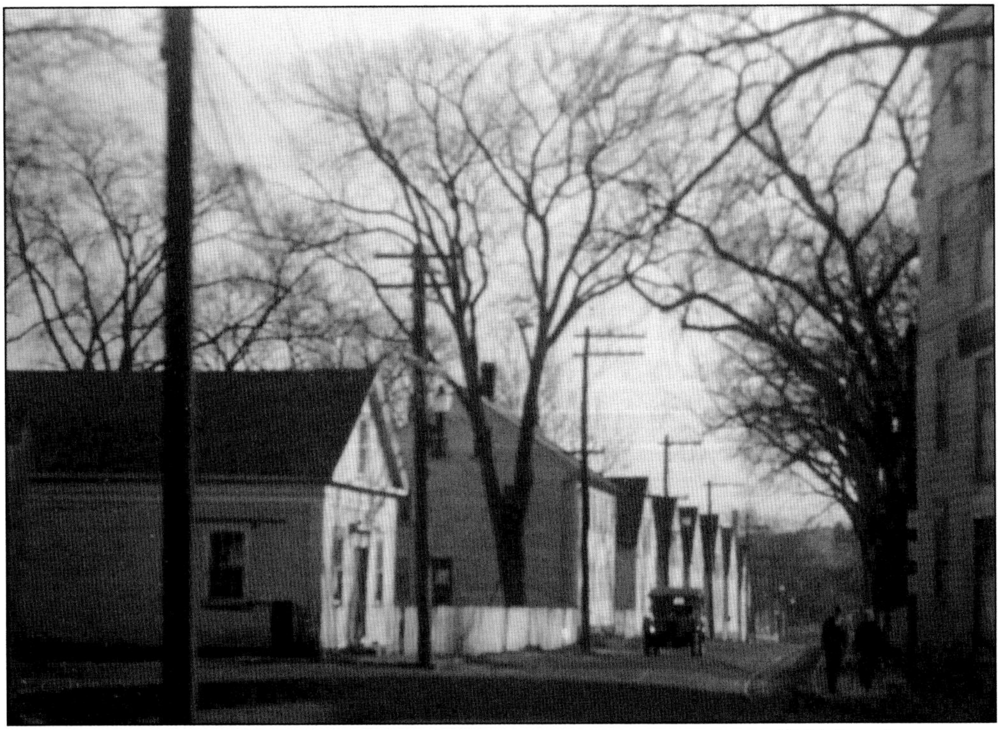

The Lippitt Mill is visible on the right, and the company store is opposite at 836 Main Street, now owned by Deanco. It was built in 1830 and still stands on the corner of Wakefield Street. The empty lot to the right of the company store is where Deanco's automotive repair shop now resides. Housing for mill workers is lined up further down Main Street. (Courtesy of Gerard Tellier Jr.)

Six

Natick Village

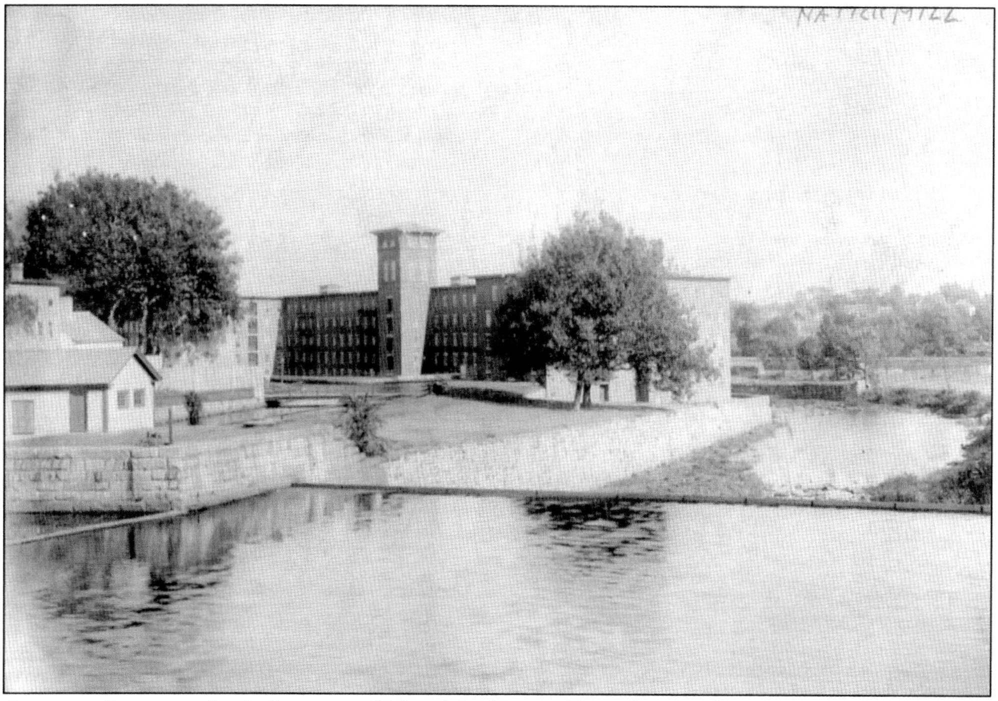

A group of investors built the original Natick Mill in 1807 on the west bank of the Pawtuxet River. In 1913, the river would become the dividing line for West Warwick on the west side and Warwick on the east side. By 1913, Natick Mills had become Pawtuxet Valley's largest mill complex.

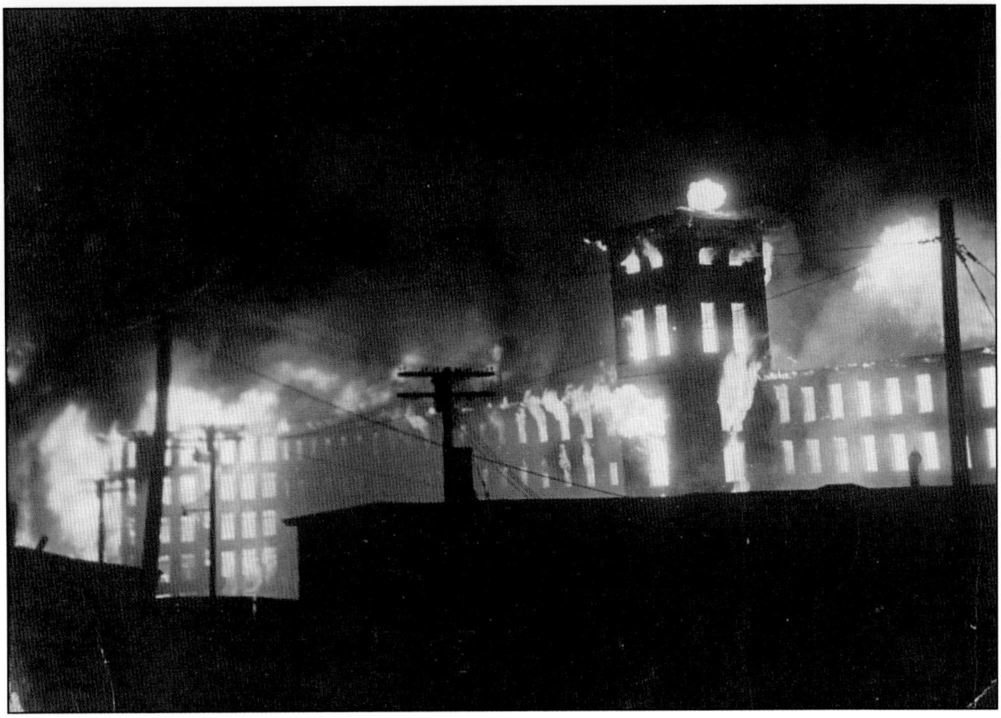

In 1815, the Rhodes Natick Company reorganized Natick Mills. William Sprague purchased two of the mills in 1821, and by 1852, he owned all of them. Sprague ran the mill complex until 1882, when he sold out to B.B. and R. Knight. The mills ran continuously until they were sold at auction in 1935. The photograph above shows the mill totally encompassed in flames on the evening of July 4, 1941. As witnessed below, it burned to the ground with only ashes remaining.

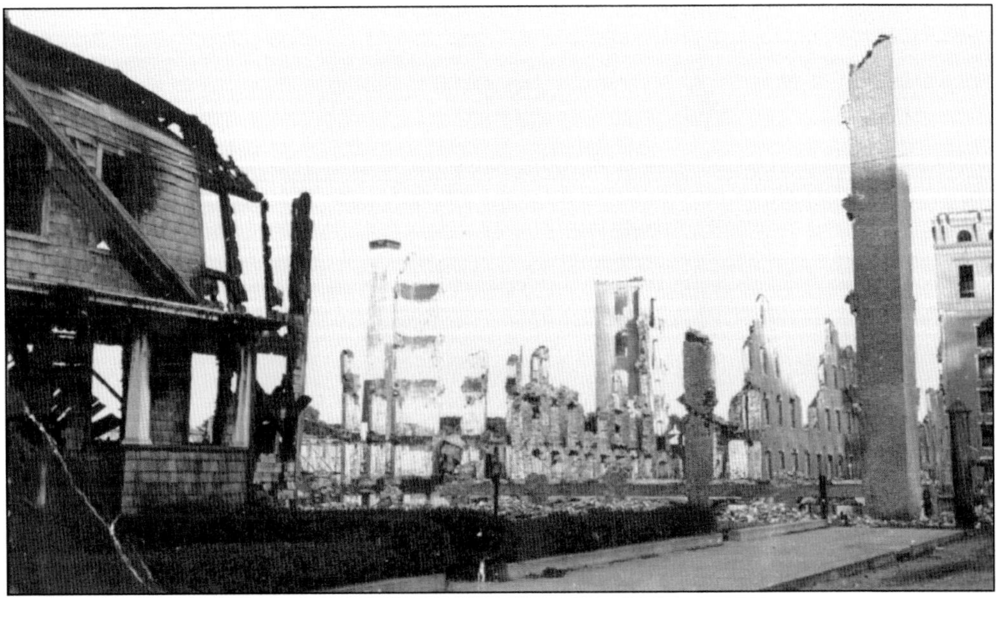

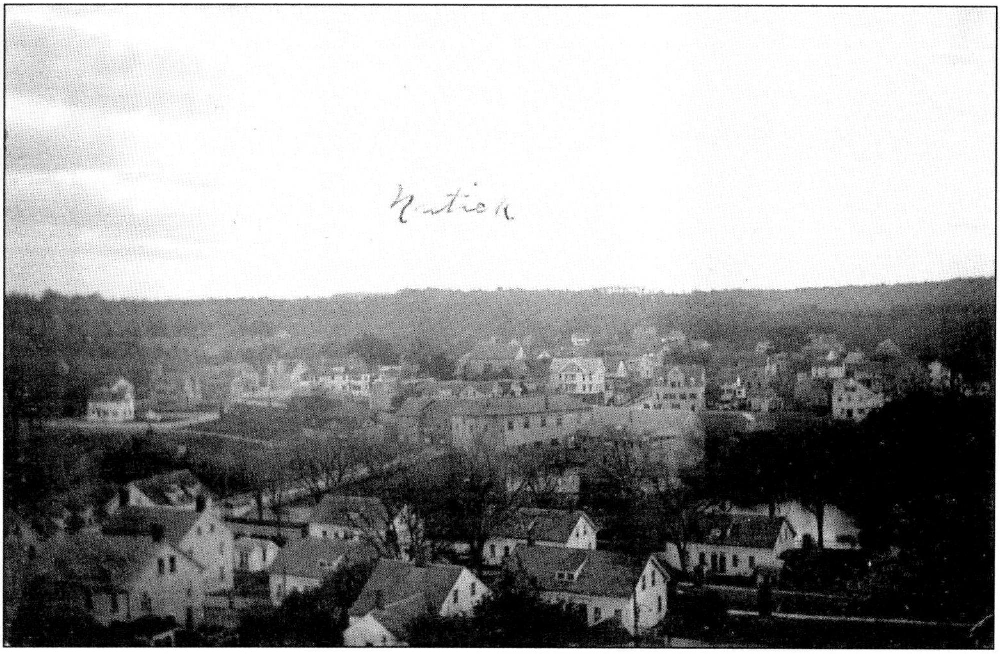

This postcard shows a bird's-eye view of Natick Village from the top of the mill water tower. It was built in 1899 on top of Prospect Hill to supply the sprinkler system for the mill. The tank was 30 feet high and held 100,000 gallons of water. This is a view looking south.

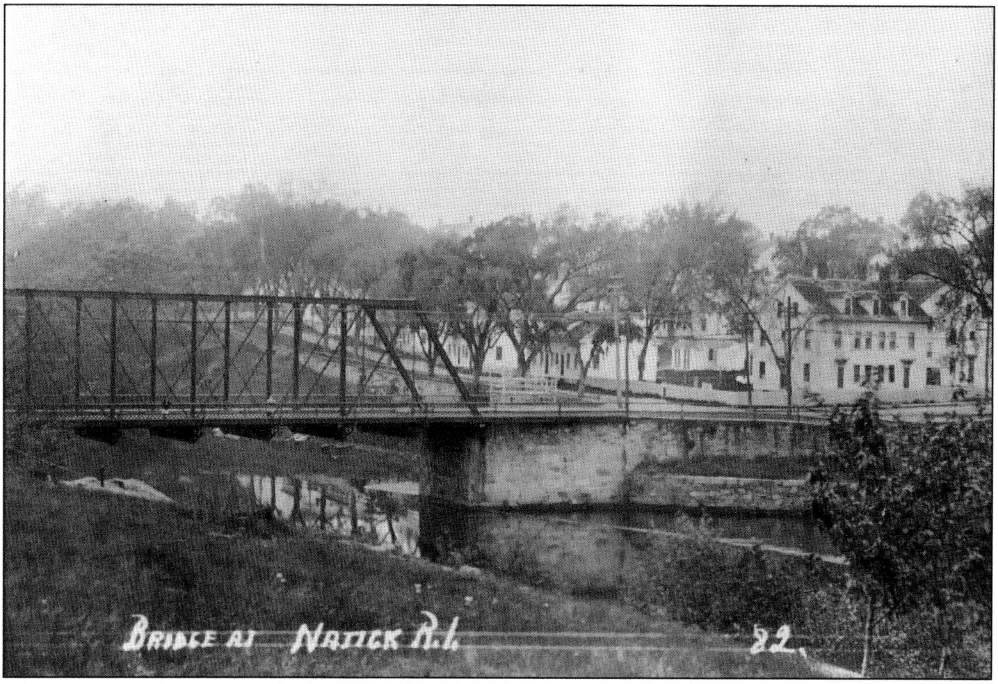

This photograph was taken looking north toward the water tower from which the above photograph was taken and displays a portion of Natick Village. The tower is to the right, just out of view. The company houses on Water Street can also be seen along the bottom of the picture at the top of the page.

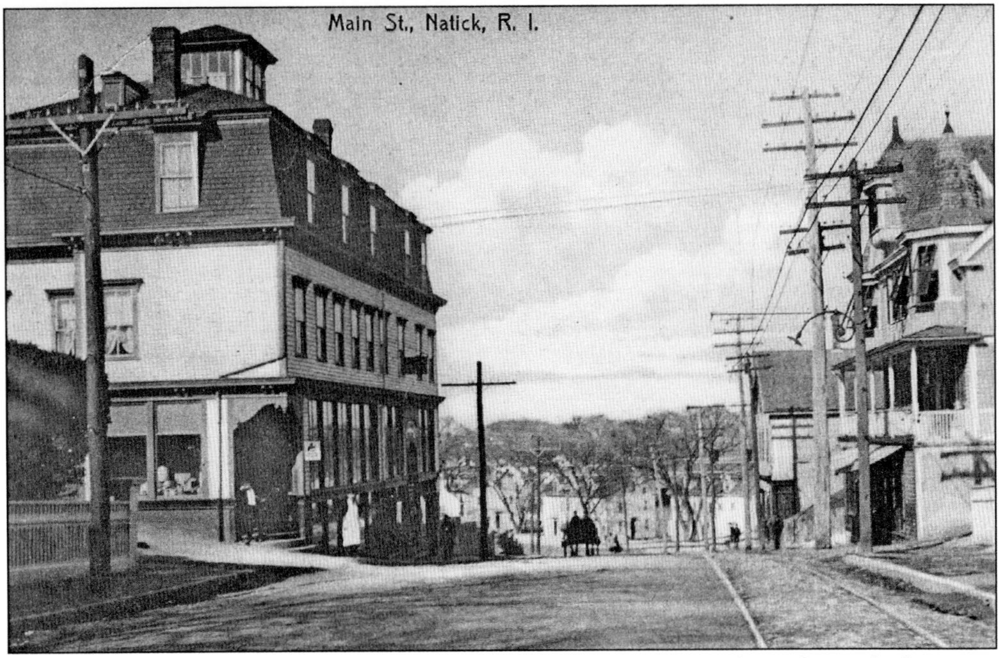

This postcard from the early 1900s is a view of Main Street, now Providence Street, looking east during the days of horses and buggies and trolleys. The building on the left no longer occupies the corner of Prospect Hill Avenue, but the three-story house on the right with the porch still stands.

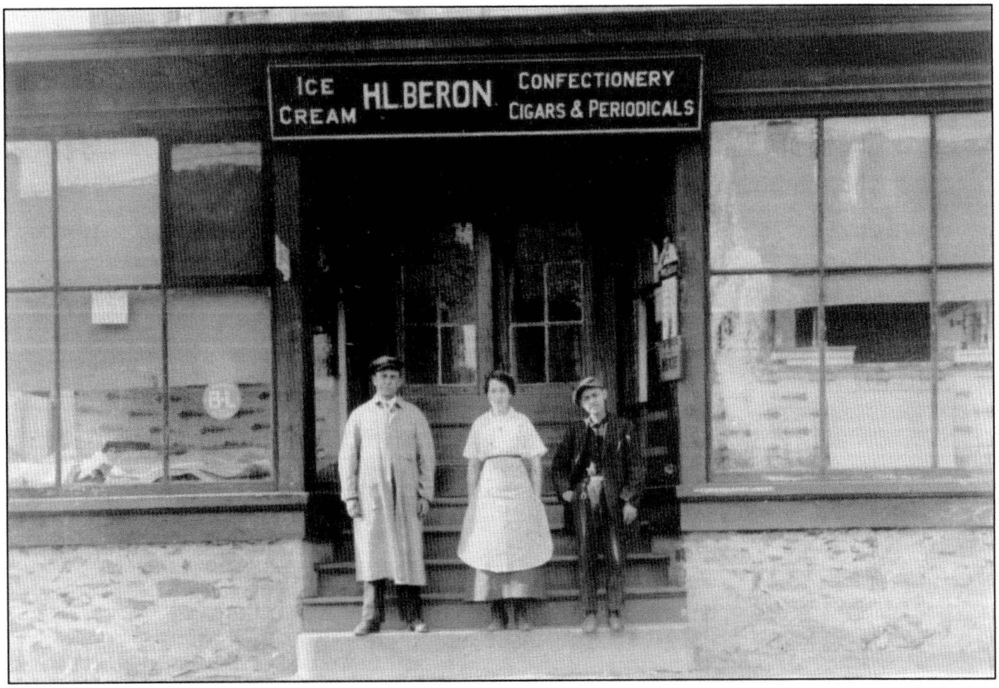

In the early 1900s, Henry L. Beron (left) ran this general store on Main Street. Most likely his wife and son are standing beside him and also worked in the store.

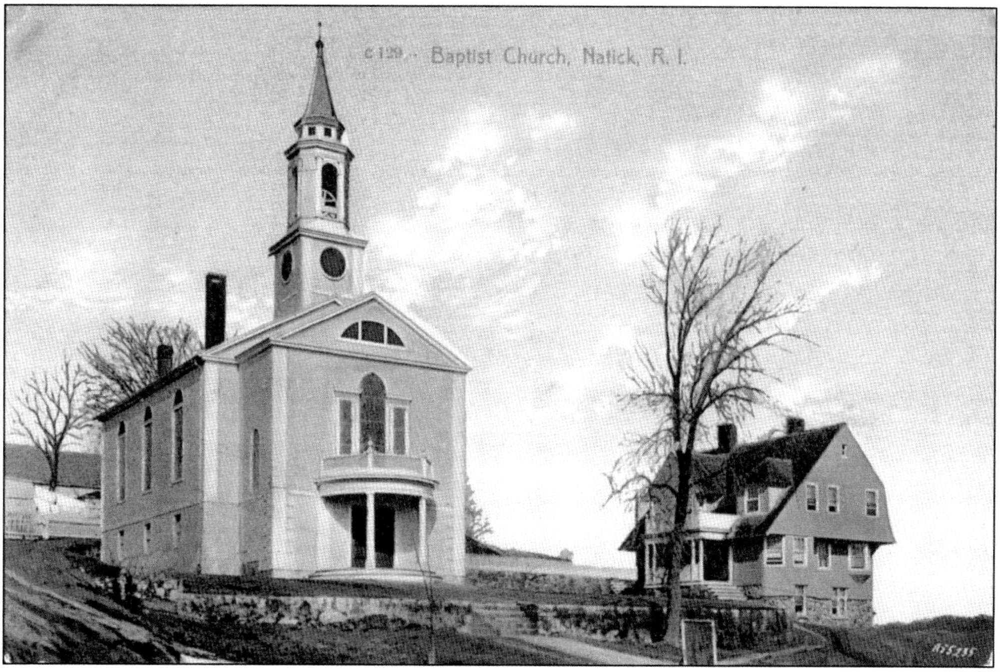

This view looking north shows the Natick Baptist Church and parsonage. The church was built in 1839 on land given by the Sprague family. It was renovated in 1890, and the parsonage was built in 1891. It still watches over the village of Natick; however, the steeple has been removed for safety purposes. (Courtesy of Donald Carpenter.)

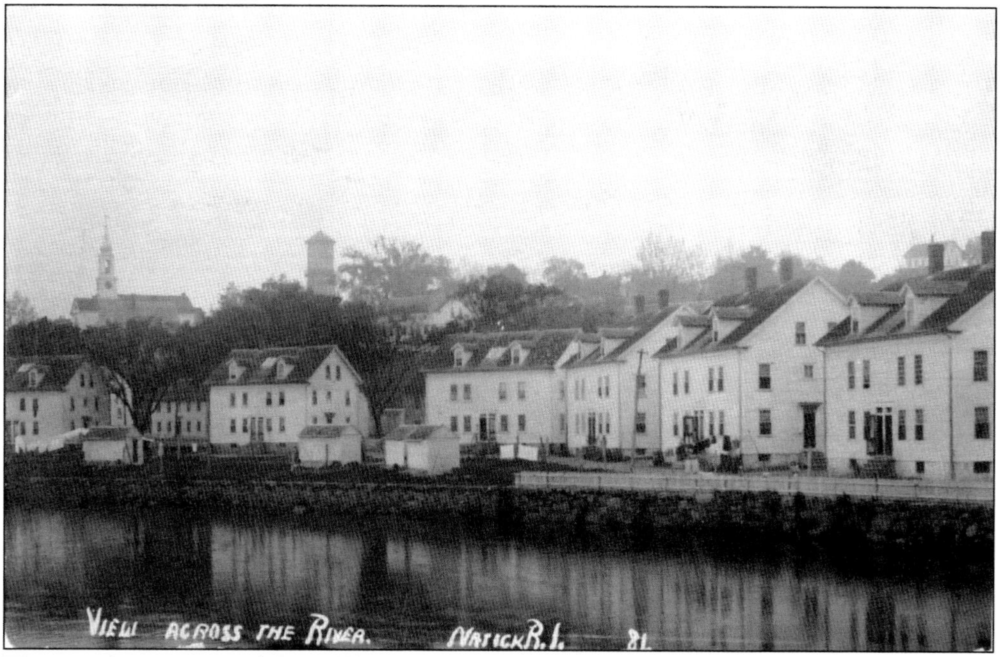

This is a close-up view of the mill houses lining River Street. It was taken from the East Avenue Bridge. The Natick Baptist Church is to the left, and the water tower for the mill is to the right of it.

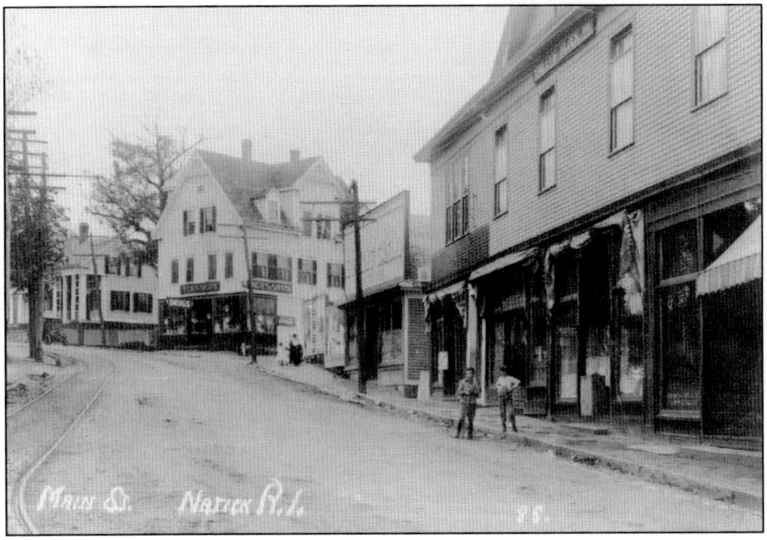

This view of Main Street, known today as Providence Street, was taken in the early 1900s. The building on the right was built in 1900 and named Dailey's Block, as the sign near the roofline states. It is also seen at the top of the next page. The large white building was home to Bernard's Drugstore.

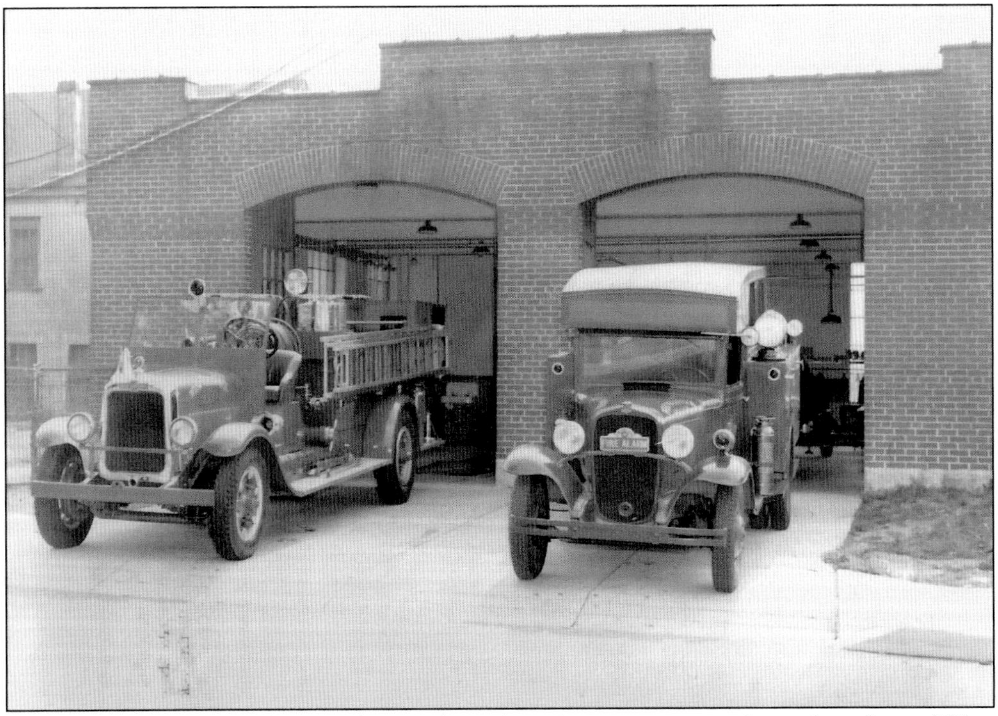

In the 1930s, when this photograph was taken, these fire engines were the pride and joy of West Warwick's Fire Department No. 3 in Natick. To start the engine on the left, a crank had to be put in the hole at the bottom of the radiator grill, and it was cranked until the engine started. The bell on top of the radiator was probably for parades. The siren behind the front fender was for fires. The open cab was convenient for parades, but not for driving to fires in rain, sleet, or snow, let alone the cold. Of course there was no power steering or heaters for that matter. But then again, those were the good old days. (Courtesy of Gerard Tellier Jr.)

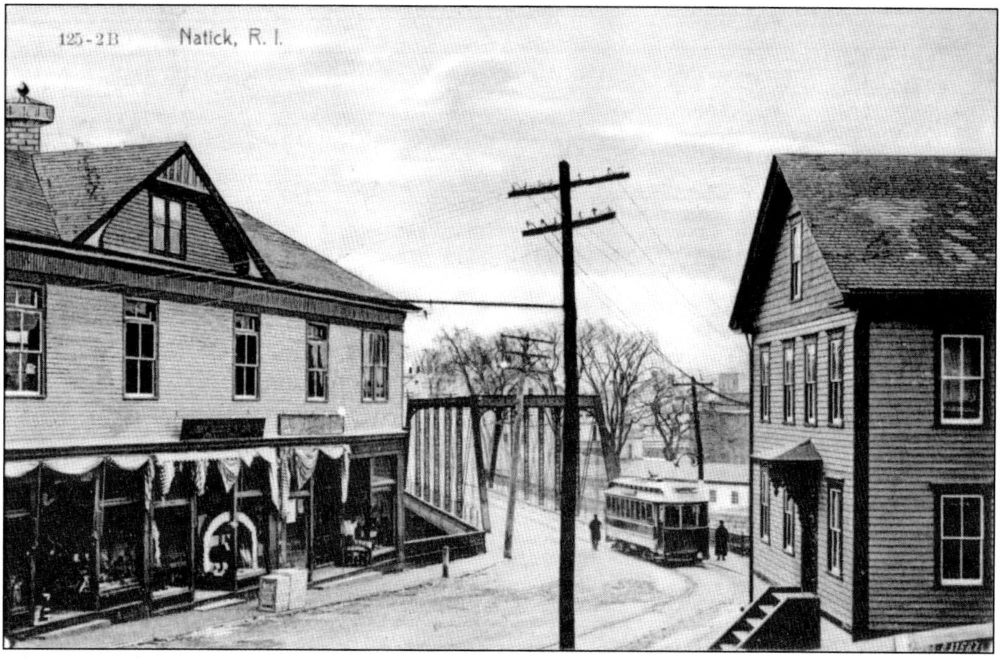

This postcard shows a view of the Dailey's Block building (left) in 1905. It contained the old Natick Theatre and a distillery. The Natick Mill and its tower can be seen to the right of the trees.

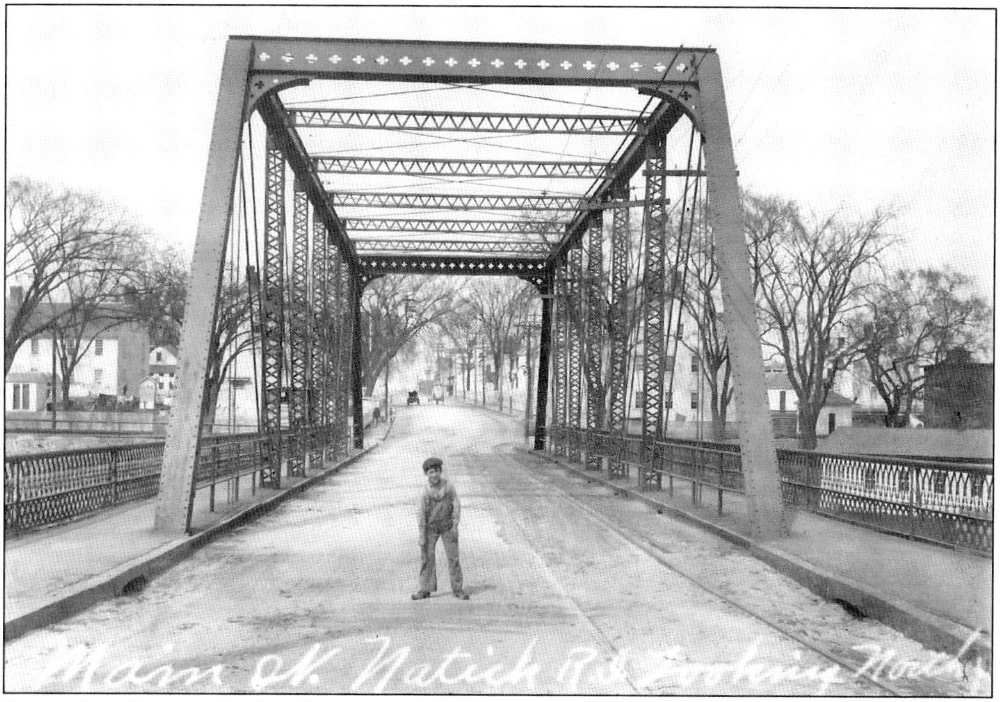

Pictured is the truss bridge that crossed the Pawtuxet River. It can also be seen above and on page 83. If the boy having his picture taken waits long enough, a car may come by. In those days, it was quite exciting to see one pass by. (Courtesy of Lawrence G. Soucy.)

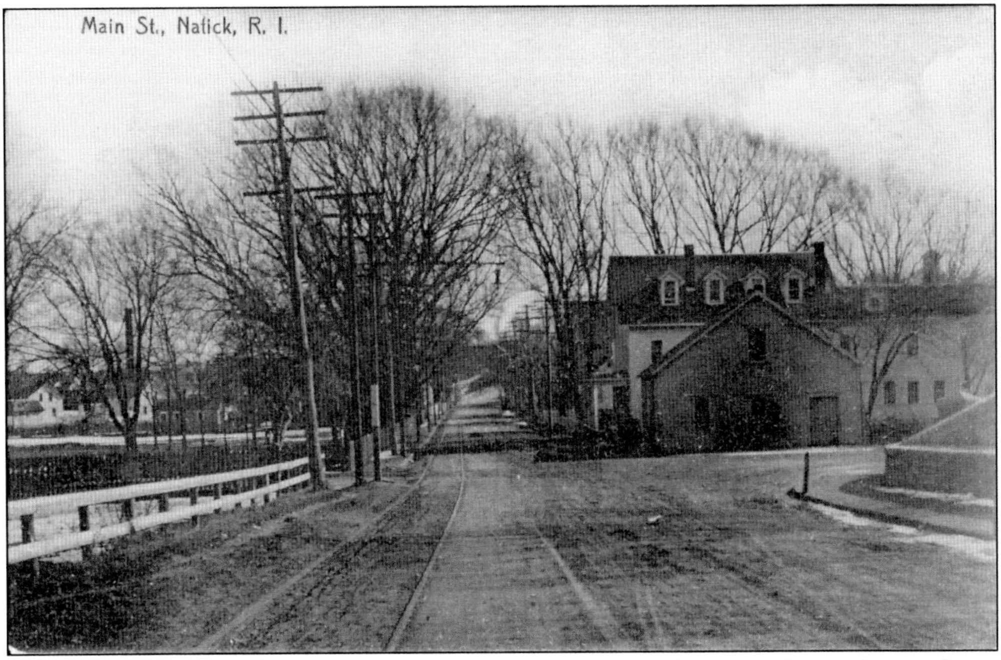

At the time this postcard was mailed on April 30, 1918, this was known as Brown Square. River Street runs to the left, and Wakefield Street turns to the right. A wall of St. Joseph's Church is in the corner. Later, when Barber's Auto Sales occupied this lot, it became known as Barber's Corner. Today, a Consumer Value Store is here. (Courtesy of Lawrence G. Soucy.)

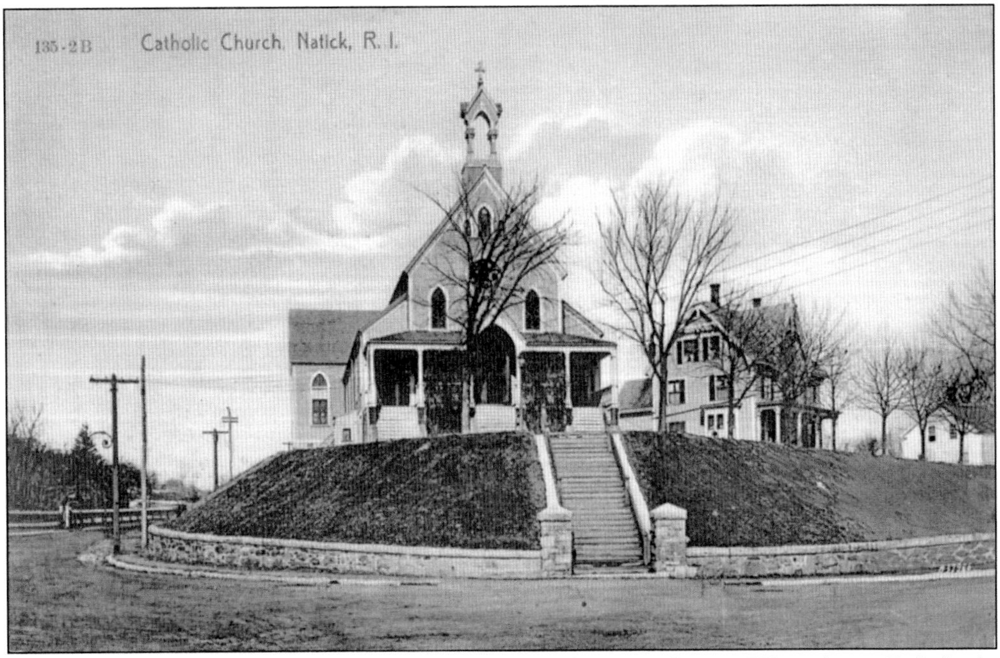

This postcard was mailed in September 1907 from Anthony to Thomas Whittaker in Rehobeth, Massachusetts. It shows St. Joseph's Church, which was built in 1873 on a lot donated by the Sprague family and altered in 1908. The rectory to the right was demolished in October 1984. (Courtesy of Donald Carpenter.)

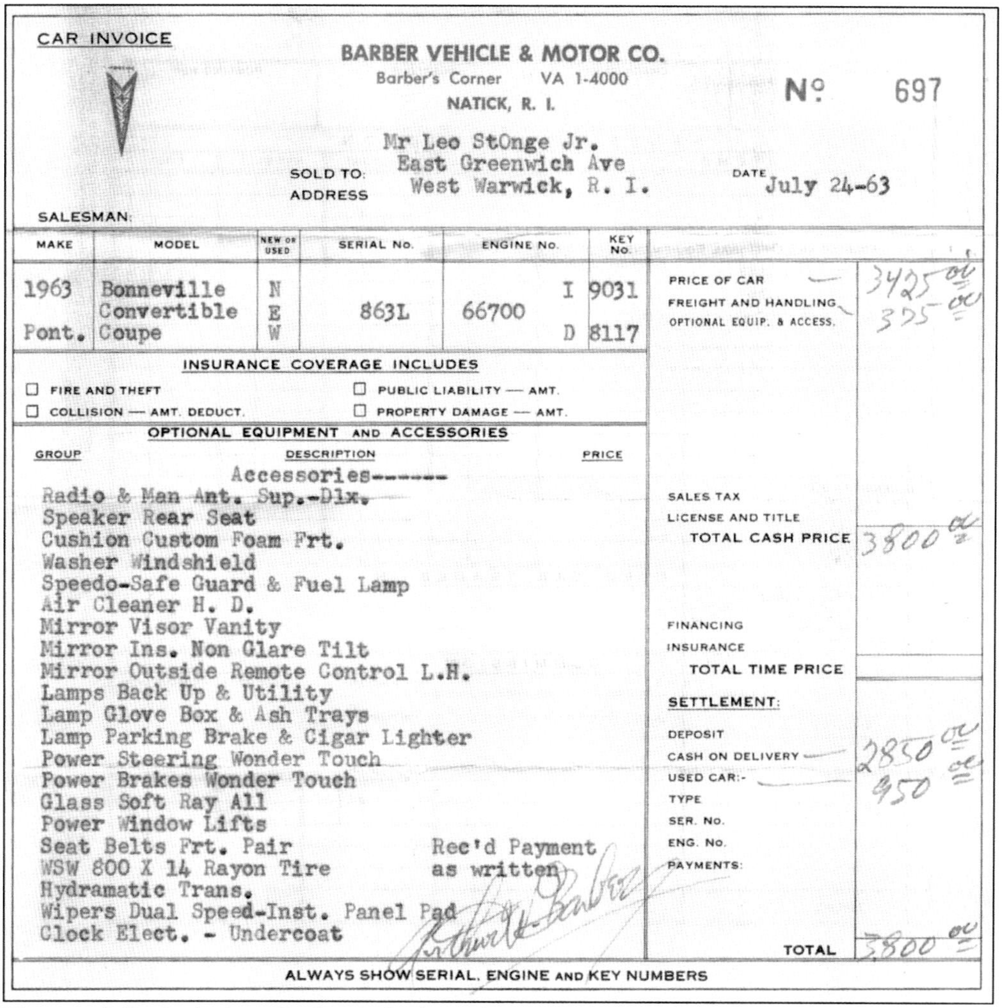

CAR INVOICE

BARBER VEHICLE & MOTOR CO.
Barber's Corner VA 1-4000
NATICK, R. I.

Nº 697

SOLD TO: Mr Leo StOnge Jr.
ADDRESS East Greenwich Ave
West Warwick, R. I.

DATE July 24-63

SALESMAN:

MAKE	MODEL	NEW OR USED	SERIAL No.	ENGINE No.	KEY No.
1963 Pont.	Bonneville Convertible Coupe	NEW	863L	66700	I 9031 D 8117

PRICE OF CAR — 3425 00
FREIGHT AND HANDLING — 375 00
OPTIONAL EQUIP. & ACCESS.

INSURANCE COVERAGE INCLUDES

☐ FIRE AND THEFT
☐ PUBLIC LIABILITY — AMT.
☐ COLLISION — AMT. DEDUCT.
☐ PROPERTY DAMAGE — AMT.

OPTIONAL EQUIPMENT AND ACCESSORIES

GROUP DESCRIPTION PRICE

Accessories------
Radio & Man Ant. Sup.-Dlx.
Speaker Rear Seat
Cushion Custom Foam Frt.
Washer Windshield
Speedo-Safe Guard & Fuel Lamp
Air Cleaner H. D.
Mirror Visor Vanity
Mirror Ins. Non Glare Tilt
Mirror Outside Remote Control L.H.
Lamps Back Up & Utility
Lamp Glove Box & Ash Trays
Lamp Parking Brake & Cigar Lighter
Power Steering Wonder Touch
Power Brakes Wonder Touch
Glass Soft Ray All
Power Window Lifts
Seat Belts Frt. Pair
WSW 800 X 14 Rayon Tire
Hydramatic Trans.
Wipers Dual Speed-Inst. Panel Pad
Clock Elect. - Undercoat

Rec'd Payment as written
Arthur H. Barber

SALES TAX
LICENSE AND TITLE
TOTAL CASH PRICE 3800 00

FINANCING
INSURANCE
TOTAL TIME PRICE

SETTLEMENT:
DEPOSIT
CASH ON DELIVERY — 2850 00
USED CAR:- — 950 00
TYPE
SER. No.
ENG. No.
PAYMENTS:

TOTAL 3800 00

ALWAYS SHOW SERIAL, ENGINE AND KEY NUMBERS

This is a bill of sale from Barber Vehicle and Motor Company, located at Barber's Corner in Natick. On July 24, 1963, Leo St. Onge Jr. bought a 1963 Pontiac Bonneville convertible for his wife, Marion. It must have been loaded with options for the price of $3,800. He even received $950 for his trade. Barber's company occupied this corner for many years, and it now resides at 334 Providence Street in Westcott; today, the CVS drugstore occupies this corner. (Courtesy of Leo St. Onge Jr.)

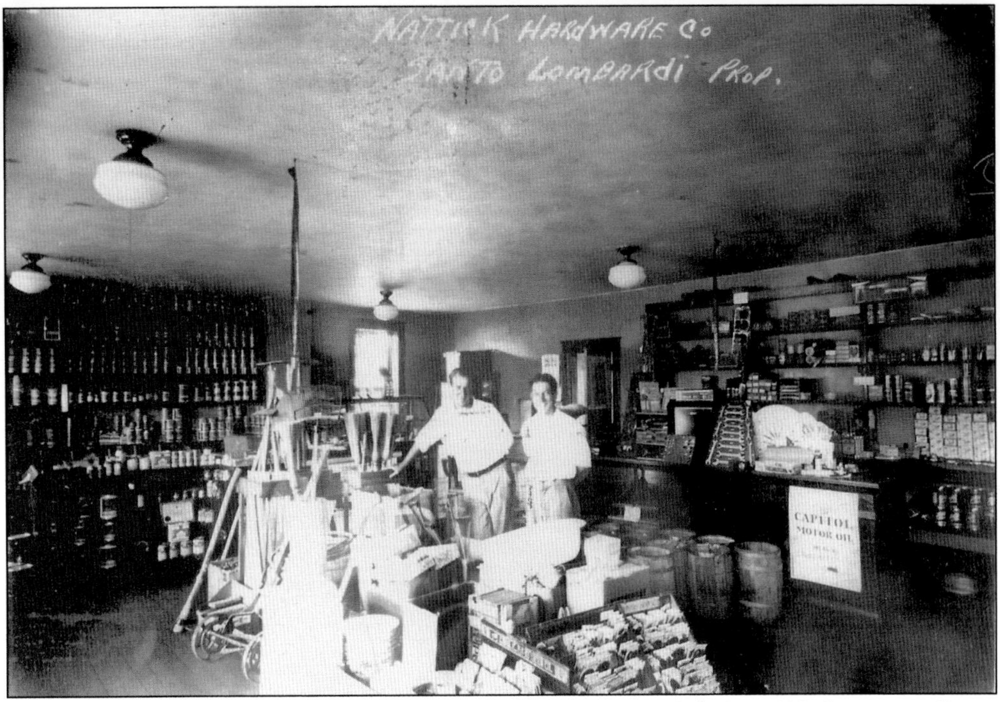

This is the interior of the Natick Hardware Company store on July 21, 1932. Proprietor Santo Lombardi (left) and his helper pose for the cameraman. To the right of them on the counter is a display of wrenches; on the floor are kegs of nails sold by the pound. The sign on the front of the counter announces that they sell Capitol Motor Oil, and on the left is a Reo push lawn mower. In the 1950s, Lombardi was arrested for breaking the Sunday blue law. He was warned not to be open on a Sunday again.

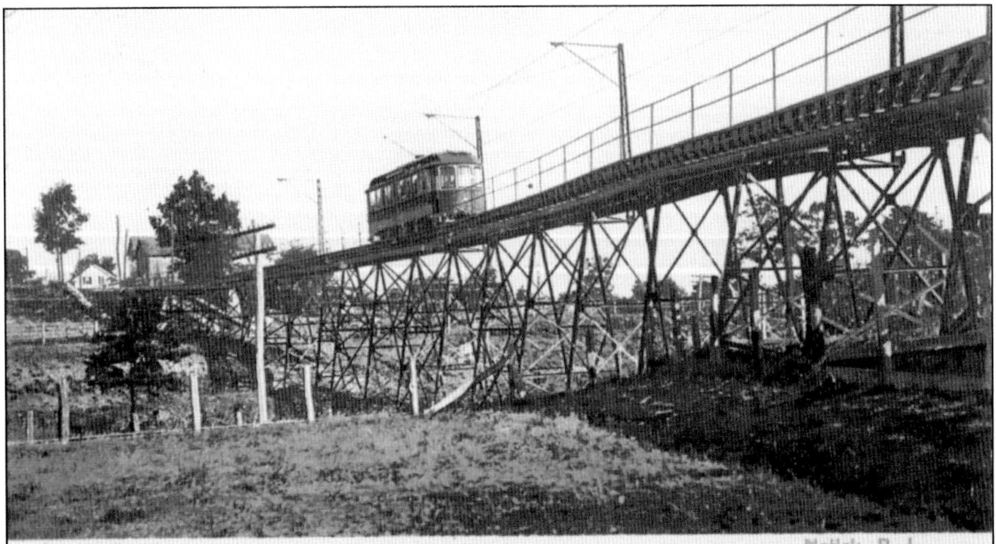

This postcard was mailed from Arctic to Anthony on July 20, 1906. It shows a trolley crossing the trestle that branched off at Brayton Avenue, crossed the tracks of the Hartford, Providence & Fishkill Railroad, and connected with Tollgate Road on the right. (Courtesy of Donald Carpenter.)

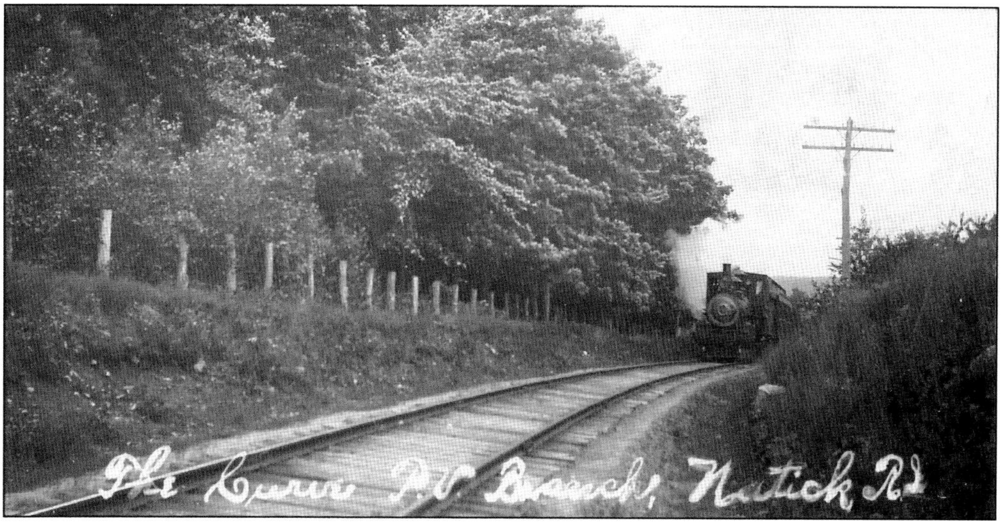

This postcard pictures a train traveling on the Pawtuxet Valley branch through Natick on the way to River Point and other points west. It will soon be passing under the trolley trestle pictured on page 90. (Courtesy of Lawrence G. Soucy.)

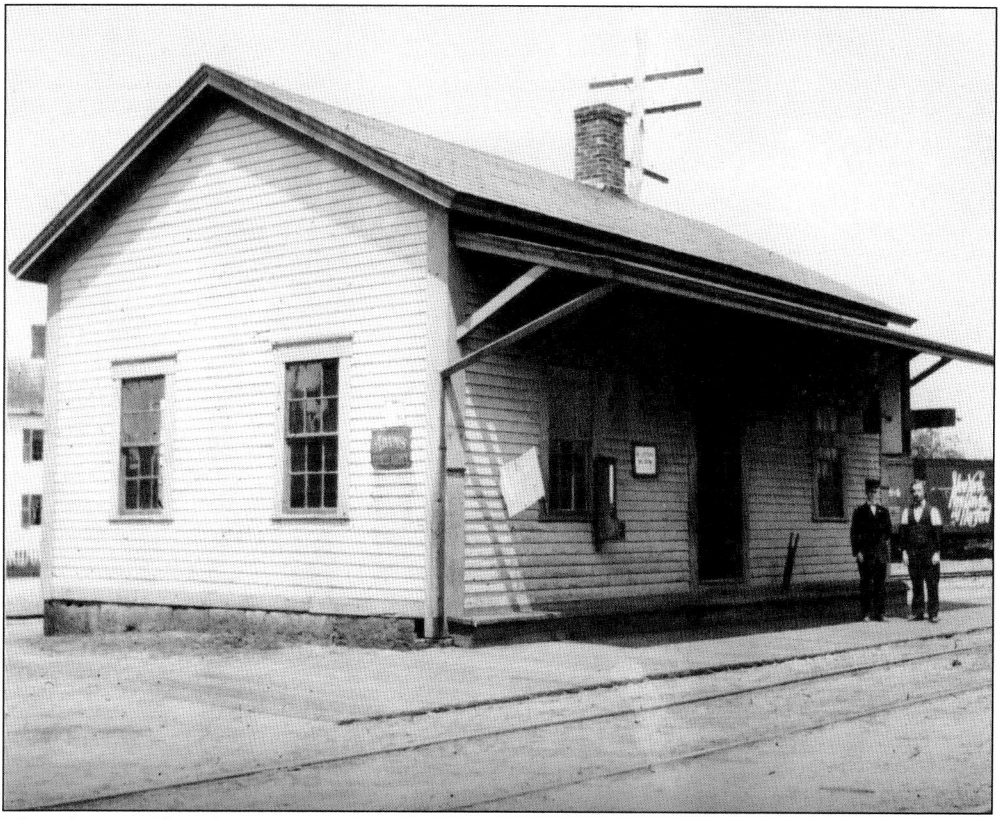

This photograph, taken in 1917, shows the East Natick train depot of the Hartford, Providence & Fishkill Railroad. The gentleman on the left is Yalva Matteson. He was the agent-operator. When West Warwick broke away from Warwick in 1913, this busy depot remained in Warwick's territory. The station was located where the bike path now crosses East Avenue.

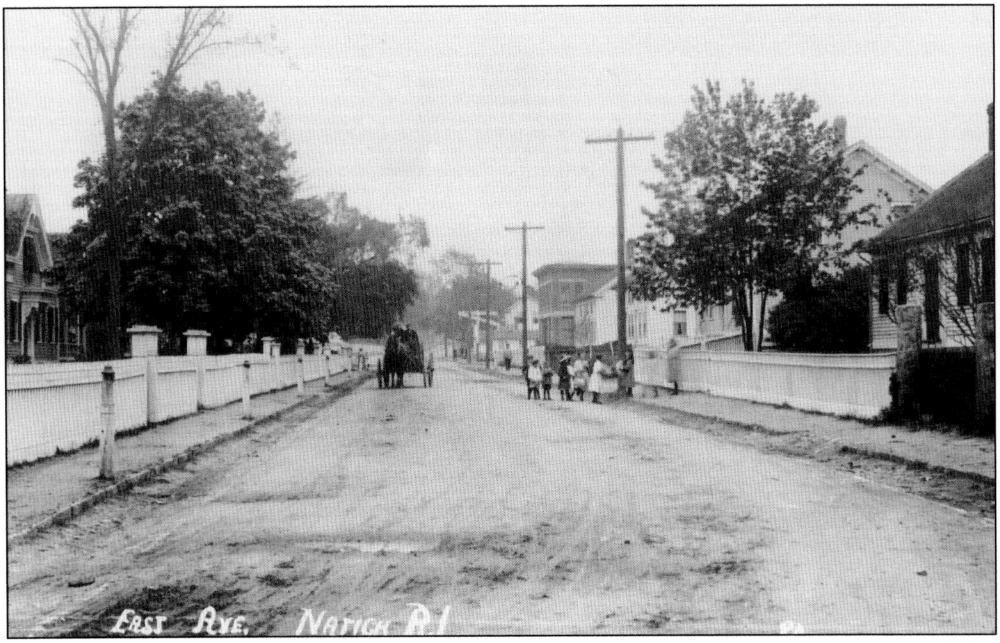

This photograph shows East Avenue in 1920. The road is still gravel, and there are no automobiles in sight. The white picket fence on the left goes continuously from house to house with hitching posts in front of each home. The two-story brick building on the right beyond the group of young girls was originally part of the Natick Mills Complex. It later became the Bowen Grain Mill and Store. The train crossing can be seen farther east, and the depot was opposite it.

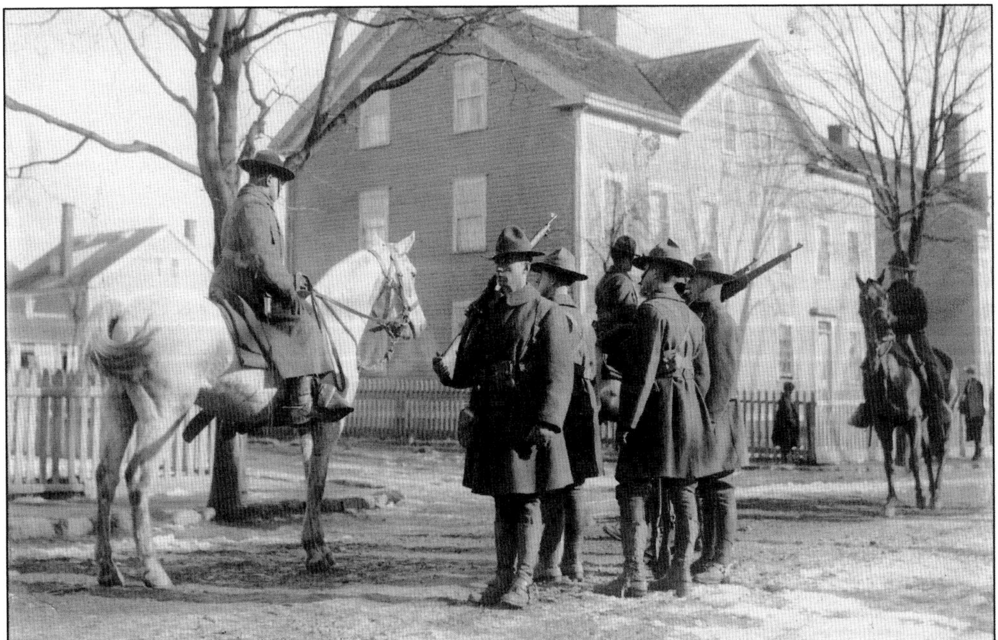

In 1922, a devastating strike of New England textile workers lasted for 33 weeks. State troopers and the National Guard were brought into Natick to maintain order, as the strikers had become unruly. The strike turned out to be the beginning of the end of the Natick Mills.

Seven

Phenix Village

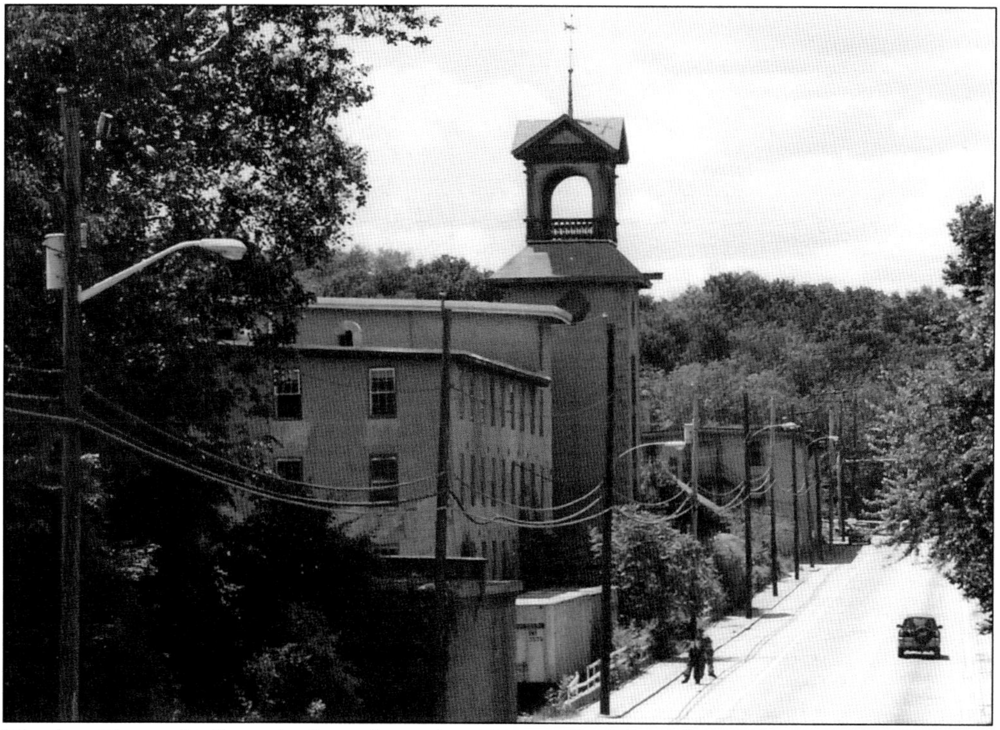

The first Phenix Mill was built in the early 1800s on the left of the road. It was constructed of wood and burned in 1821. In 1822, a small stone mill was built at the near end of this photograph to replace it. A second stone mill was constructed at the far end in 1825. In 1882, they were connected to create the mill and its impressive tower. The brick mill building hidden by the trees on the right was built in 1909. The overhead walkway that connected the two mills was removed on June 19, 1997. (Courtesy of Gerard Tellier Jr.)

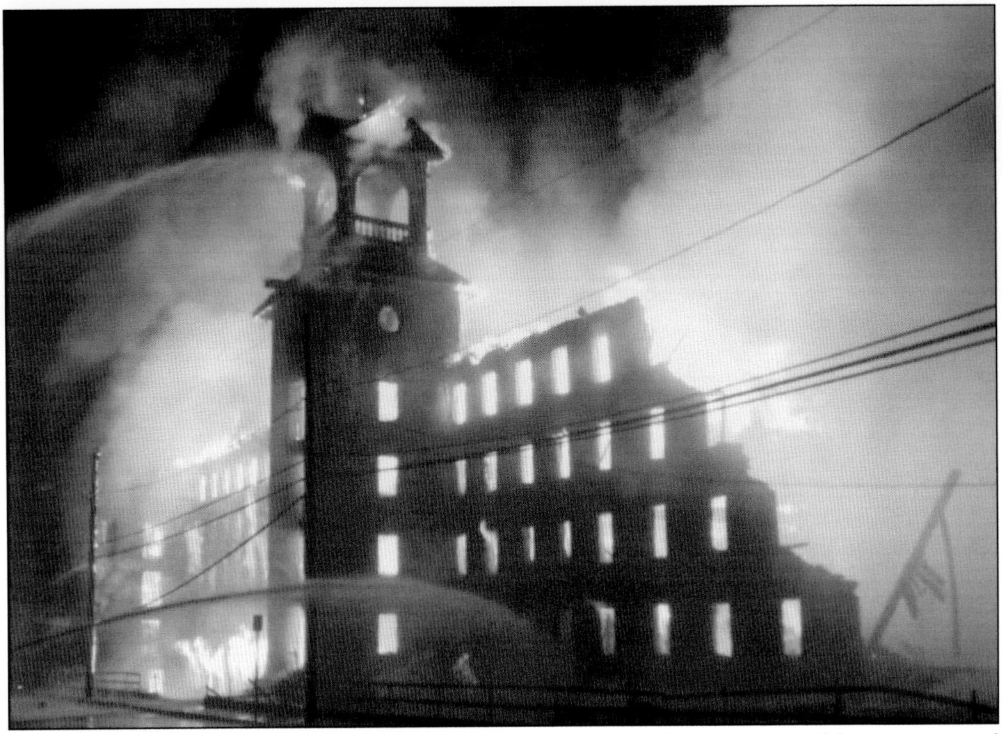

Textiles were manufactured in this five-story stone structure, which was later used for spinning and weaving operations. At one point, over half of the residents of Phenix worked 13-hour shifts in the mill. Scott Laboratories, a pharmaceutical research company, bought the building in the 1960s. A number of other businesses used the mill buildings through the years after Scott Laboratories moved out. In 1995, a fire destroyed one of the small buildings, and on March 30, 2005, the fire pictured destroyed the entire complex. The photograph below was taken on April 1, 2005, the morning after the blaze. In it, the fire companies are still pouring water on the smoldering ashes. (Both, courtesy of Gerard Tellier Jr.)

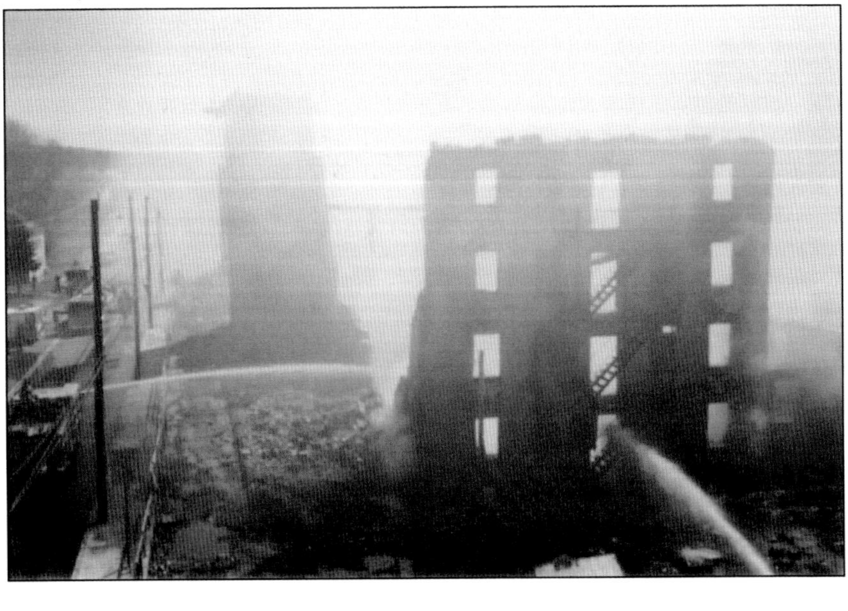

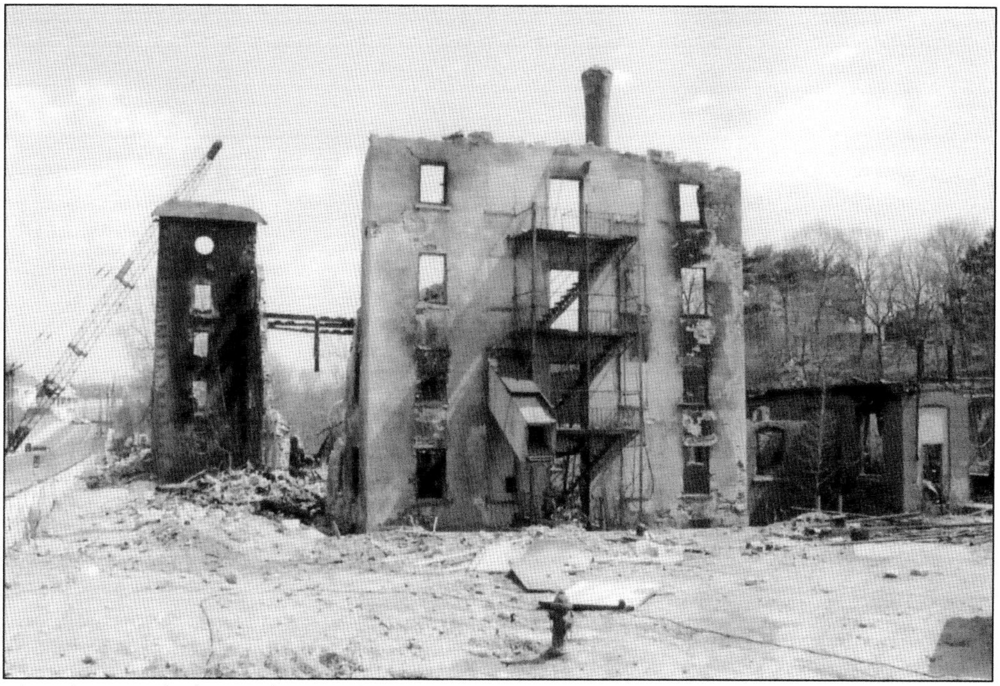

This photograph shows what was left of the 183-year-old mill building just before the wrecking ball finished leveling it on April 6, 2005. The complex had been bought by Mill Conversions of Woonsocket. The plan had been to transform the old mill into condominiums, as the company had done to a mill in Woonsocket. (Courtesy of Gerard Tellier Jr.)

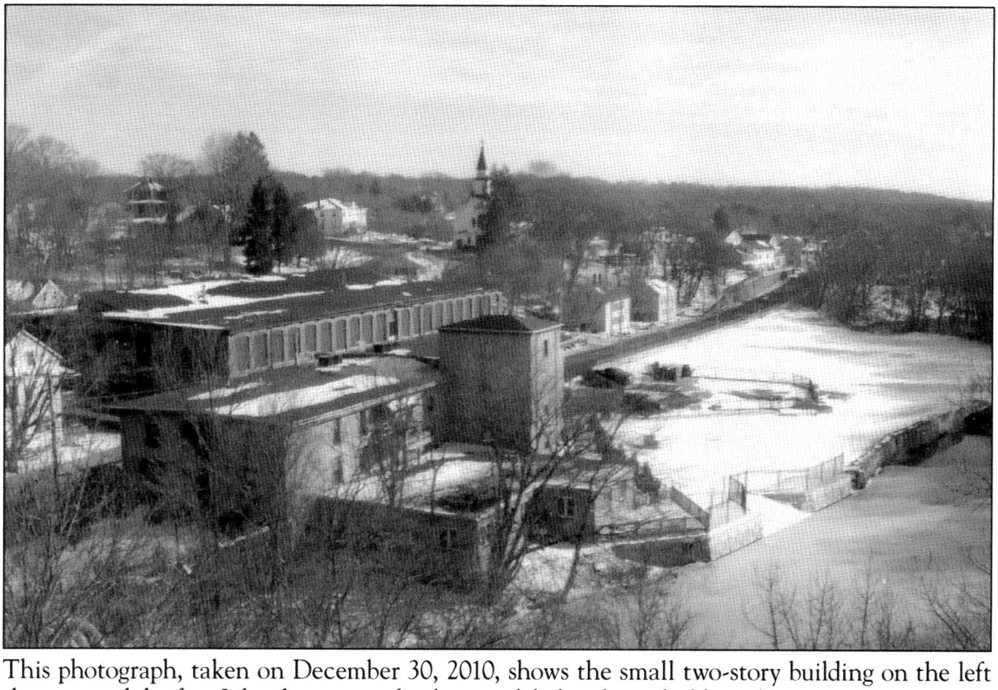

This photograph, taken on December 30, 2010, shows the small two-story building on the left that escaped the fire. It has been completely remodeled and now holds six housing units. SS Peter and Paul Church stands in the distance overlooking the village. (Author's collection.)

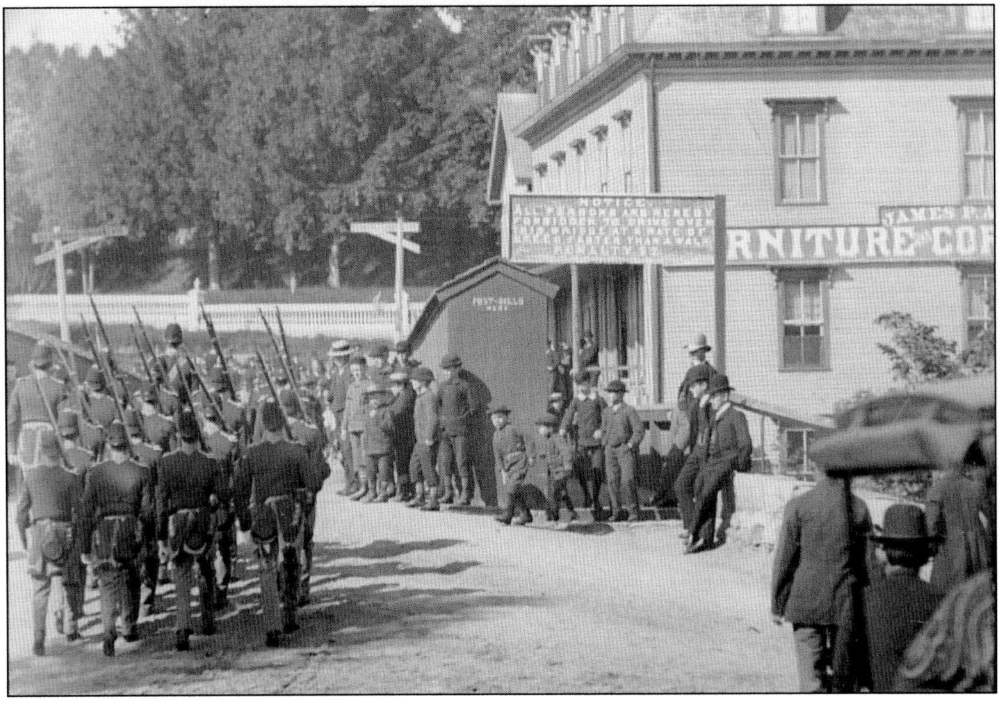

This is a view of the Grand Army of the Republic (GAR) after crossing the Phenix Bridge on their way up Fairview Avenue, perhaps to the Greenwood Cemetery. The sign on the Mumford building reads: "James F. Arnold Furniture and Coffin Warerooms." The large sign states: "Notice, All persons are hereby forbidden to drive over this bridge at a rate of speed faster than a walk. Penalty $2.00." William B. Spencer built a house behind the white fence in 1850 (see page 99). (Courtesy of Lawrence Soucy.)

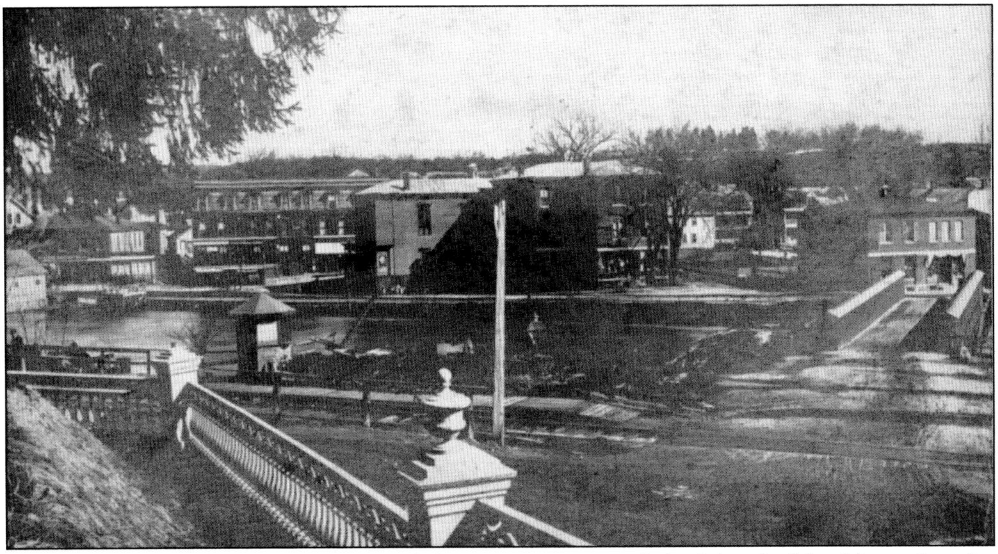

This photograph shows the remains of the train station and the Mumford building after the fire of March 12, 1888. Tickets were temporarily sold out of the little building next to the ashes. Later, the depot would be built on this side of the tracks, as seen on page 97. (Courtesy of Donald Carpenter.)

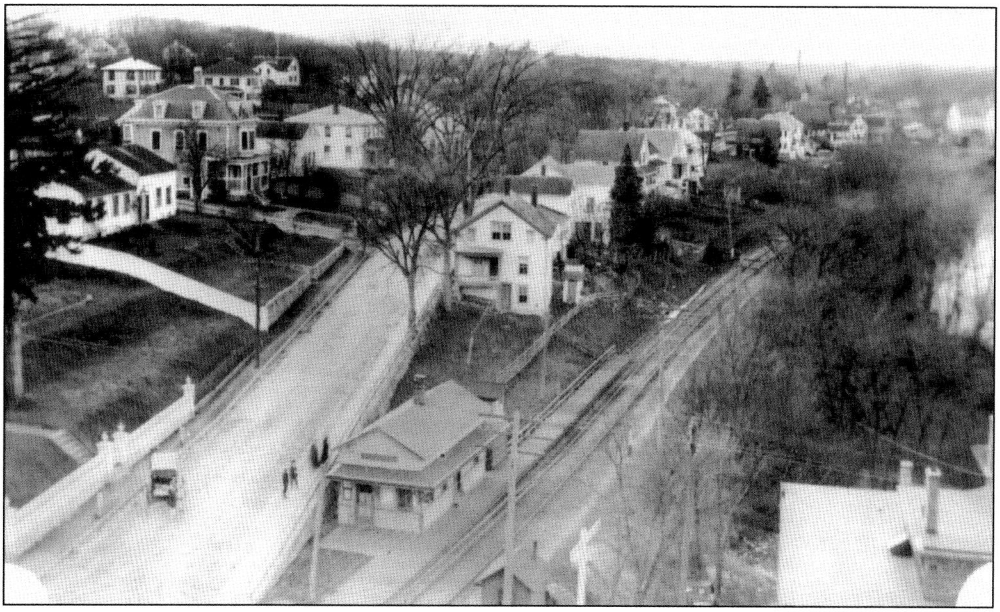

The Pawtuxet Valley Railroad train, traveling from Hope, would approach the relocated Phenix station beside Ames Street. The railroad bed was converted to the Phenix-Harris Riverwalk trail in the 1960s. The following verses are from "River Walk" by Helen O. Larson: "In the spring they'll walk by the river, for a river walk has been made / They'll be shielded from the hot Sun, for the trees will give them shade. A teenage boy will be laughing and so carefree / He will say to the young girl, come walk the river walk with me." This view was taken from the Phenix Baptist Church steeple in 1918. (Courtesy of Donald Carpenter.)

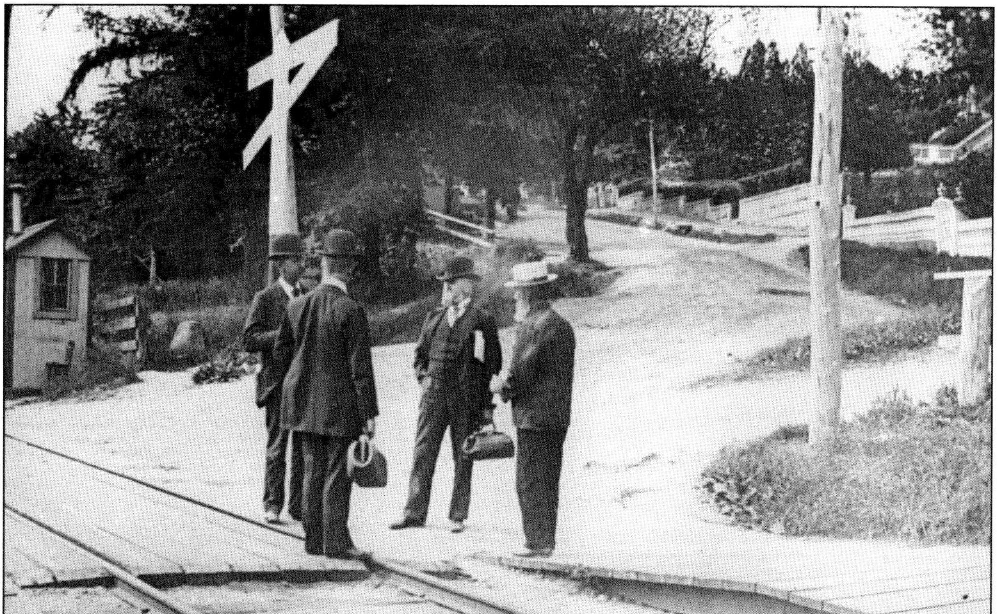

This photograph from 1905 shows, from left to right, J. Ellery Hudson, David Clark, Presbery Hoxie, and Harvey Spencer. They are waiting on Fairview Avenue to board the train to Providence. The building to the left is the crossing-guard cabin. (Courtesy of Lawrence G. Soucy.)

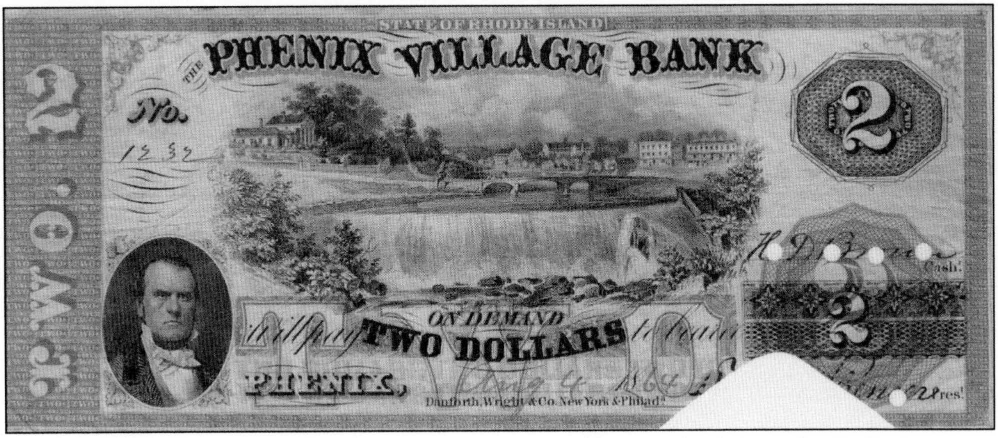

This $2 bill of the Phenix Village Bank was engraved by Danforth, Wright & Company in 1864. It displays a detailed central vignette. The house on the hill on Fairview Avenue (left) is William B. Spencer's first house, built in 1849 and seen on the facing page. The bill also pictures the second bridge built across the Pawtuxet River in Phenix. The four buildings pictured above the bridge are, from left to right, Lanphear Machine Shop (built in 1848), Harris Mill (1850), the first Capron Block, and the second Spencer Block (1855). The view ends with the Pawtuxet River spilling over the Phenix Dam. The gentleman pictured is bank president William B. Spencer. (Courtesy of Gerard Tellier Jr.)

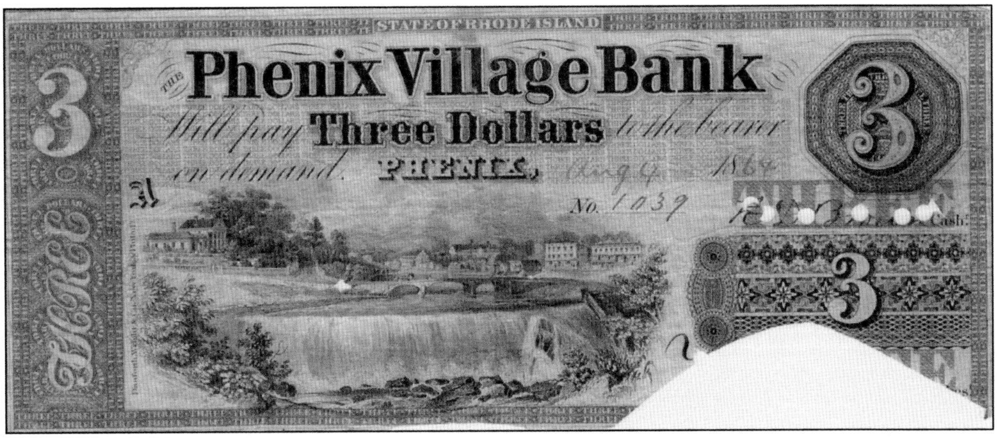

The original Phenix Village Bank was incorporated in 1856. The Phenix Savings Bank was chartered in 1858. A fire destroyed much of the business area and the bank. A *New York Times* article dated March 16, 1897, reads: "The Phenix Savings Bank of Phenix, Rhode Island suspended payment yesterday [March 15] and refused deposits. It did not affect the Phenix National Bank located in the same building." This was a time when they really did make $3 bills. (Courtesy of Gerard Tellier Jr.)

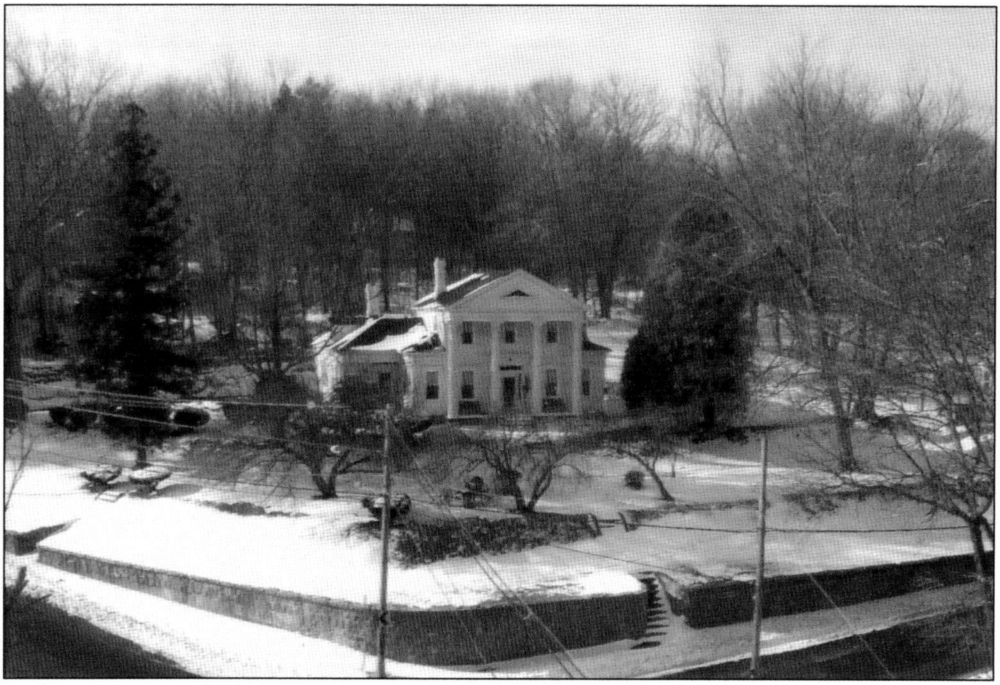

William B. Spencer built this imposing two-story Greek Revival home in 1847. It still survives today, as this photograph was taken on December 30, 2010. It is located at 2 Ames Street and overlooks the Pawtuxet River and the village of Phenix. Below is the beautiful Italianate-style home he built next door at 11 Fairview Avenue. It sits on a hill atop a massive granite-block wall. Spenser and his family moved in after it was completed in 1870. This photograph was taken February 8, 2011. Both houses have been well maintained for over 100 years. (Both, author's collection.)

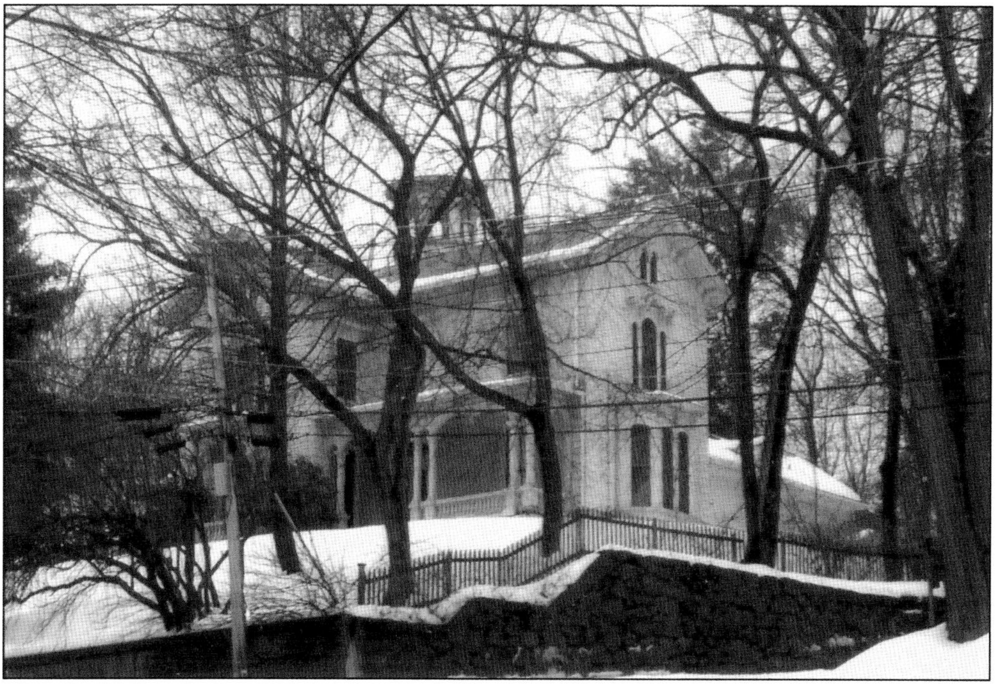

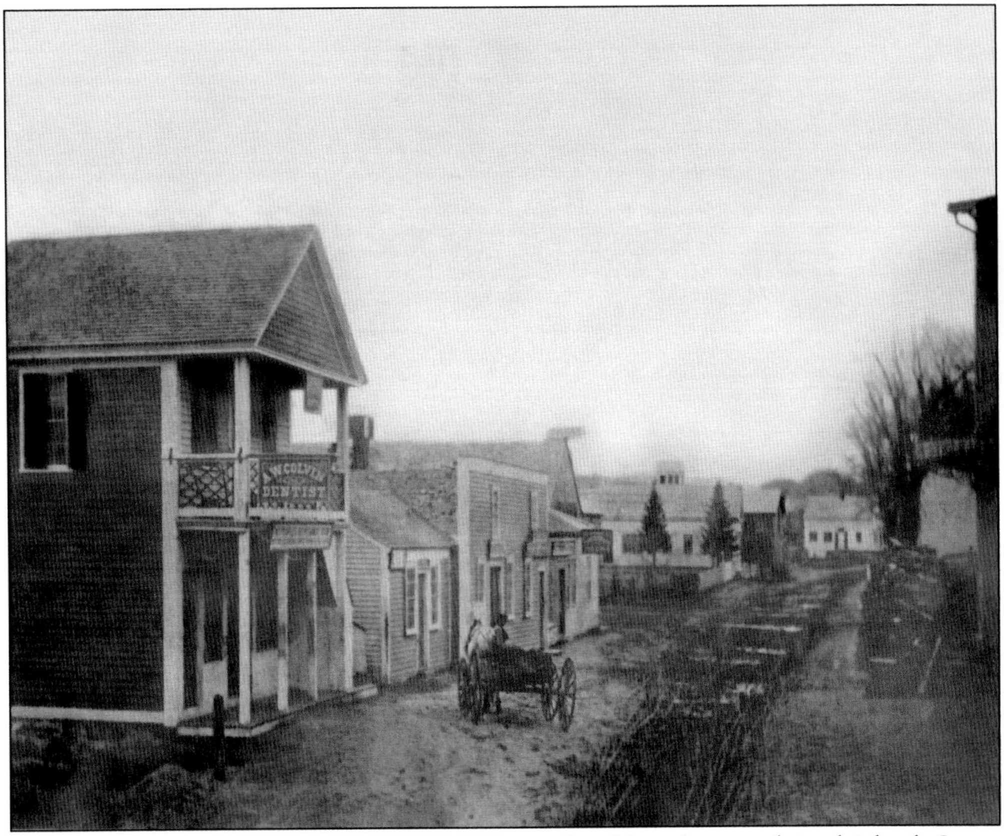

This image of Phenix holds the distinction of being the oldest photograph in this book. It was taken in 1861 and given to Donald Carpenter by his aunt Mabel Wheelock. The local dentist, A.W. Colvin, practiced in the first building on the left and eventually moved to the second floor of the Lawton building. The road was still dirt, and trolley tracks had yet to be installed. (Courtesy of Donald Carpenter.)

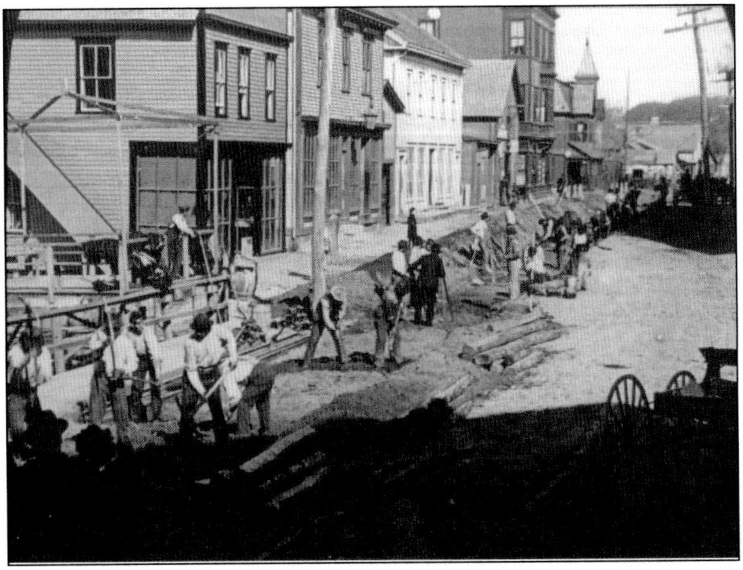

This photograph shows men laying the tracks for the trolley in 1894. The buildings are, from left to right, the original livery stable with a second floor added, John Conley Liquor, Phillip Duffy's store, Steven Card's Livery, the Gleaner building, and the fire station. (Courtesy of Lawrence G. Soucy.)

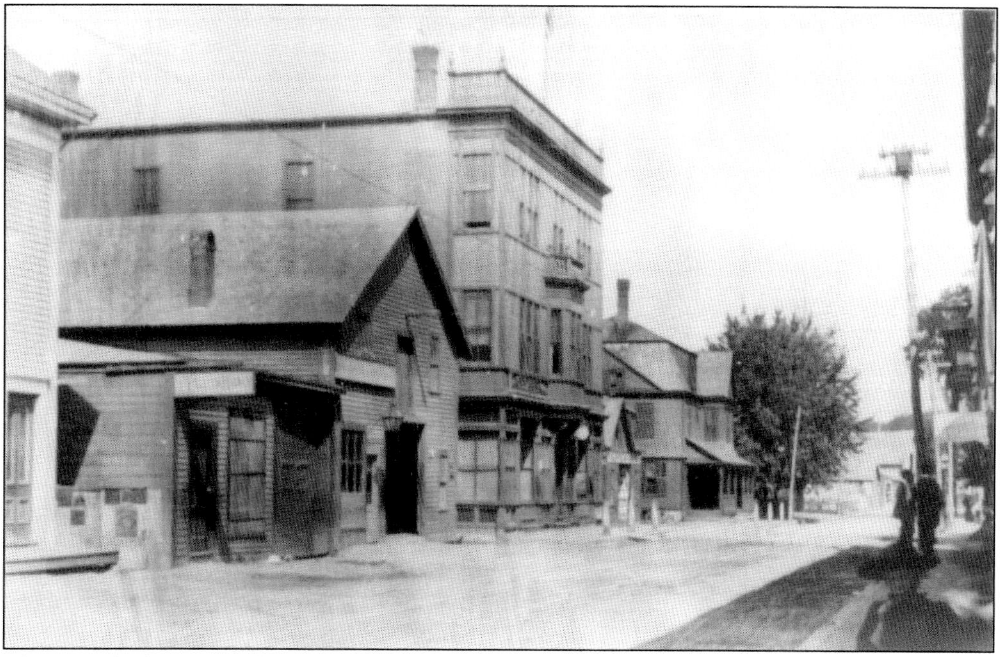

This view looking west shows Steven Card's Livery followed by the Gleaner building, which was home to the GAR hall. The McGregor Post No. 14 met on the top floor. The Briggs Hotel appears after the small building in between. (Courtesy of Lawrence G. Soucy.)

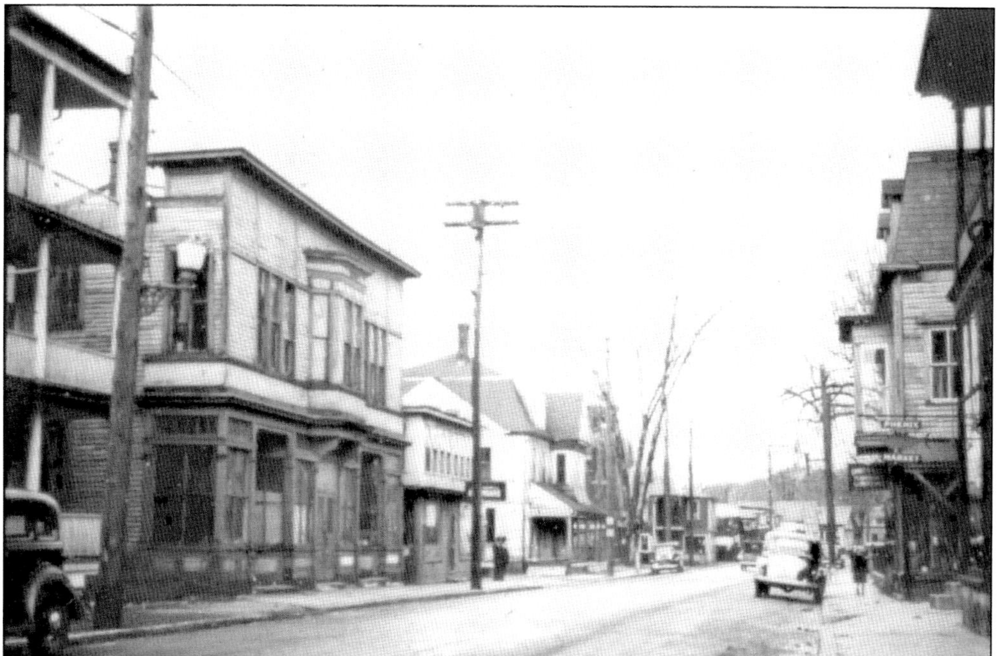

By the 1930s and with the popularity of the automobile, the livery appears to have been replaced with a three-story tenement house. A fire has burned off the top floor of the Gleaner building seen above, and the tower of the fire station is visible after the Briggs Hotel. (Courtesy of Lawrence G. Soucy.)

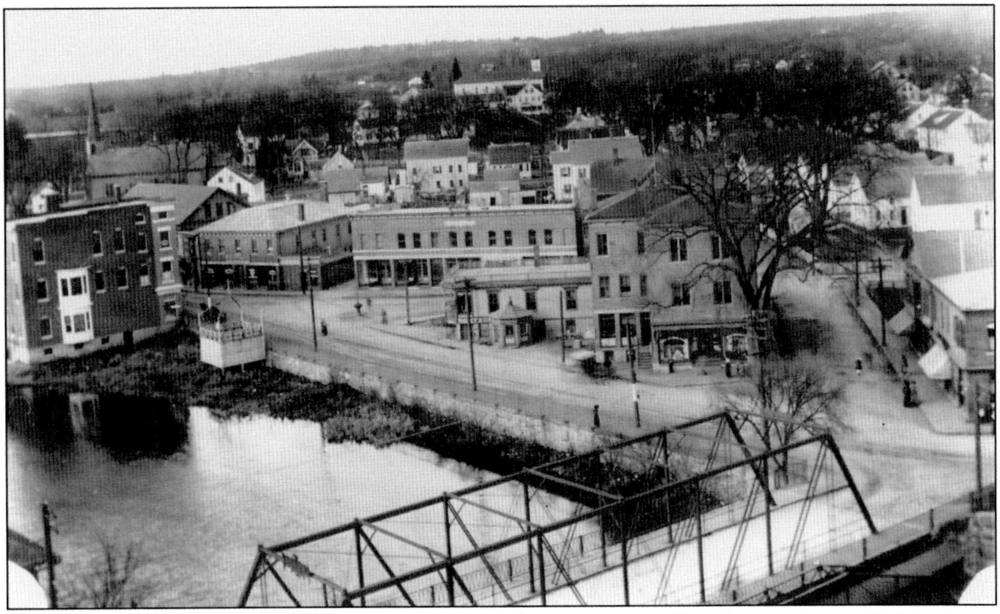

This view of Phenix Square was taken from the Phenix Baptist Church steeple in 1907. It shows the bandstand on the bank of the Pawtuxet River with the Capron building above it. To the right is the Arnold Block, built in 1898 after the fire of 1894 destroyed the Spencer building. The building in front of it was the music hall. Its top floor burned off in a fire on February 23, 1897. William Lewis ran his peanut shop in the small octagonal building beside it. The Phenix Methodist Church can be seen in the upper left corner. (Courtesy of Lawrence G. Soucy.)

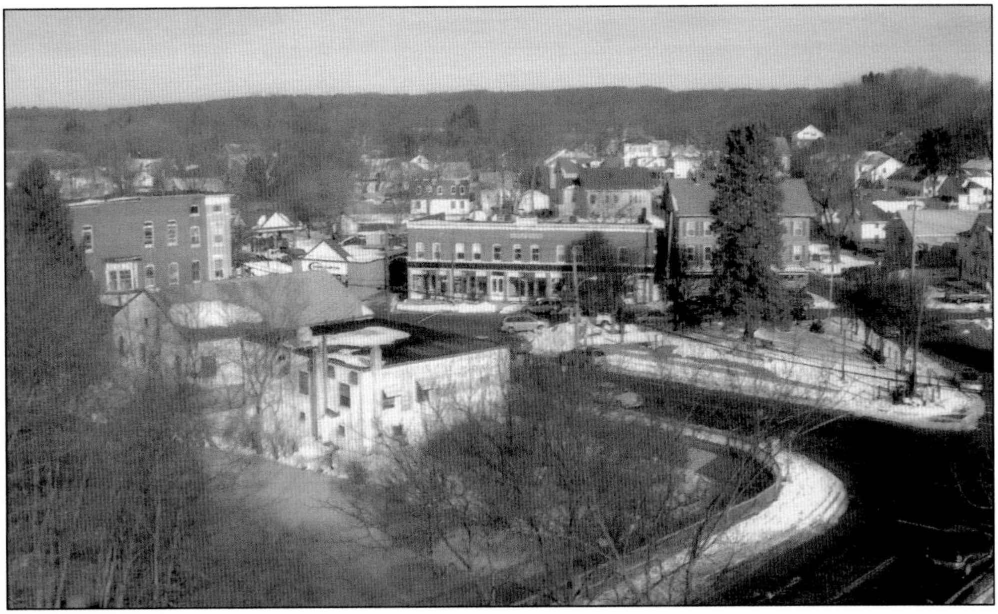

This photograph was taken 103 years later, on December 30, 2010. Rob Burton, the Tree Guy, was gracious enough to allow the author use of his bucket truck to obtain this picture. The Phenix Hotel, beside the Arnold building, is hidden behind the Christmas tree. The Himes building is to the left beside two new buildings built on the river. The closest structure is Hudson's Cleaners. (Author's collection.)

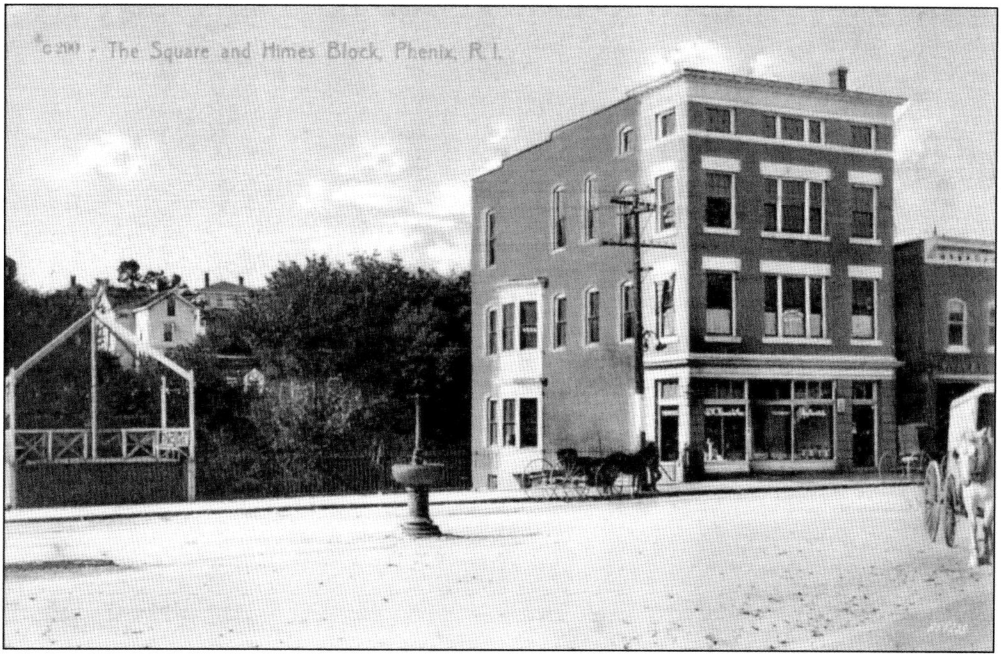

This postcard was mailed June 22, 1908. It shows the four-story S.W. Himes building. The bandstand is to the left, where Hudson Cleaners is today. The water fountain for the horses is at the intersection of Main and Highland Streets. It was installed on May 2, 1889, and removed in the late 1930s. (Courtesy of Lawrence G. Soucy.)

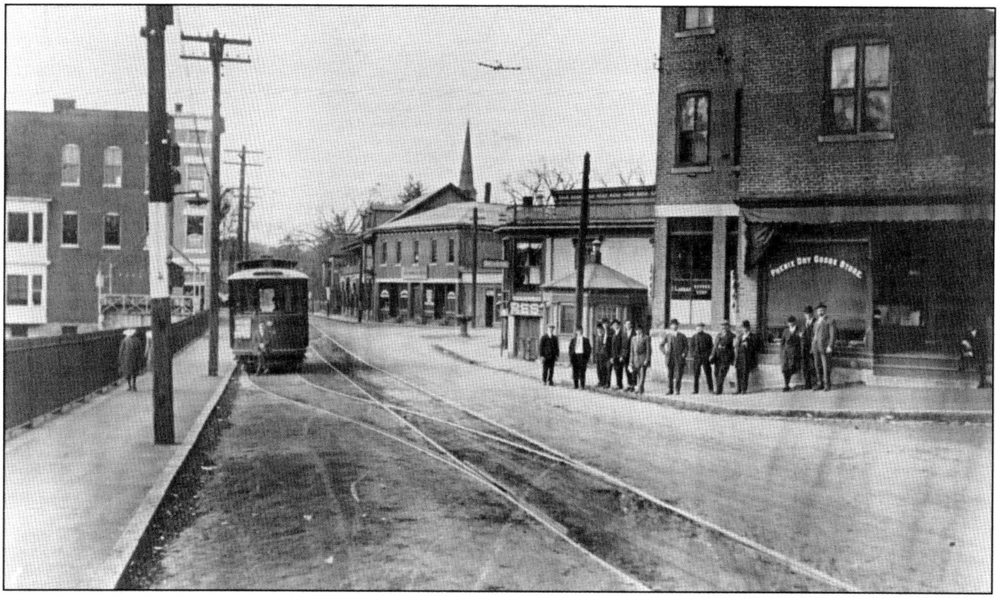

A Pawtuxet Valley Electric Street Railway trolley has pulled off to a siding in this photograph from 1920. The railway opened service to the valley in 1895. William Lewis's peanut shop is visible along with the music hall behind it, minus the top floor. The building that the Phenix Dry Goods store is in was the Lawton building, which is now gone. A beautiful pine tree that is decorated and lit every Christmas has replaced it. The Phenix Methodist Church steeple can be seen reaching for the sky above the Capron building.

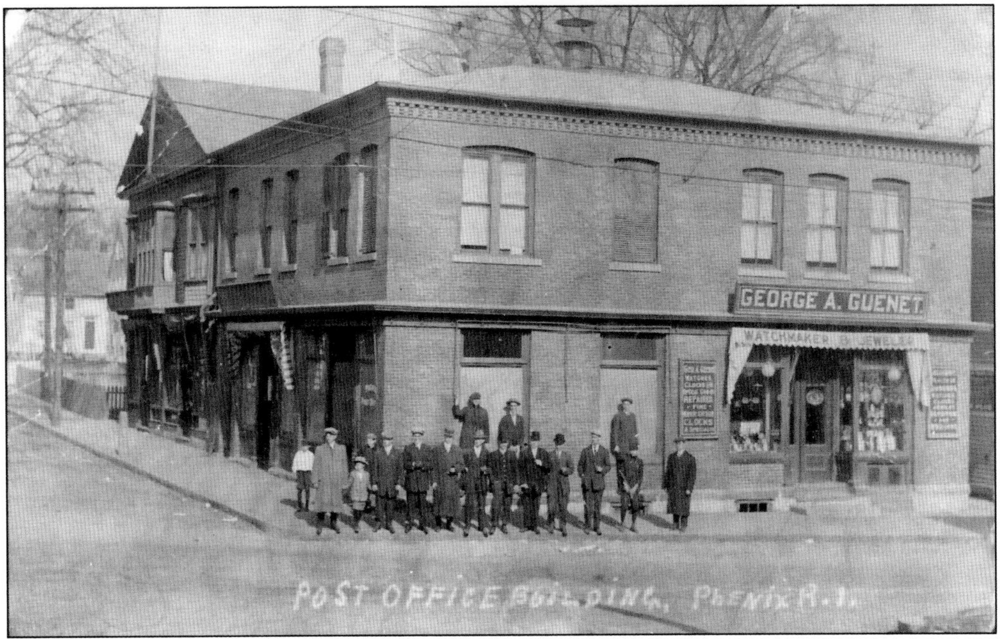

This photograph shows the post office building on the corner of Main and Pleasant Streets. George A. Guenet ran a jewelry store there also. The building behind it is the Spalding Block. At one time, the first floor was home to an IGA grocery store run by the Leveillee family. (Courtesy of Lawrence G. Soucy.)

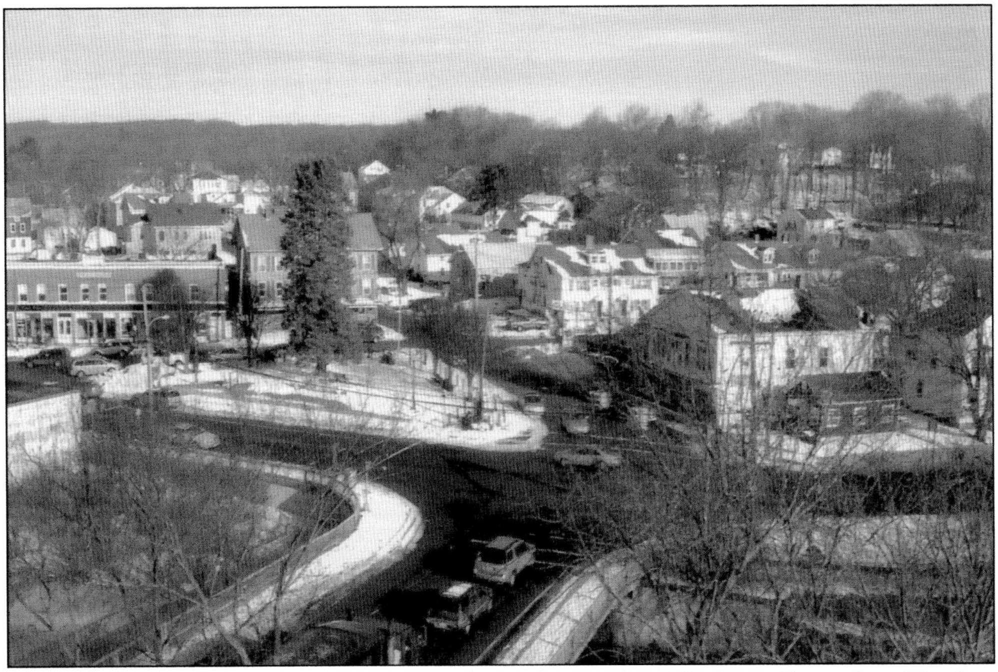

This photograph, taken in December 2010, shows the Spalding Block is still standing. The first floor is occupied by the Phenix Square Restaurant, which advertises its location "In Beautiful Downtown Phenix." The post office building on the corner has been replaced with a small building that houses William's Barber Shop. (Author's collection.)

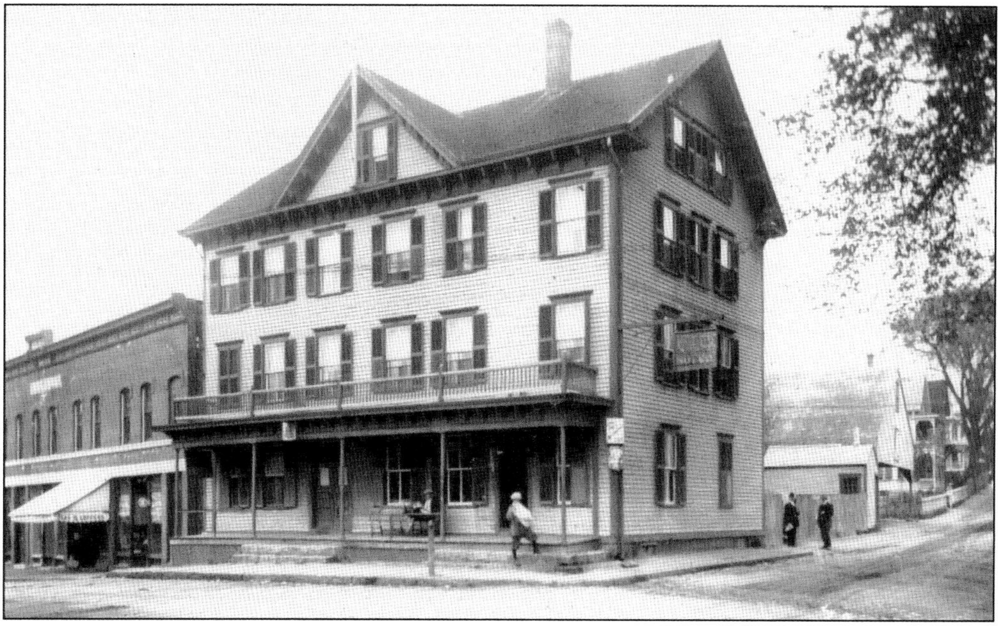

The first Phenix Hotel, run by Harrison and Emmanuel Collins, was built on this site in 1847. It was destroyed in the great fire of May 24, 1871. This photograph, taken in 1945, shows the present Phenix Hotel, which was rebuilt in 1871. Today, it still operates as a hotel on the corner of Highland and Pleasant Streets. The Arnold building is to the left. (Courtesy of Donald Carpenter.)

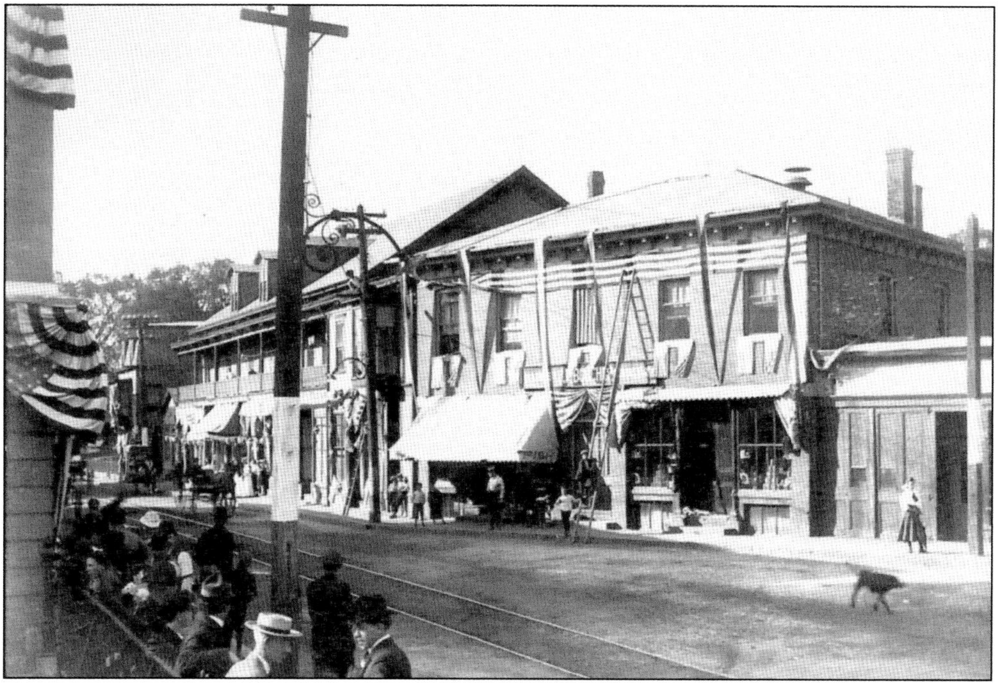

It appears that when this photograph was taken in 1901, the village merchants were decorating for the Fourth of July. A ladder is still against the side of the Capron building that was built in 1883. The Arnold building seen at the top of page 102 would be to the right. (Courtesy of Donald Carpenter.)

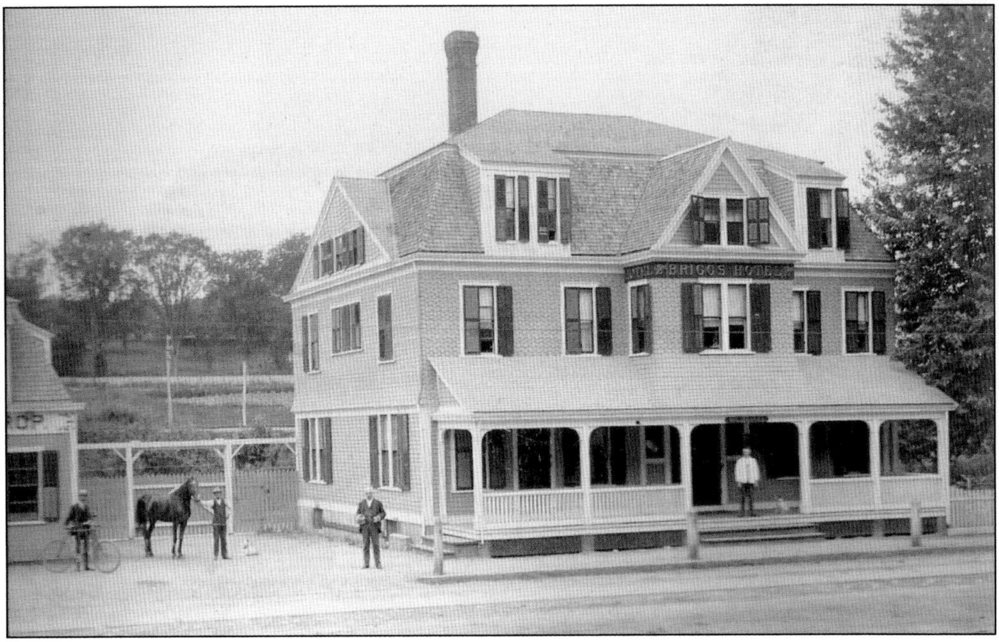

On April 11, 1860, Stephen C. Briggs bought a lot with a house from John Lippitt. He later bought two more lots in 1861. By 1870, he had built an addition to the house, and in February, he opened it as a hotel. On July 13, 1885, it was destroyed by fire. Son Willet G. Briggs built this beautiful house and stable in 1886 and continued business as the W.G. Briggs Hotel and Stable. Later, Sternbach's Oil Company, located across the street from the fire station, stored its trucks in the barn. (Both, courtesy of Lawrence G. Soucy.)

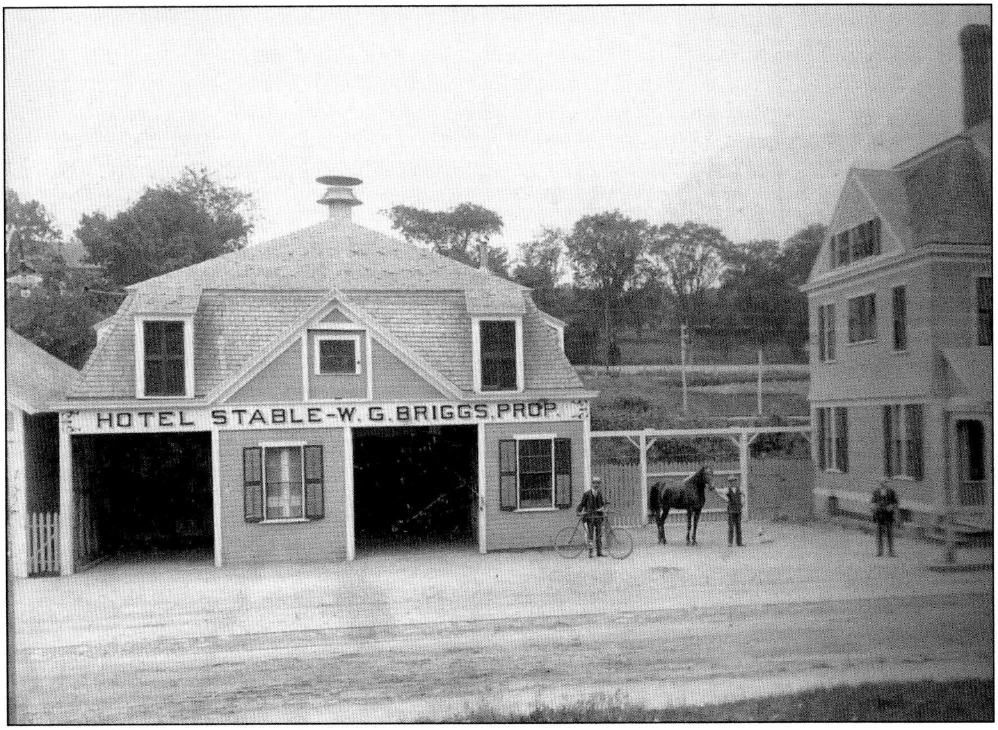

Even though most of this building was in the village of Harris and the town of Coventry, it was named the Phenix Fire Station. The following verses are from "Dedicated to Firemen" by Helen O. Larson, written in 1980 at age 70: "Let's have a large parade, let's tie ribbons on the trees / For what would we ever do, without dedicated men like these. Let's line both sides of the street, let's applaud as they go by / Because while fighting fires, some of them could die." (Courtesy of Gerard Tellier Jr.)

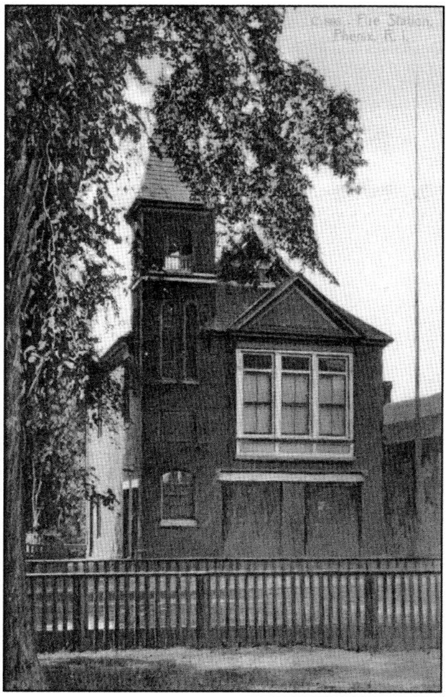

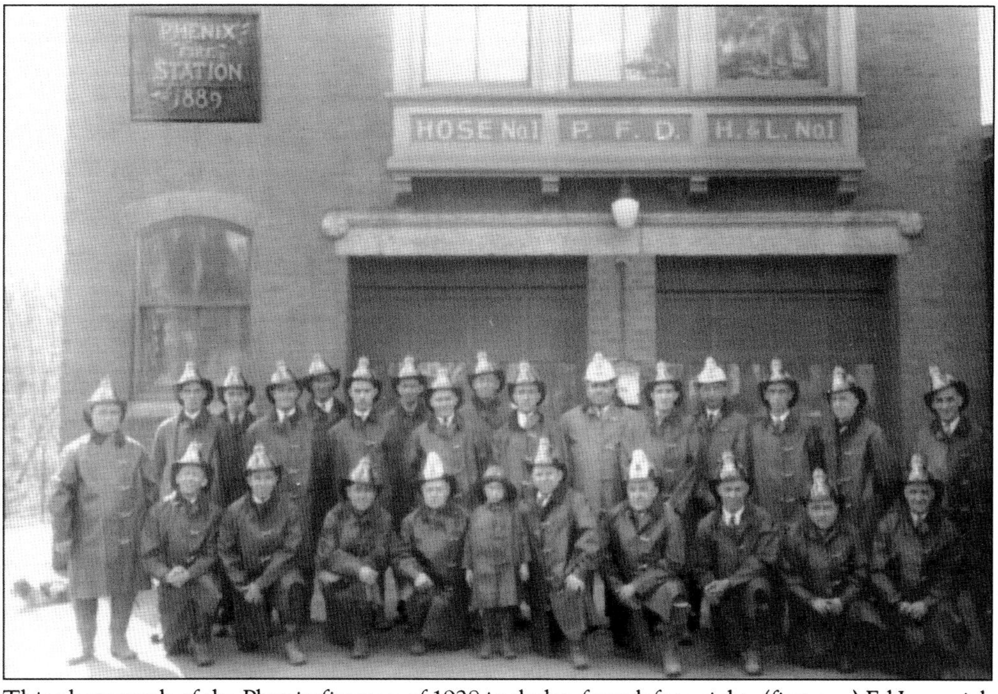

This photograph of the Phenix firemen of 1928 includes, from left to right, (first row) Ed Lemerick (standing), Donat Demers, Camille Arcand, Bud Duffinae, Charles Hopkins, Joseph Arcand, Albert Peltier, Gerard Trudeau, A. Hopkins, and Pete Theroux; (second row) Joe Miclette, Ernest Fercente, Don Richotte, Leo Landroch, Ernest Jabot, Chief Fred Colvin, Donat Lamothe, First Assistant Chief Oscar Arcand, Jim Leveillee, Donat Theroux, and Jack Picard; (third row) Donald Trudeau, Henry Hudson, Richard Picard, and Doria Lebrun. The five-year-old little boy, their mascot, is Roger Chabot. He is now 87 and the only person in the photograph who is still living. (Courtesy of Gerard Tellier Jr.)

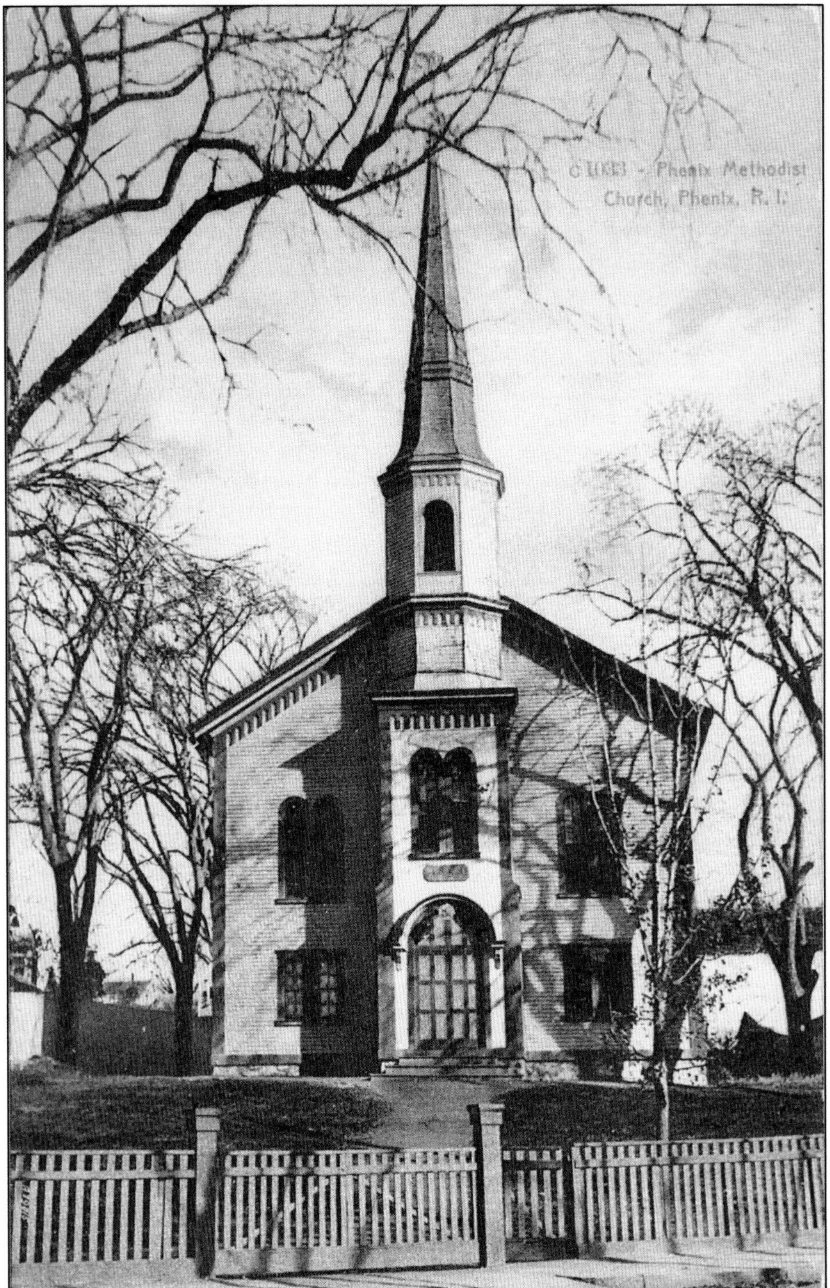

The Phenix Methodist Church was built by Pardon Spencer in 1859. In the 1970s, the congregation joined with the Hope Methodist Church. They built a new church in Hope and named it the Shepherd of the Valley. A Cumberland Farms store now occupies the property. The following verses are from "The Shepherd of the Valley," written by Helen O. Larson in 1996 at age 85: "There's a church by the side of the highway, where the faithful go to pray / And each Sunday my son Raymond, worships there with his Ashlee Rae. The Shepherd of the Valley Church, draws people far and near / They love to sing and pray there, to the Shepherd they love so dear. Each and every Sunday, as the people go in, they realize Shepherd of the Valley, was named after Him."

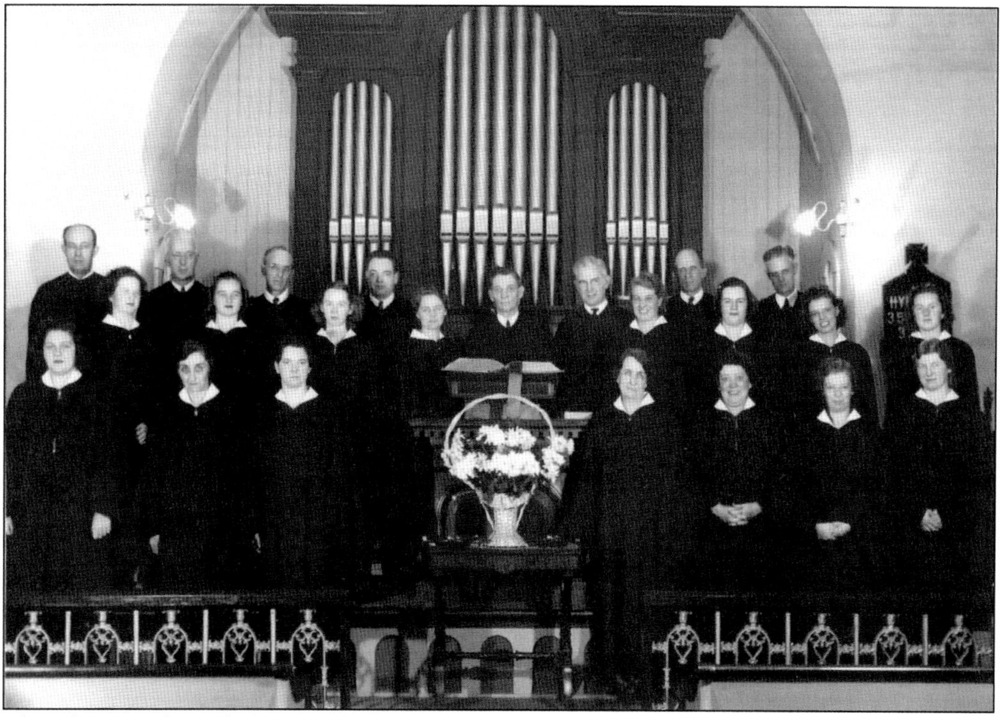

This photograph spotlights the Phenix Methodist Church choir on December 15, 1939. From left to right are (first row) Clarice Greaves, Lucille Gibson, Lucille Manning, Marion Hudson, Mrs. James Lindsay, Esther Bodwell Northup, and Cora Richardson; (second row) Marjorie Cowen, Beth Folsom, Norma Johnson, Irene Carney, (organist), Rev. George W. Manning (pastor), Eliza Johnson, Marjorie Campbell, Nina Lindsay, and Shirley Thornton; (third row) Albert S. Hudson, James M. Lindsay, Ellery E. Hudson, Raymond Manning, William Gibson, John Buckley Hudson, and Earl R. Handy. (Courtesy of Donald Carpenter.)

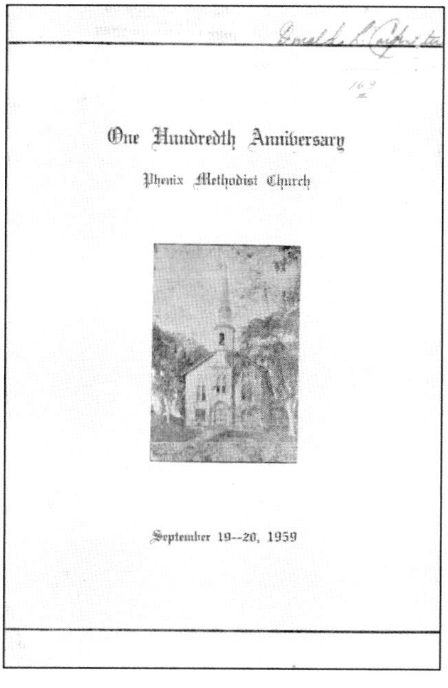

Almost 20 years after the top photograph was taken, the congregation celebrated its 100th anniversary on Saturday and Sunday, September 19–20, 1959. This program announces the services. The organ pictured was built in 1859 by George Stevens of Cambridge, Massachusetts. (Courtesy of Donald Carpenter.)

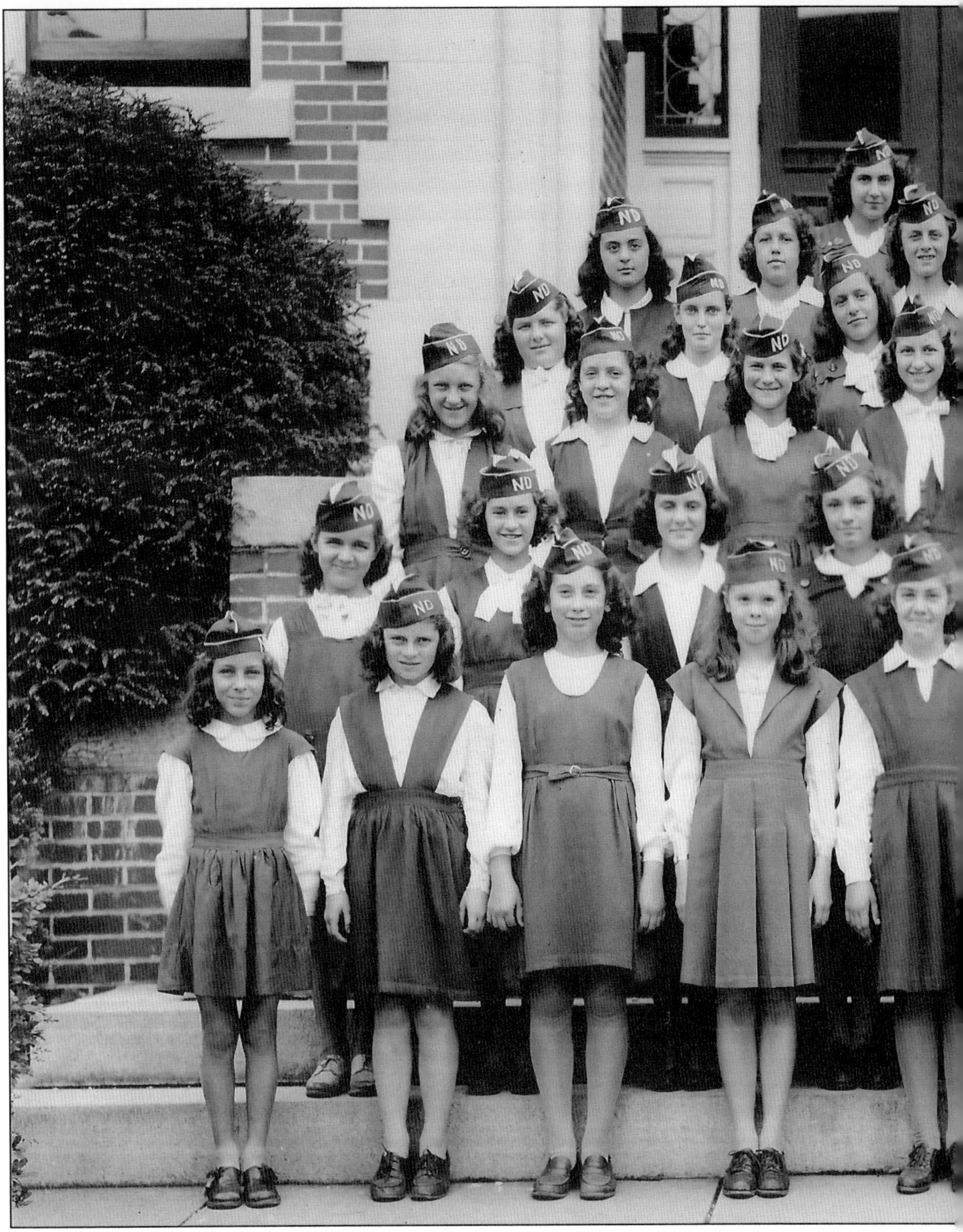

This photograph of the Notre Dame School chorale was taken on the steps of the school in 1947. From left to right are (first row) Claire Martin, Joan Joubert, Helen Provost, Margo Hebert, Pauline Chabot, Estelle Heroux, Reinette Detonnancourt, Doris Vallerian, Roberta Lavallee, and Jacqueline Gourd; (second row) Helen Dupuis, Claire Theroux, Francois Touchette, Ferdenande Theroux, Lucile Heroux, Claire Peletier, Pauline Chapdelaine, Yvonne Gouguen, and Jacqueline Brouillard; (third row) Gloria Boudreau, Pauline Desrosiers, Jennine Lavigne, Pauline Goulet,

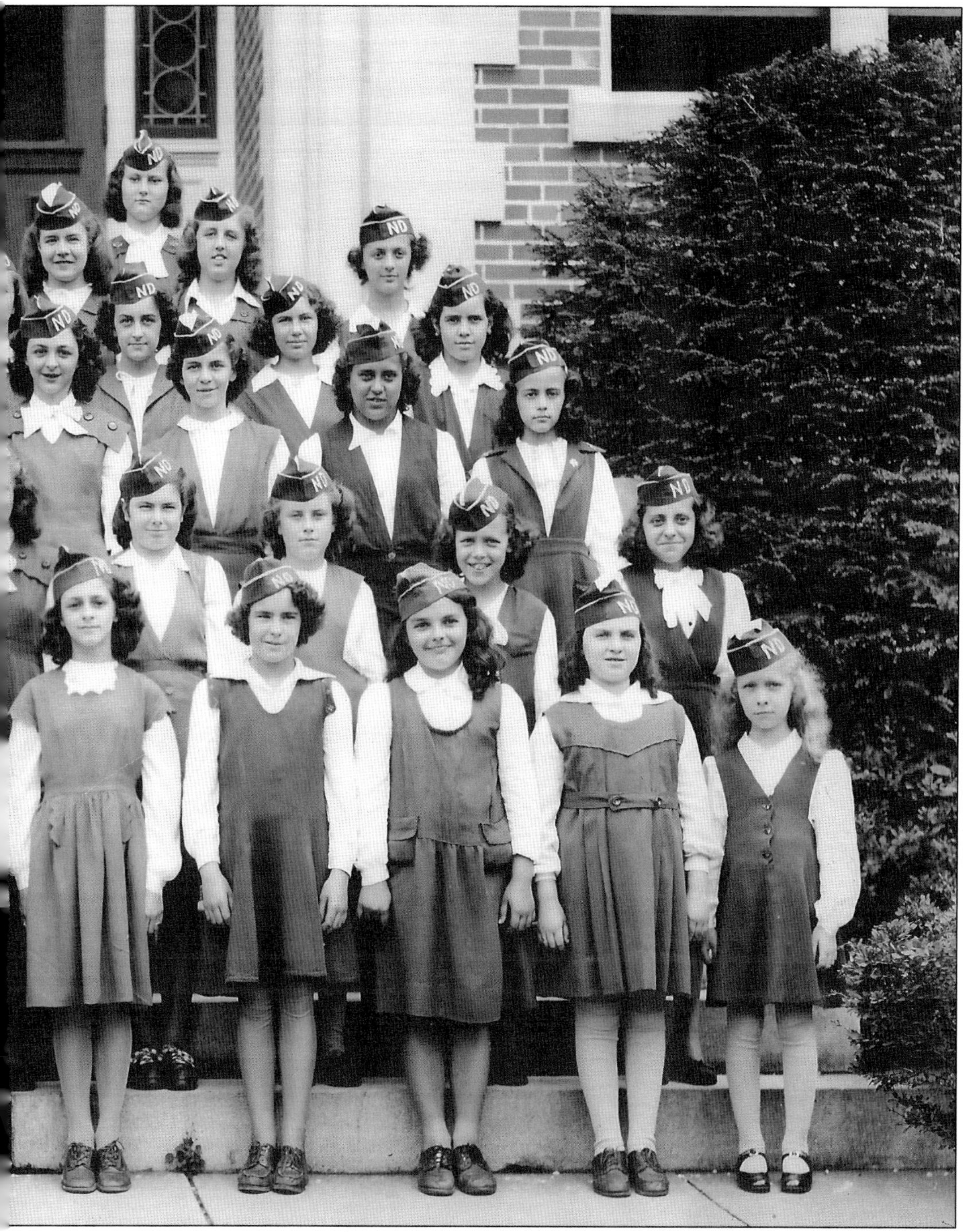

Ninette Bousquet, Jannette Plante, Irene Limerick, and Sylvia Bouchard; (fourth row) Annette Parenteau, Theresa Dube, Pauline Hebert, Jacqueline Miller, Jean Russi, Margaret Provost, and Carol Blanchette; (fifth row) Georgette Maguira, Alice Lebrun, Henrietta Nadeau, Claire Masse, Irene Lefebvre, Lucille Lavigne, Natalie Lebrun, and Dorothy Trudeau. (Courtesy of Gerard Heroux.)

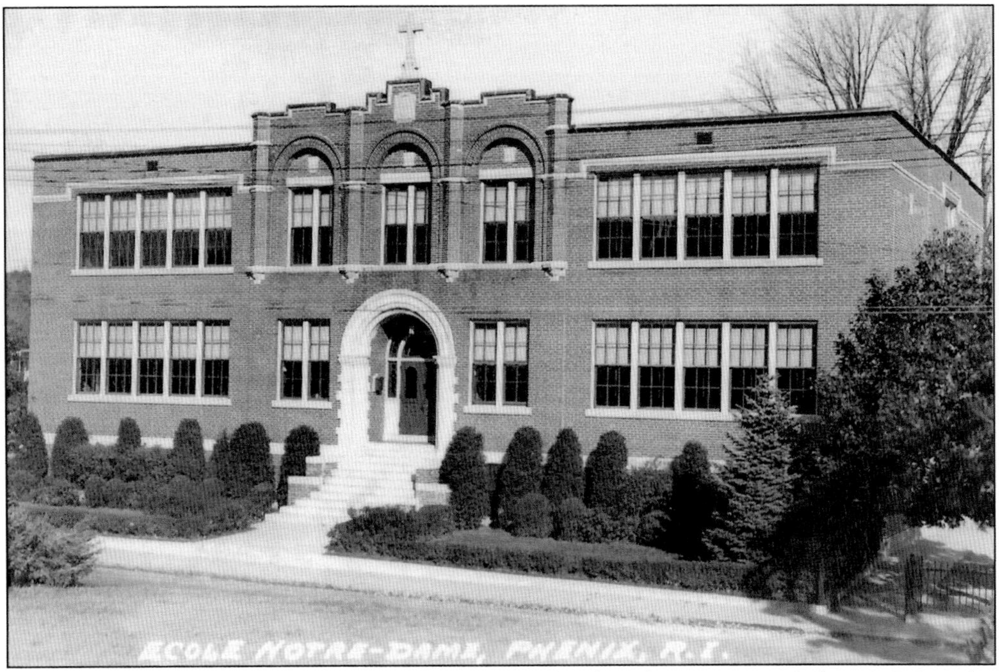

This is the Notre Dame School, built in 1926, which the chorale group attended in 1947. It is also the school the author's children attended in the 1970s. (Courtesy of Gerard Tellier Jr.)

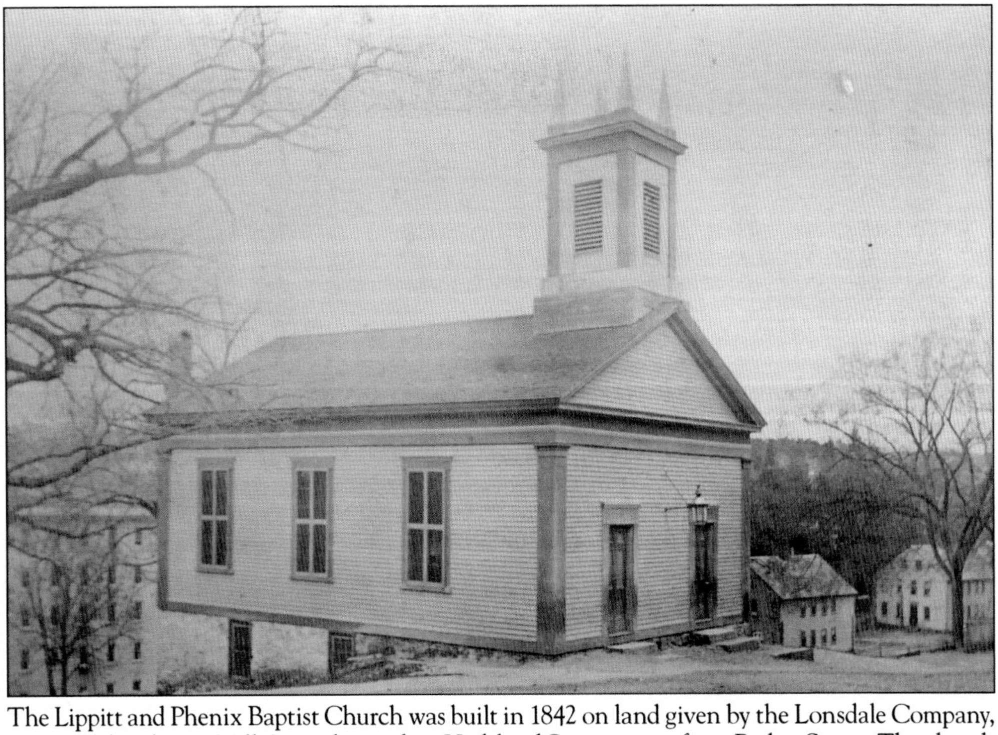

The Lippitt and Phenix Baptist Church was built in 1842 on land given by the Lonsdale Company, owner of the Phenix Mill. It was located on Highland Street across from Parker Street. The church was removed in 1892 to build SS Peter and Paul Church. The Phenix Mill can be seen in the distance to the left. (Courtesy of Donald Carpenter.)

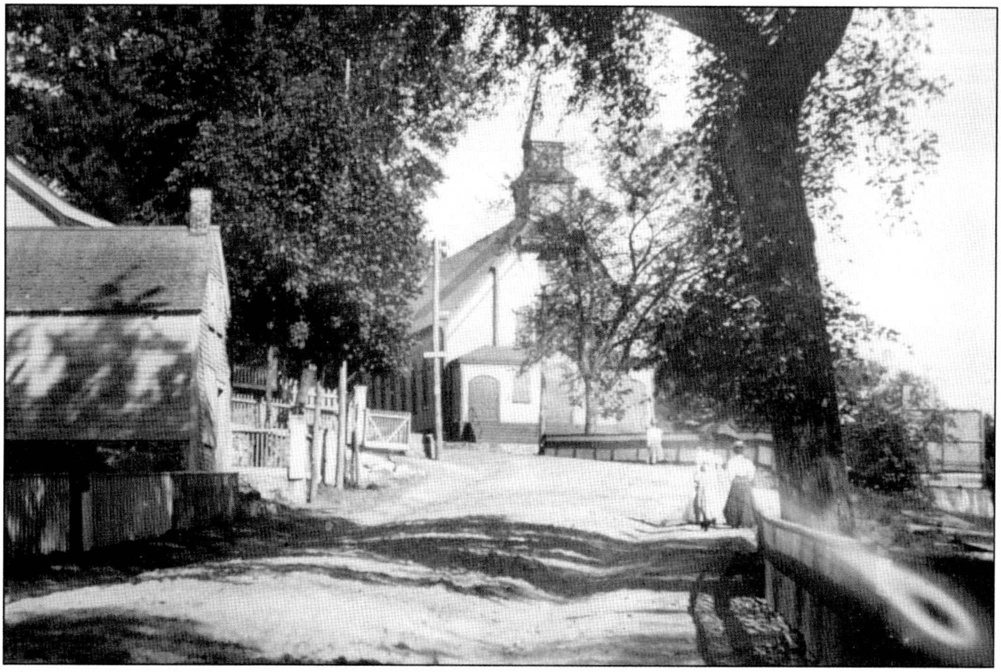

This is a view of SS Peter and Paul Church on Highland Street looking east. It was built in 1892 and set sideways on the narrow lot. George H. Page of Centreville built it at a cost of $17,000. Perhaps the lady on the sidewalk with her daughter is walking to church.

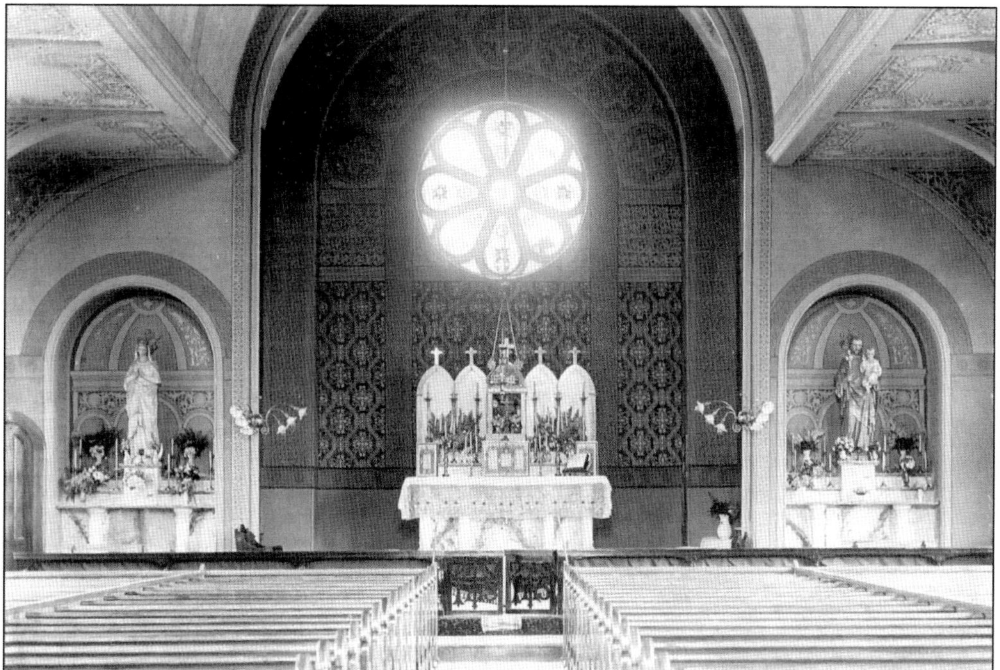

This is the interior of SS Peter and Paul Church. Extensive detail work appears both on the ceiling and all across the front. This church is still in existence after 119 years. (Courtesy of Donald Carpenter.)

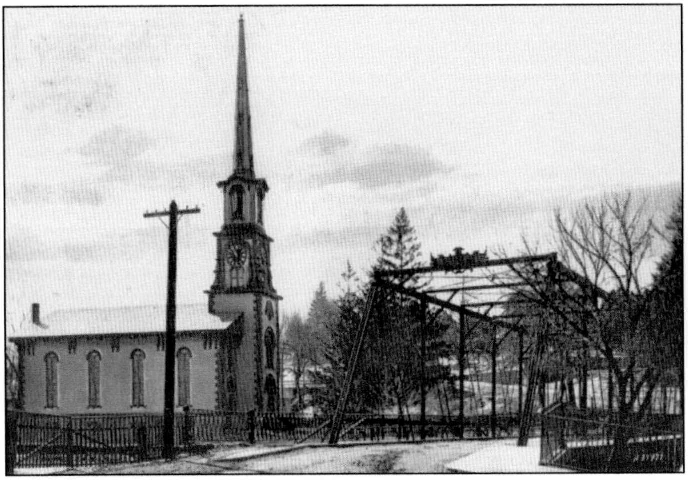

This photograph is of the Phenix Baptist Church, built in 1869 on land donated by William Bennett Spencer. The steeple stood an impressive 162 feet, pointing toward Heaven. In 1933, it became unsafe and was removed. The pictures on the tops of pages 97 and 102 were taken from the tower above the clock. The church was torn down in 1978, and a new one was erected beside it.

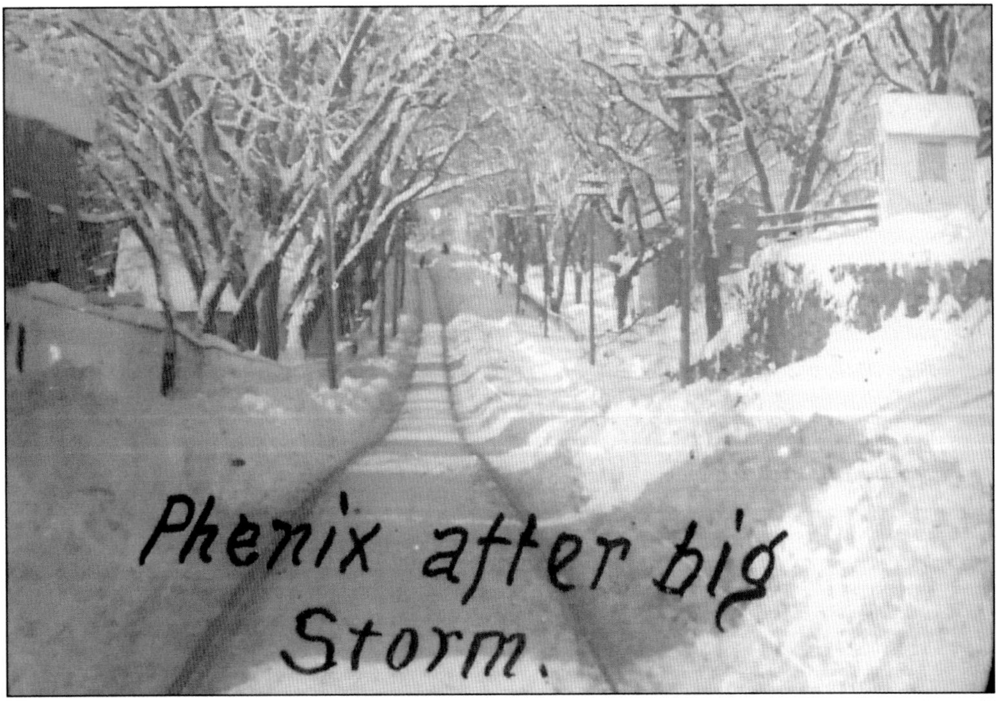

This is a view of Main Street leaving Lippitt looking west, just after Highland Street branches off. The Phenix Mill complex would be at the bottom of the hill on the left. Today, the traffic light would be straight ahead. The following verse is from "Winter Wonderland," written by Helen O. Larson on January 16, 1978, at age 77: "The little snow birds, were nibbling away / On the cracker crumbs, I threw out today." (Courtesy of Lawrence G. Soucy.)

Eight

River Point Village

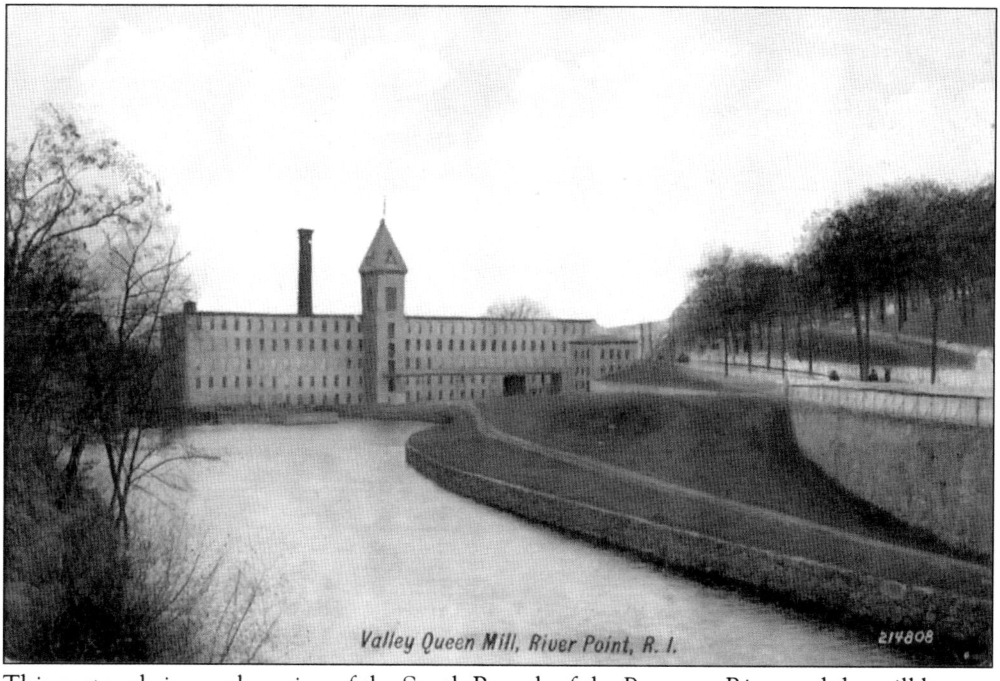

This postcard gives a clear view of the South Branch of the Pawtuxet River and the mill known as the Valley Queen. This five-story structure was built in 1835 and enlarged in 1889. All of the granite to build it was quarried from a ledge on the opposite side of the river. It is known today as the Original Bradford Soap Works, established in Rhode Island by James Rogers and William Murgatroyd of Bradford, England. (Courtesy of Richard Hughes.)

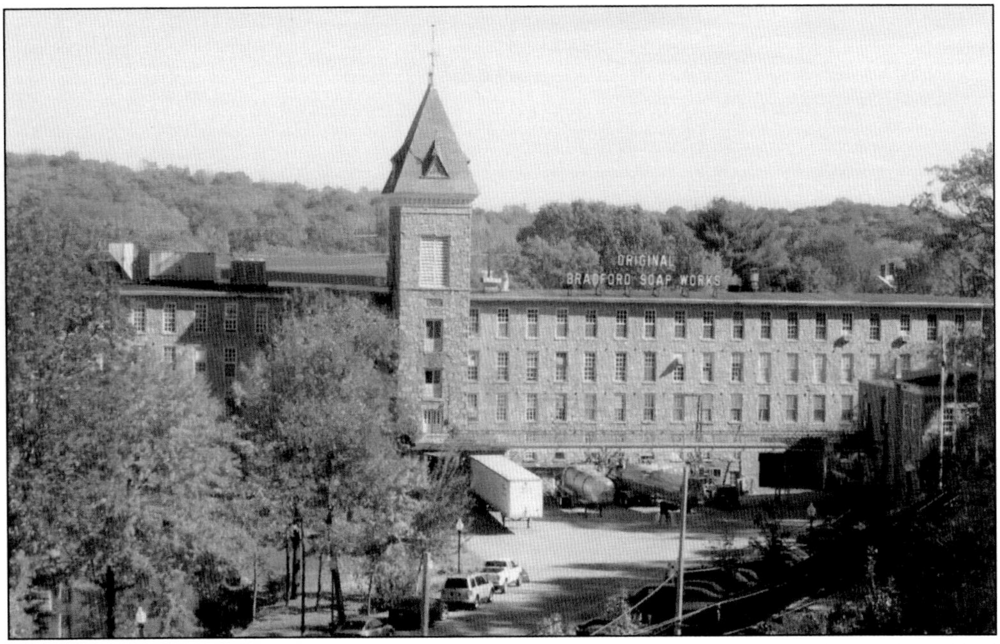

This photograph was taken in 2008 from the Royal Mills complex. It shows the Original Bradford Soap Works, founded in Providence in 1876 and relocated here in 1931. After 134 years, it is the world's largest manufacturer of specialty soap. (Courtesy of Gerard Tellier Jr.)

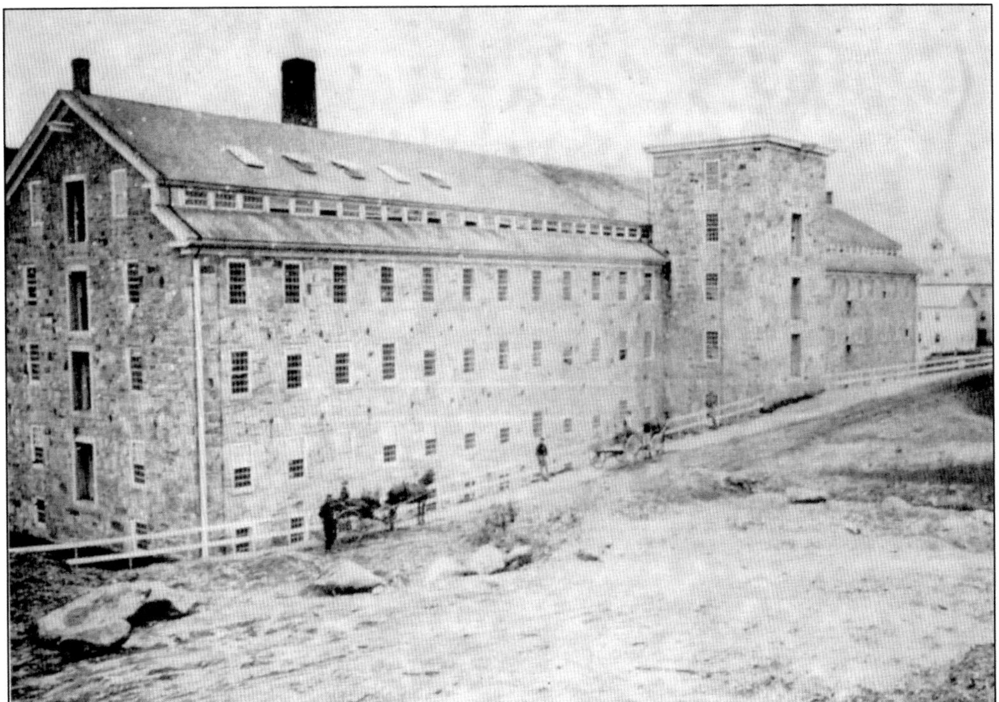

This photograph is of the original stone mill built on this site in 1821 and known as the River Point Mill. In 1890, Royal Mills was built on this site. The trail along the fence became Providence Street, as it is known today. (Courtesy of Donald Carpenter.)

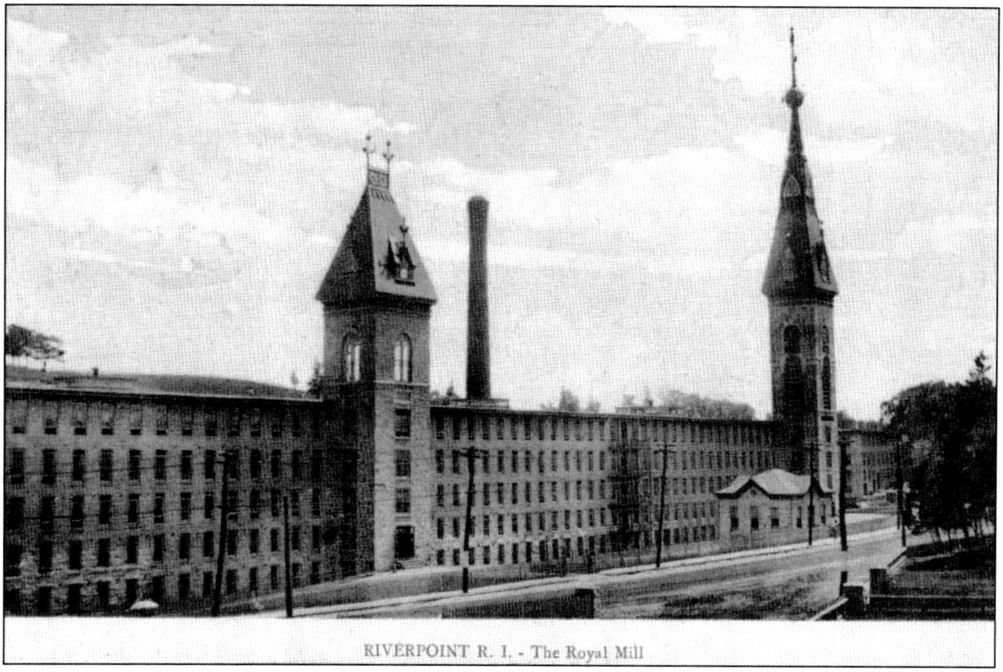

This postcard was mailed on August 7, 1922. Benjamin Brayton and Robert Knight purchased the property in 1885 and built this Royal Mills in 1890. It was partially destroyed by fire in 1919. Consequently, it was rebuilt in 1920, as pictured below. (Courtesy of Lawrence G. Soucy.)

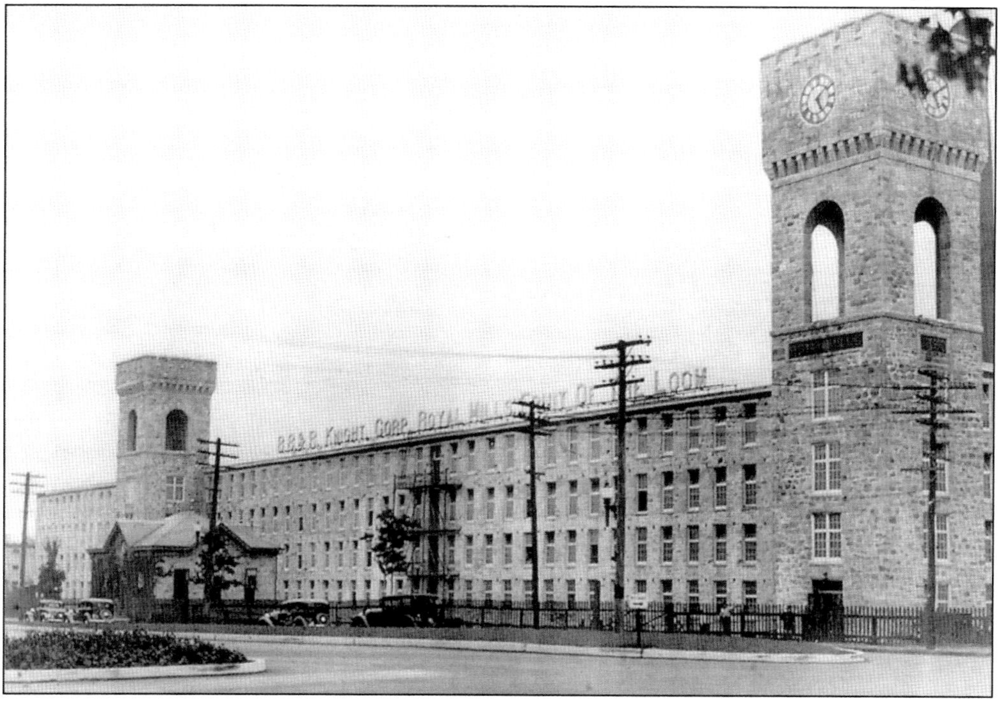

In 1921, the Knights moved their Fruit of the Loom production to this location. The Knights were proud to place their name, the mill's name, and their famous product name on the top of the mill for all to see. This is a photograph from the 1930s. (Courtesy of Gerard Tellier Jr.)

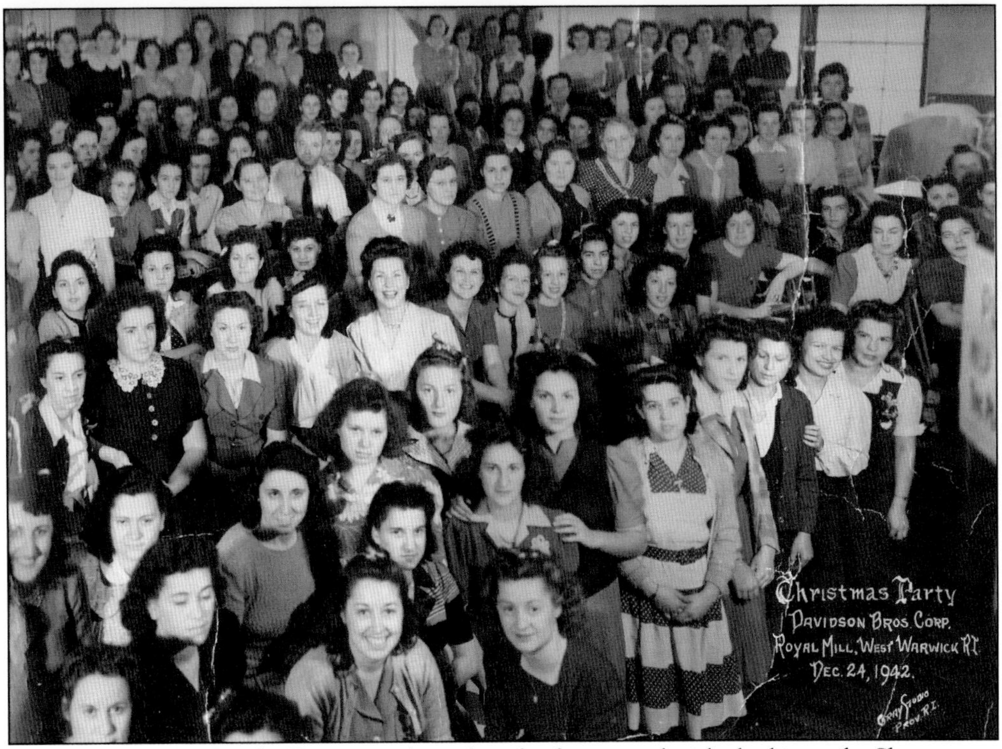

The author's aunt, Cecelia Francis, is the girl in the foreground with the big smile. She appears to be enjoying the Davidson Brothers Corporation's Christmas party in this 1942 photograph. (Courtesy of Ruth Jean Francis-Servant.)

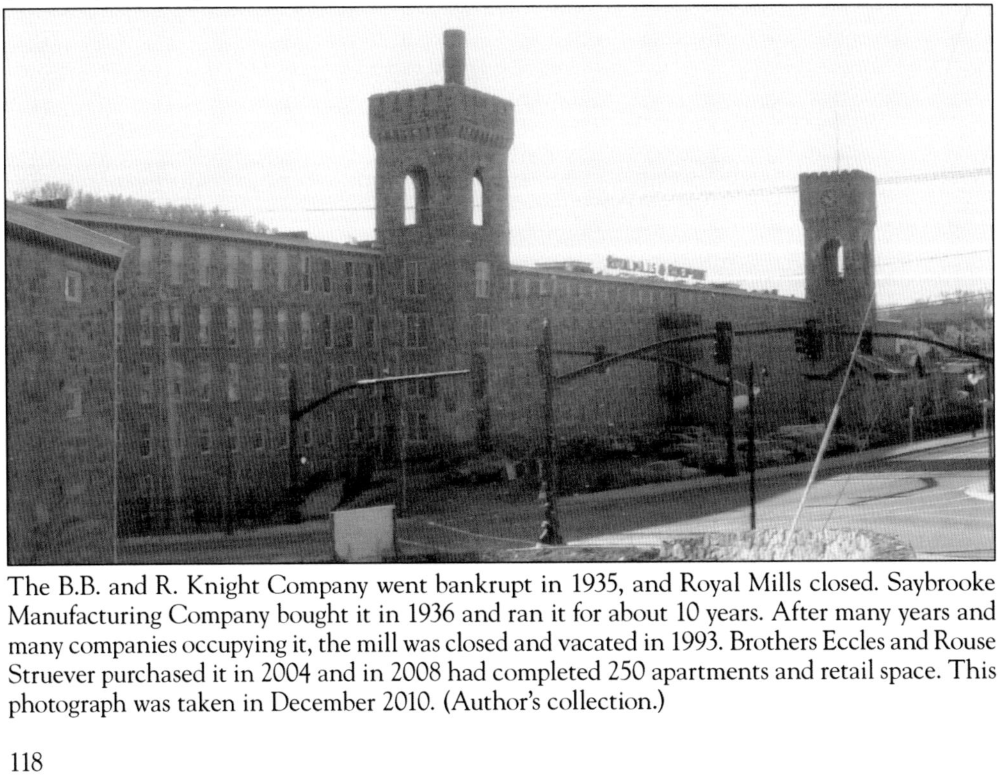
The B.B. and R. Knight Company went bankrupt in 1935, and Royal Mills closed. Saybrooke Manufacturing Company bought it in 1936 and ran it for about 10 years. After many years and many companies occupying it, the mill was closed and vacated in 1993. Brothers Eccles and Rouse Struever purchased it in 2004 and in 2008 had completed 250 apartments and retail space. This photograph was taken in December 2010. (Author's collection.)